Praise for *Downton Abbey and Philosophy*

"As Violet might say, 'Forgive these writers for getting you even more addicted to Downton Abbey? Perhaps. Forget all the philosophical gold gathered? Never.'"

> — ROBERTO SIRVENT, author of *Embracing Vulnerability: Human and Divine*

"Downton Abbey and Philosophy *captures just what is so rich about* both Downton Abbey *and philosophy. So much of the greatness of* Downton Abbey *is often lost on viewers. And that's what good philosophy does so well: it brings out the subtleties of life, regardless of the time period. So, whether it's major issues you grapple with such as death, love and meaning, or life's more daily intricacies like manners and money, this book is for you. Cheers.*"

> — JACK BOWEN, author of *If You Can Read This: The Philosophy of Bumper Stickers*

"The world of Downton Abbey *is the perfect vehicle for exploring issues of class, work, gender, warfare, and more.* Downton Abbey and Philosophy *is a must for any fan of the program with an interest in the world around them. Whether you live upstairs with the aristocrats or downstairs in the servant's quarters with the rest of us, this book will get you thinking.*"

> — GREG LITTMANN, Associate Professor of Philosophy, SIU Edwardsville

"Whether you are upstairs sipping tea in the salon with the ladies in your finest dress and hat or you dwell downstairs and only appear to scrub floors, set tables, and answer the door, this book will be your bedtime companion. It's your philosophical love who keeps you warm with wisdom, that great secret you needn't worry about keeping . . . unlike that other love you kiss quietly behind closed doors."

> — KIMBERLY BALTZER-JARAY, author of *Doorway to the World of Essences*

"Fans of Downton *will find much food for thought in this book. It looks at the characters, their relationships, and life at the Abbey in ways that are not only enlightening, but that will also help fans enjoy the show in deeper ways.*"

> —MIKE AUSTIN, editor of *Virtues in Acti*

D1299138

"In a time of cell phones, disruptive social networks, and rapid technological change, it's boggling how much we can learn from a time when etiquette, stoicism, and rigorous class structure were the norm. Downtown Abbey is a natural fit for exploring modern-day issues like drones, rapidly changing technology, and a society caught up in change that we can remarkably relate to. Barkman and Arp have done a splendid job!"

— WAYNE YUEN, editor of *The Walking Dead and Philosophy: Zombie Apocalypse Now*

"Violet Crawley, the Dowager Countess of Grantham, once said to Lady Edith, 'all life is a series of problems which we must try and solve.' This book delves into many of the philosophical problems posed by Downton Abbey. What the Dowager also says about a good pudding applies to this book: it would be a pity to miss!"

— BRETT GAUL, Associate Professor of Philosophy, Southwest Minnesota State University

"Although only a passing fan of Downton Abbey, I had never watched enough of it to develop the habit. The book Downton Abbey and Philosophy however, has reintroduced me to it in an exciting way. Touching on the moral, psychologic, religious, historic, social, and political aspects of the Abbey and its inhabitants, the chapters were written in a readable and informed way that drew me back to the series. I have to imagine that this is how really smart people sound when they aren't worried about looking smart."

— DAN MIORI, author and medical practitioner

"Downton Abbey is our generation's window to a deeply divisive post-Edwardian social world, where everyday occurrences challenge acknowledged ideals of chivalry and modesty. This fine volume assembles together philosophers' responses to the wildly popular television series, addressing questions of the moral, epistemic, and logical matters arising from the juggernaut of distinct social classes represented by the Crawley household."

— JOSEPH ULATOWSKI, University of Texas at El Paso

Downton Abbey
and Philosophy

Popular Culture and Philosophy® Series Editor: George A. Reisch

IN PREPARATION:

For full details of all Popular Culture and Philosophy® books, visit www.opencourtbooks.com.

Popular Culture and Philosophy®

Downton Abbey and Philosophy

Thinking in That Manor

Edited by

ADAM BARKMAN AND ROBERT ARP

OPEN COURT
Chicago

Volume 95 in the series, Popular Culture and Philosophy ®, edited by George A. Reisch

For more information, visit our website at www.opencourtbooks.com.

Open Court Publishing Company is a division of Carus Publishing Company, dba Cricket Media.

Copyright © 2016 by Carus Publishing Company, dba Cricket Media

First printing 2016

Printed and bound in the United States of America.

Library of Congress Cataloging-in-Publication Data

Downton Abbey and philosophy / edited by Adam Barkman and Robert Arp.
   pages cm. — (Popular culture and philosophy ; Volume 95)
   Includes bibliographical references and index.
   ISBN 978-0-8126-9903-6 (trade paper : alk. paper) 1. Downton Abbey
   (Television program) I. Barkman, Adam, 1979- editor.
PN1992.77.D735D79 2015
791.45'72—dc23
                                                                2015019273

Contents

Of the Simple and Complex

Watched today by over 100 million viewers in over 200 countries, *Downton Abbey*, a UK period drama set in the early twentieth century, is a TV series that the uninitiated think only appeals to older ladies or British conservatives. Indeed, the show is unashamedly quaint, domestic, and homey, which is not the stuff of other international hits such as *Baywatch, Lost,* and *CSI.* But just as there are many levels to the actual Abbey—the world of masters above, and the world of servants below—so, too, are there many levels of meaning to *Downton Abbey* the show.

The genius of *Downton*—if just one feature had to be pointed to—would be its ability to incarnate historical accuracy while at the same time raising universal concerns of an ethical, social, and political nature. Haters sometimes claim that the series is a melodramatic, bogus vision of England at the time; their common charge seems to be that the show is beautiful but dumb, or well-acted but superficial in concern. Now certainly it's true that some episodes revolve around seemingly trivial, gossipy issues such as who stole the snuffbox, but these particular issues—while certainly being not less—are also much more than what they appear, and, if you are reading this, then you know this as well.

Take the snuffbox incident, for example. Thomas the servant steals some wine from the cellar, and is discovered by another servant, Bates, who happens to be the valet—the personal servant—of Lord Grantham. Thomas attempts to silence, or at least cast doubt on the character of, Bates, by stealing something that presumably only Bates would have easy access to: one of Lord Grantham's snuffboxes. In the end, Bates is vindicated and Thomas gets his just deserts— 'nuff said. On the surface, this *does* seem like pretty weak tea, right? Not exactly.

First, through a superb performance by Robert James-Collier, Thomas manages in the small to conjure up classic villainy. He takes something that doesn't belong to him for purely selfish purposes (stealing), and then he tells lies about an innocent man for purely selfish purposes (defaming). Although the scope of these injustices is small, they are universally understood. Every culture has its figure who has performed these acts and, as a result, is properly booed: Satan, Ahriman, Ravana, Mara, and Iblis to name just a few. Likewise, actor Brendan Coyle's Bates is the archetypally innocent and clever, and as such plays the Christ-, Socrates-, or Confucius-type. Now, unless one wants to argue that such universal types and themes are the same as the superficial— which, in turn, would suggest their ignorance of Plato's *Republic* or Kant's *The Critique of Pure Reason*—we should conclude that the bursting forth of the universal in the particular is something to celebrate when it is done in such a clear way as it is done with the snuffbox incident. In terms of moral clarity, this episode might be simple, but it's far from superficial and it is certainly beautiful and valuable since moral clarity is beautiful and valuable.

Second, the three characters relevant to this incident— Thomas, Bates, and Lord Grantham—are more than bare moral beings: among other things, each exhibits important social differences. In this scene we are subtly reminded that there is a social hierarchy among the three men, and regardless of whether one agrees with *this* social hierarchy, we are reminded of hierarchy as such and that "propriety" (Confucius), "dharma" (Brahmin), or "justice" (Aristotle) partly consists in paying attention to hierarchy and differences therein. Most non-Western viewers of *Downton* recognize this, which is part of the appeal of the show for them; but those raised in Western democracies—where justice is often reduced to equality—we tend to see this all as foreign, odd, and yet intriguing. Certainly, if pressed we'd agree, for example, both that parents and children are human (equal) and that parents have an authority that children do not (different), but, generally, we are not encouraged to *think* about differences of "greater and lesser." Yet the snuffbox incident *does* encourage us to think about this: we know that Bates is the valet, for example, and that he is expected to do certain things that Thomas and Lord Grantham aren't. Here the particular— Bates the twentieth-century valet to Lord Grantham— inspires viewers to think of a larger reality, and we are better for it as a result.

And this is just one simple incident where we are encouraged to think of greater things and are rewarded for doing so. There are countless other incidents in the five seasons of *Downton Abbey* covered in this book where more complex matters lie just below the surface. In fact, if one of the strengths of *Downton* is that it's a taproot to a vast reality beyond the world of the show, another of its strengths is also highlighting—not necessarily at the same time—the incredible complexities that make up concrete persons in time. That is, while Thomas does play the Satan-figure and Bates the Christ-figure (and many of us love the show for this), few who have watched the first five seasons would dispute that as concrete persons, and not as types, Bates, Thomas, and even, or especially, Lord Grantham are neither purely hateful, nor purely sympathetic. Thomas constantly plots evil to be sure, yet is also willing to take a beating to spare Jimmy from one. Bates gives money to help a desperate Molesley, but, though questions remain, might have killed at least one person outside of the law. Lord Grantham, too, is virtuous in his concern for the tenants on his land, but cold toward the prospect of his daughters' flourishing as genuine individuals. We love these complexities as windows into our world, and thinking about such complexities—and pointing out contradictions and problems with many of these complexities—is what helps us also think about our own state as such.

The chapters in this volume discuss the many other instances where universal and particular matters arise with great force. The oft-neglected matter of etiquette or "small morals" as Hume calls them are a constant theme, as are women's rights. Philosophies of work and place are brought to our attention with surprising depth. Wartime ethics and the constant challenge to adapt basic moral principles to very particular, changing battlefields is another important theme, as are philosophies about what a just socio-political order should look like. And the list goes on. But enough of us already; let's get to the chapters themselves.

Finding Your Place

1
Finding the Meaning of Life in *Downton Abbey*

KIMBERLY BLESSING

Anxiety-ridden college students are plagued with the question: What am I going to do with my life? One of the most successful entrepreneurs of the modern era is Steve Jobs, creator of Apple. He told the Stanford University class of 2005:

> You've got to find what you love. And that is as true for work as it is for your lovers. Your work is going to fill a large part of your life, and the only way to be truly satisfied is to do what you believe is great work. And the only way to do great work is to love what you do.

Confucius (551–479 BCE) offered similar advice, "Choose a job you love, and you will never have to work a day in your life." Similarly, talk-show-host-turned-spiritual-guru Oprah Winfrey preaches "Follow your bliss." Winfrey is a fan of Joseph Campbell (1904–1987), an American mythologist whose work greatly influenced *Star Wars* director George Lucas. In *The Power of Myth*, Campbell explains that his general formula for his students is "'Follow your bliss.' Find where it is, and don't be afraid to follow it."

Few characters from *Downton Abbey* do this. Instead, the rigid class structure of post-Edwardian England prescribes them certain roles. Many of their jobs are far from blissful, much less the result of their choosing to DWYL (Do What You Love). Most obvious are the servants. However, when the head maid, Anna, asks Edith Crawley, "What would you like me to get you?" even Edith responds, "A different life."

So, it's not just the underprivileged servants who don't do what they love. Lady Mary Crawley, Matthew Crawley (Mary's husband), and everyone affected by the law mandating that a woman can't inherit a title or estate, are not doing what they love. In the first minutes of the first episode, we learn that the heirs to the *Downton* estate sank with the *Titanic*. The head of the estate, Lord Grantham, has three daughters (Mary, Edith, and Sybil), and no sons. British law says only a man can inherit a title. One servant says to another, "I thought Lady Mary was the heir." The other responds, "She's a girl, stupid. Girls can't inherit." Eventually the estate comes down to Matthew, with whom Lady Mary eventually—and quite predictably—falls in love:

> **Lord Grantham**: You do not love the place yet.
>
> **Matthew**: Well, obviously, it's . . .
>
> **Lord Grantham**: No, you don't love it. You see a million bricks that may crumble, a thousand gutters and pipes that may block and leak, and stone that will crack in the frost.
>
> **Matthew**: But you don't?
>
> **Lord Grantham**: I see my life's work. (1:2)

Happiness

In spite of Job's assertion that it's all about DWYL, many of *Downton*'s characters are able to find meaning and happiness. Meaningfulness and happiness are very closely related to each other, but they are not synonymous. Matthew's war experiences, which resulted in serious injuries that he thought were going to leave him paralyzed, were certainly not happy days. But it would seem odd to suggest that his experience as a soldier in World War I was not deeply meaningful. He even suggests that those painful experiences were beneficial: "War has a way of distinguishing between the things that matter and the things that don't" (2:1).

Later on, in season 4, we see Lady Mary work her way through her profound grief over losing her husband in a car accident. At one point she observes, "I'm not unhappy. I'm just not quite ready to be happy" (4:1). Any of us who has lost a loved one would never invite such pain and sorrow into our lives if we could help it. But we'd never look at the loss of a loved one as meaningless. Though religion plays a minor role in the lives of the characters in *Downton Abbey*, the Christian narrative offers one way to think about how pain and suffering are an important and meaningful part of one's life.

Meaningfulness

Meaningfulness, like morality, is a value that only applies to human lives, be they ordinary or extraordinary. Like morality, meaningfulness varies and comes in degrees. Some actions, such as defending your country in battle, strike us as more meaningful than others such as attending a society ball. The beautiful and spirited Lady Sybil longs to find more meaning in her life: "Sometimes, it feels as if all the men I have ever danced with are dead. I just feel so useless, wasting my life while they sacrifice theirs" (2:1).

When we consider the relative meaningfulness of a person's life we might consider the life as a whole, or we may isolate some part of that life, including an individual action or set of actions, project, or endeavor. Young Lady Sybil and Violet, Dowager Countess of Grantham, seem to disagree as to whether certain endeavors, say, learning to speak French, make a person's life more more or less meaningful. Lady Sybil exclaims: "No one ever learned anything from a governess except for French, and how to curtsy." To which Lady Violet responds, "What more do you need?" (1:7). Downstairs, Mr. Carson, who has worked at Downton since he was a boy, represents the old guard. As head butler the success of a society ball is a very meaningful part of his work and daily life: "Miss O'Brien, we are about to host a society wedding. I have no time for training young hobbledehoys" (3:1).

Purposefulness

Lots of folks believe that in order for a life to be meaningful, it must be goal-driven. Lord Grantham, for example, says in season 3, "The estate must be a major employer and support the house or there's no point to any of it." For both aristocrats and their servants, there is a very rigid class structure and social plan in place at Downton. Everyone knows his or her roles and purpose. Lord Grantham, again, says, "We all have different parts to play, Matthew, and we must all be allowed to play them" (1:2). The aristocratic women of the older generation, Cora, the American wife of Lord Grantham, and Violet, are resigned to their roles. Yet the Crawley daughters seem to resist, and in some cases rebel against, their roles as heiress or wife. Lady Mary wonders, "How many times am I to be ordered to marry the man sitting next to me at dinner?" To which Lady Cora Grantham responds, "As many times as it takes" (1:5). In another scene Lady Mary defends her sister Sybil, who eventually runs off with Branson, their father's Irish-Marxist chauffeur, saying, "Sybil is entitled to her opinions." Without missing a beat Violet retorts, "No. She isn't until she is married. Then her husband will tell her what her opinions are" (1:6).

Oddly the very people who seem to have the least freedom in determining their lot in life, namely the servants, still experience freedom in their personal lives. The bright and virtuous Anna would probably not have chosen a life of servitude. Still, she is able to craft a meaningful life within this rigid social structure that has been imposed on her. This is most clearly exemplified in what is the most powerful love story of *Downton*, that of Anna and Mr. Bates. Anna: "I love you, Mr. Bates. I know it's not ladylike to say it, but I'm not a lady, and I don't pretend to be." Mr. Bates: "You are a lady to me. And I never knew a finer one" (1:5).

Freedom

Downton's characters suggest that it's possible to find meaning in spite of the fact that they're forced into a line of work or life that was not their choosing. In one of Maggie Smith's priceless deliveries, just after discovering that Lady Mary's Turkish lover died of a heart attack while in bed with Mary, Lady Violet suggests the extent to which the individual, even an English aristocrat, has control over his will.

> **Violet**: Oh, my dears! Is it really true? I can't believe it. Last night he looked so well! Of course, it would happen to a foreigner. It's typical.

Mary: Don't be ridiculous!

Violet: I'm not being ridiculous. No Englishman would dream of dying in someone else's house, especially someone they didn't even know.

Sybil: Oh, Granny, even the English aren't in control of everything.

Violet: Well I hope we're in control of something, if only ourselves. (1:3)

Next to the long-suffering demoted butler and valet, Mr. Molesley, John Bates must be the most unlucky chap on the show. Still he maintains, "You can change your life if you want to. Sometimes you have to be hard on yourself, but you can change it completely. I know" (1:3). Even Lady Violet is willing to concede that women have some freedom, "I'm a woman, Mary. I can be as contrary as I choose" (2:4).

Finding One's Passion

What all of this suggests is that if a life or line of work is to be meaningful, it is up to the individual subject to find or create meaning in his or her life. Advocates of this point of view argue that we can find meaning in life or activities if we are passionately interested or invested in them. Accordingly it is up to you, the individual subject, to discover what is in your nature to do. Once you find your passion, you will find meaning in your life. In other words, you can find anything meaningful because it is up to you, the subject, to invest your lives and actions with meaning.

Existentialists, among others such as Jobs and Winfrey, embrace this subjective view of meaningfulness. Friedrich Nietzsche (1844–1900) thinks meaning arises from the creative, passionate *process* of an activity, not by achieving goals. Nietzsche thinks that if you live in the moment with passion simply for what it is, then life can be meaningful. The strength of meaning-subjectivism lies in the fact that any individual can find or create meaning in any situation or life. This is also the greatest weakness of this theory. For if anything counts, then "trivial" things like counting bottle caps or hairs on one's head could be meaningful. This is also true of dastardly deeds such as those carried about by the dark and mischievous footman Thomas and his co-conspirator, O'Brien.

Moreover, it may be asked whether or not it is necessary to be passionately invested in a project, endeavor, life, in order for it to meaningful. It seems plausible to suppose that a scientist might work for years in a laboratory, never really getting excited about her day-to-day work and activities. Then one day she makes an important discovery. Wouldn't that confer her work and life with meaning? Passionate love affairs, both licit and illicit, abound in *Downton Abbey*. It's not clear, however, whether it is the passion per se that is doing the meaning-work, or whether it is something else, such as love and commitment. Additionally, if meaningfulness requires passion, what about people who are just not very passionate by nature? People like the British, for example?

> **Mary**: [*Referring to an unwelcome guest.*] We can't make a scene.

> **Edith**: I sometimes feel we should make more scenes about things that really matter to us.

> **Anthony Gillingham**: It wouldn't be very English.

> **Edith**: No, but I envy it . . . all those Latins screaming, and shouting, and hurling themselves into graves. I bet they feel much better afterwards.

> **Mary**: I wonder. I think once you've let it out, it must be hard to get it back in. (4:9)

Objective Meaning

For reasons like these, many philosophers reject subjectivism as a sound theory of meaningfulness. Some philosophers are objectivists. Robert Nozick views meaningfulness in terms of permanence, which gets cashed out in terms of transcending limits, "A significant life is, in some sense, permanent; it makes a permanent difference to the world—it leaves traces. To be wiped out completely, traces and all, goes a long way toward destroying the meaning of one's life." Lord Grantham's life is meaningful because he is able to pass on the legacy of Downton Abbey. On the other hand, Hitler's life certainly "left traces." But that doesn't seem to be the kind of life that Nozick would want to hold up as meaningful.

Susan Wolf offers a hybrid view of meaningfulness. She agrees that meaningfulness requires a subjective element. But Wolf thinks that meaningfulness additionally requires an objective component because there are certain projects and not others that are "fitting for fulfillment," or worthy of love. For example, no human being should be fulfilled counting bottle caps. Or what about eating excrement? Being fulfilled or satisfied isn't all there is to meaningfulness. For it also matters what *kinds* of actions and projects you choose. Wolf argues that "meaning arises when subjective attraction meets objective attractiveness." This hybrid view of meaning is expressed in a pithy slogan: "loving objects that are worthy of love."

The Holy You

Ross Douthat uses Robert Bellah's phrase "expressive individualism," describing it as the view that "the key to the good life lies almost exclusively in self-discovery, self-actualization, the cultivation of the unique and holy You." Authenticity language, which gets a lot of play in existential thought among others, encourages this view that the key to a meaningful life lies in finding your true self and expressing it.

The holy You is noticeably absent in *Downton Abbey*. Instead, the characters put aside their passions and self-interest in order to serve some larger purpose, in occupations such as caretaker, servant, soldier, or nurse. It's hard to imagine how Jobs's advice would fall on the ears of Lord Grantham, who seems immune from considering his own wants and desires:

> You are my darling daughter, and I love you, hard as it is for an Englishman to say the words. If I had made my own fortune and bought Downton for myself, it should be yours without question. But I did not. My fortune is the work of others, who labored to build a great dynasty. Do I have the right to destroy their work, or impoverish that dynasty? I am a custodian, my dear, not an owner. I must strive to be worthy of the task I have been set. (1:4)

Even the stubborn and single-minded Lady Mary eventually realizes her duty to Downton: "Papa, you're always saying how we're not the owners of Downton, but the caretakers. Very well, now let's take care of it" (4:3).

German philosopher Immanuel Kant (1724–1804) would maintain that it's irrational to will a world that abided by the law DWYL. In his *Metaphysics of Morals,* Kant argues that a person cannot let his or her talents wither on the vine for the sake of pleasure:

> A system of nature conforming with this law could indeed exist, with everyone behaving like the Islanders of the south Pacific, letting their talents rust and devoting their lives merely to idleness, indulgence, and baby-making—in short, to pleasure . . . As a rational being, he necessarily wills that all his abilities should be developed, because they serve him and are given to him for all sorts of possible purposes.

For a brief time there is a distance between Lord and Lady Grantham as the result of a painful miscarriage caused by O'Brien forcing Lady Cora to fall. During this time Lord Grantham finds himself attracted to a maid who lost her husband in the Battle of Somme. He eventually comes to his senses, however, realizing that duty trumps desire:

JANE MOORSUM: Will you be happy? Really?

ROBERT CRAWLEY: I have no right to be unhappy, which is almost the same.

JANE MOORSUM: Almost. Not quite. (1:8)

Downton's hard-working servants are likewise hardly concerned with personal fulfillment and self-actualization. The fatalistic Mr. Carson observes, "But what does it matter anyway? We shout and scream and wail and cry, but in the end we must all die." The less dire Mrs. Hughes keeps him in check: "Well. That's cheered me up. I'll get on with my work." Mr. Carson and Mrs. Hughes, pillars of virtue and propriety, take great pride in their work, exemplifying virtues of industry and integrity. For Carson, his work ethic is a matter of patriotic duty, "Keeping up standards is the only way we can show the Germans we will not be beaten in the end." "Well," responds Mrs. Hughes, "give me some warning the next time we're expecting Germans at Downton and I'll see what I can do!" (2:1). The same hard work ethic is evident in Mrs. Patmore, the proud and perfectionist cook. She is unrelenting in terms of what she expects from her poor underling Daisy, saying, "Daisy! What's happened to you? I said you could go for a drink of water, not a trip up the Nile!" (1:3). In another episode, the all-too-timid Daisy is determined to prove herself worthy of Mrs. Patmore's respect, "I was only trying to help." But Mrs. Patmore is not one for excuses, saying, "Oh, Judas was only trying to help I suppose, when he brought the Roman soldiers to the Garden!" (1:5).

Doing What You Don't Love

Jobs's seemingly uplifting view that urges young people to ponder what they most enjoy doing and then turn that activity into a wage-earning enterprise, keeps them focused on themselves "to the point of narcissism," Miya Tokumitsu argues. Just count how many times Jobs uses the word "you" in the four sentences from his Stanford speech, she suggests (the answer is eight). And by focusing on ourselves, are absolved of "any obligation to . . . the wider world."

The DWYL ethos that is so ubiquitous in our culture requires workers to be passionate about their work. As a result, a great deal of work is degraded and devalued. In this sense DWYL is elitist. Gordon Marino points out that "it ignores the idea that work itself possesses value." It might also be a way to exploit workers, for it persuades people to work for little or no money. A great example is adjunct professors and unpaid interns whose academic research should, by this logic, be done out of pure love.

Tokumitsu observes that Jobs's view creates two opposing classes of work: (i) that which is lovable (creative, intellectual, socially prestigious) and (ii) that which is not (repetitive, unintellectual, undistinguished). We might expect that these same work-class lines would cut across the social-class lines of Downton. But this is not the case. For both servants and their masters unlovable work is viewed as socially necessary. The ethos of *Downton Abbey* suggests that hard and honest work is an end in itself, not a means towards personal fulfillment. Mr. Carson: "To progress in your chosen career William, you must remember that a good servant at all times retains a sense of pride and dignity that reflects the pride and dignity of the family he serves. And never make me remind you of it again" (1:2). By exercising virtues of integrity, pride, and industry *Downton's* characters validate work that is not their passion.

This suggests that it is possible to find meaning in life and work even if a person is not DWYL.

Pursuing socially necessary work provides meaning for many real people living real lives. It's not clear, however, how to encourage young people to get outside themselves so that they can, as Marino says, put their passions "aside for the benefit of a larger circle, be it family or society" for this "does not come naturally to everyone." Testing and intensive career counseling might help young people to hone in on their talents, which might track them into meaningful work. We might also explore apprenticeships along the lines of a German model. This would mean that we need to elevate our views of vocational and professional training, which would result in correcting our views about liberal education. On this model, liberal education is not merely or primarily a means to getting a job, but rather is something that is intrinsically valuable. And, given the increasing costs of higher education, it should only be pursued by those who want to learn, not those who are chiefly looking for a job. Finally we need to be honest with young people: only a very lucky few get to DWYL. And for those of us who do, we are only able to follow our bliss on the backs of many others who are not afforded such a luxury. Do we really want to say that their less-than-lovable work is not valuable?

Find Something to Do

Liberals criticize *Downton Abbey* creator Julian Fellowes because his melodrama celebrates British aristocracy and endorses conservative values. Indeed this post-WWI series challenges some very popular conceptions of meaningfulness, such as those put forward by celebrity icons such as Steve Jobs and Oprah Winfrey. Young undergraduates would eschew the work of *Downton*'s servants, as well as the rigidly defined roles of their aristocratic masters. Fortunately they have every opportunity to DWYL. It remains to be seen whether or not their lives are any more meaningful for it. And in this spirit, let's give the last word to Lady Violet, who says in season 3, "Edith dear, you're a woman with a brain and reasonability. Stop whining and find something to *do*."

2
I May Be a Socialist, But I'm Not a Lunatic

JOSEPH WALDERZAK

In the second season of *Downton Abbey*, socialist and chauffeur Tom Branson laments the assassination of the Russian Czar. Hopeful for a peaceful socialist revolution, Tom admits "sometimes a hard sacrifice must be made for a future that's worth having" (2:5). As the show progresses and Tom becomes romantically involved with Lady Sybil, married to her, and eventually accepted as part of the noble family after Sybil's death, Tom's remark takes on a new meaning. Tom's fervent socialist beliefs slowly erode as he becomes accustomed to his new life and welcoming to aristocratic values. As it turns out, Tom's beliefs were the hard sacrifice he made in order to secure a future worth having.

What makes *Downton* so exceptionally entertaining is its persistent use of conflicts. Past and present. Present and future. Upstairs and downstairs. Love and duty. Commonly, the series allows for characters to embody these conflicts. For instance, the conflict between past and present is personified through the relationship of Violet Crawley and Isobel Crawley. In this way, complex social and political issues are to be identified by each character and all conflicts are developed through character interaction and interplay.

One of the most dynamic, and philosophically interesting, is the conflict among Matthew Crawley, Tom Branson, and Robert Crawley regarding the duty and responsibility of the aristocratic caretakers of Downton to the estate. At face value, Branson represents socialist values, Robert represents aristocratic values, and Matthew represents capitalist values. What makes these conflicts so important is that the series is able to characterize each of the economic and political beliefs in a particular light, possibly influencing audience views and adding to our historical imagination. Ultimately, as the friendship between Tom and Robert grows the differences in their viewpoints dissipates, suggesting a shared viewpoint exists between the two seemingly opposed views. So, who's the real socialist here?

Robert Crawley: Classic Conservatism and Noblesse Oblige

The viewer's introduction to Robert makes his sense of duty to both the estate itself and those below him in social rank blatantly obvious. His personal and familial relationship with Downton is expressed in these early episodes when he claims "Downton is in my bones" (1:1) and that it is his "life's work" (1:2). Robert's father started the hospital and established an endowment to keep it running, and the estate funds the Downton Fair (1:4), the Grantham Cup flower contest (1:5), and even transitions the estate into a wartime convalescent home in the second season, and hosts fundraising events for the troops and a concert to lighten their spirits (2:2). Other episodes focus on the servants' ball (2: Christmas Special) and the village bazaar (4:8), both provided by the estate headed by Robert. The communal aspect of the estate is what legitimizes its very existence according to Robert.

In the first episode of the series he expresses the responsibility he feels towards Bates, despite his perceived inadequacies, and in the following episode shames Matthew for viewing his butler, Molesley, as being superfluous to his lifestyle. Robert explains that Matthew's part is to allow for others to play their part and for ensuring that each individual is able to achieve a sense of self-worth. This view is reiterated throughout the series perhaps most plainly when he explains to Mary that he is not the owner of Downton but merely its custodian (1:4). This becomes such a common refrain that Mary says "You [Robert] always say we're the caretakers of Downton not the owners" in order to remind Robert of his core beliefs (4:4). Robert's duty to his employees can't be overstated. In fact, Robert comes to the personal aid of nearly every principal employee. Beyond those mentioned above, he helps Mrs. Patmore locate a relative during the war (2:2), pleads for John Bates to return during his blackmail-inspired exile (2:4) and provides him with legal aid, gets William transferred to Downton after his war injury, and consistently shows forgiveness to Thomas.

In these attitudes and efforts Robert embodies the concept of noblesse oblige, a French phrase referring to the "obligation of nobility." Basically, nobility is not simply a status of entitlement but requires the fulfillment of social responsibilities. Robert's responsibility to his employees, the estate and its tenants, and the surrounding village is his fulfillment of the obligation of nobility. When faced with the prospect of possibly having to sell Downton, Robert laments, "I couldn't do that. I have a duty beyond saving my own skin. The estate must be a major employer and support the house or there's no point to it. To any of it" (3:1). Nowhere else is Robert's observance of noblesse oblige so bluntly stated. Robert's politics come out of the dominant aristocratic conservative politics of the eighteenth and nineteenth century. At times, Robert's conservatism appears radically antiquated for the early twentieth century. He views the aristocracy as vital to keeping the values of the pastoral world, in which the working class was elevated through being offered meaningful work and basic living conditions. It was the duty of the nobility to give meaning and self-worth to individuals, not legislation, which is why it was so essential to maintain the aristocracy and mitigate the power of the rising business class. Even as the conservative (Tory) political party became less influenced by aristocratic conservatism and more so by liberalism and business interests in the interwar period, Robert's conservatism remained.

Tom Branson: Fenian and Socialist

When Tom is first introduced to Robert, they share a cordial exchange in which Robert offers the use of his expansive library to Tom (1:4). In this conversation Tom expresses his interest in history and politics, something that will come to solely define his character prior to his relationship with Sybil. Tom's politics is what initially brings him and Sybil close to one another and in those early episodes Tom's sense of insecurity about his politics and profession is apparent. In the fourth episode of season 1 he explains, "I'm a socialist, not a revolutionary. And I won't always be a chauffeur." At other times, Tom is more adamant about his views and rallies against the "gap between the aristocracy and the poor" as well as labeling Robert a "representative of an oppressive class" (1:6). In these impassioned moments, Tom's socialist politics appear to be impossible to compromise despite his somewhat contradictory appraisal of Robert as a good man and a decent employer. Likewise, his plan to conscientiously object to his call-up for service suggests his views are entirely serious (2:3). His anger over failing to be medically cleared, thus rendering his planned peaceful protest nonviable, further demonstrates his earnest and somewhat radical beliefs. His radicalism comes fully to the surface when he nearly publicly embarrasses a military captain visiting Downton. His love for Sybil convinces him to pen an apology which, when intercepted by Anna, results in his scheme being interrupted. Ultimately, Branson must promise to butler Carson to forgo any protests (2:4). This promise upsets Sybil who views Branson's politics as central to his being. He assuages these fears by ensuring her of his plans to join the Irish revolution once the war concludes.

It is Tom's politics concerning Ireland's independence that pit him against the Crawley family, and Robert particularly. After hearing of Sybil's pregnancy, Robert jests "we're to have a Fenian grandchild" (2: Christmas Special). Cora playfully undermines the seriousness of the issue by retorting that it may be beneficial to have someone on "the other side." Tom is further patronized at a dinner and interrogated over Ireland's politics and subsequently drugged, leading him to act indignantly. "Fenian," a derogatory term introduced in the early nineteenth century referring to the radical independence-seeking Fenian Brotherhood, is not a fair description of Tom. While he firmly believes in Ireland's natural right to independence, he does not support an armed revolution.

He frequently reiterates his interest and hope in a non-violent revolution and when he inadvertently becomes involved in a violent episode he expresses sincere grief to the Crawley family (3:4). Tom often borrows directly from the language of Karl Marx (1818–1883), such as the passage above when he describes Robert as a representative of class oppression. Marx, a nineteenth-century philosopher who criticized the capitalist system, developed an economic theory to describe oppressive class relations. However, when prodded, Tom self-identifies as a republican, rather than a Marxist (3:1). Tom's agricultural upbringing and peaceful intentions have far more in common with the utopian socialist philosophy of Robert Owen (1771–1858) and Charles Fourier (1772–1837).

Owen, a nineteenth-century Welsh philosopher, established a community called New Harmony, which was based on the aims of nurturing human character and enjoying the results of one's work. Both Owen and Fourier advocated a view of human character which is entirely formed by circumstances. Accordingly, one cannot be blamed for one's actions—an idea that goes a ways towards explaining Tom's contradictory views of Robert as oppressive and decent. When Tom becomes the landlord for the agricultural properties of the estate, his embodiment of Fourier's philosophy is even more obvious. Fourier, in his *The Theory of Four Movements*, identifies poverty as the cause of disorder in society and advocates cooperation and appropriate contributions in order to improve productivity.

Tom vs. Robert

Tom and Robert's opposition to one another begins in earnest in the sixth episode of the first season in which Robert blames Tom for enabling Sybil's political activism. Robert quips, "I was amused by the idea of an Irish radical chauffeur but I see now that I've been naïve." Later, he calls Branson's character into question because he reads Marx and others but eventually allows Tom to stay on only because of Sybil's ultimatum. As Tom and Sybil's relationship becomes more serious, Robert's issues with Tom become more personal and less philosophical. Not unrelated to their political differences, Robert threatens to cut Sybil off from money if she goes through with leaving for Ireland with Tom. To do so, according to Robert, would be tantamount to "throwing her life away" (2:8).

In these threats Robert uses his aristocratic position in an attempt to distance his daughter from Tom. When he is unable to intimidate Sybil, Robert attempts to bribe Tom to leave the village and abandon his plans to wed Sybil. Tom poignantly responds, "You know your problem, my Lord? You're like all of your kind. You think you have the monopoly of honor. Doesn't it occur to you that I might believe that the best guarantee of Sybil's happiness lies with me?" Importantly, Robert and Tom's personal disagreement borrows the language of their economic and political differences. Robert's attempt to wield his financial power to manipulate Tom is resisted and Tom rebukes these efforts by challenging Robert's "monopoly of honor." Tom uses the opportunity to proclaim his genuine love for Sybil to also challenge Robert's, and the aristocracy's, perceived monopoly on virtue. When Robert ultimately, albeit reluctantly, grants his blessing to Sybil and Tom, Violet attempts to lessen Robert's concerns by explaining "the aristocracy has not survived by its intransigence, oh no no, we must work with what we got to minimize the scandal" (2:8).

Robert's fears have as little to do with Sybil and as much to do with how Tom may compromise his noble status. Once Tom and Sybil wed, Tom comes further into conflict with the expectations of his new noble status. He refuses to wear the expected morning coat and dress jackets claiming he doesn't "approve of these costumes" and sees "them as the uniform of oppression" and would "be uncomfortable wearing them" (3:1). When visiting Downton Place as a prospective new home given Robert's financial missteps, Branson belittles the family's grief claiming most people would still consider it "a fairy palace" (3:3). These conflicts will eventually wane, and he comes to accept his guilt as misplaced. Through this process his socialism is ultimately abandoned.

Matthew vs. Robert

Matthew's role in the conflict over civic duty and social politics is largely confined to the third season in which his unexpected inheritance compels him to take a more serious interest in the running of the estate. In prior seasons, Matthew took on a more reluctant role which largely catered to Robert's expertise. In one episode Matthew admires a building that he and Robert had decided to restore which led to Robert respecting Matthew's conscientiousness (1:4). However, the Matthew and Robert engagement is far more combative when Matthew's inheritance is invested into Downton. Matthew's politics are fervently capitalist, repeatedly championing "investment, increasing productivity, and reducing waste" in order to secure a self-securing level of profit (3:7).

Matthew and Robert's conflict begins in earnest when the fate of Downton is put into jeopardy due to Robert's irresponsible speculation on railroads during the war. Matthew embraces the news and proposes for them to finally live a "simpler way" (3:1). To Robert, Matthew mistakes their lifestyle as lavish for the sake of pleasure rather than for the sake of providing employment. Episodes that show the struggles of Molesley and the story line regarding Ethel's resorting to prostitution suggest the market that Matthew celebrates is failing to offer valuable employment. Violet articulates Robert's view by stressing that it is their duty to provide employment. She quips, "an aristocrat with no servants is as much use as a glass hammer" (3:1).

Humorously naïve about how their form of employment is self-serving and demeaning, Robert and Violet view their obligation as selfless and necessary. Importantly, Matthew's objection to bringing the number of servants up to pre-war levels is not related to the immorality of the servant-nobleman relationship. Rather, Matthew views servants as financially superfluous. As Matthew becomes more involved in the running of Downton he begins to detect waste. He passionately complains that swaths of land go unworked. Robert, supported by Mary, defends his decision to allow tenants to stay on the land in spite of their inability to utilize the land efficiently. Matthew proposes providing a cottage for the tenants and criticizes Robert for viewing the attempt to make money as akin to being mean. In this conflict, Robert's obligation to the people and Matthew's trust in efficiency and the capitalist system dramatically collide. As their conflict escalates, Matthew barks, "capital is leaking into the cracks caused by bad management" (3:6). He calls for investment in new machinery and new techniques in order to make Downton self-supporting. While Matthew is partially motivated by protecting the estate for Mary and their children, his primary obligation is maximizing profits from the estate. Robert would sooner sell the estate than abandon, or jettison, the people who rely upon it; his loyalty is to the tenants whom he regards as partners.

Who's the Real Socialist Here?
The Case against Tom

Through the first two and a half seasons, Tom's socialism is never in doubt. His plans to conscientiously object and embarrass a military captain may have been disrupted, but even after marrying Sybil he remains committed to his causes. The turning point is when Tom returns to Downton, fleeing Ireland after being involved in the destruction of a British mansion (3:4). He tearfully admits he doesn't want the rich to rule but he doesn't want to punish them either. His experience at Downton, and his relationship with Sybil, appear to have compromised his beliefs, although he still attempts to distance himself by pleading "we all live in a harsh world but at least I know we do" (3:4).

Branson's socialism from that point forward becomes mere lip service as Tom's acceptance into the family results in his siding predominantly with Matthew's style of management. When Tom and Matthew walk the property, Tom's concerns about an impending evicted tenant are put aside by Matthew's quick assurance that "we'll look after him" (3:5). In a similar scene in which Tom is educating Mary on the property, he ensures her that a tenant is keeping their land because they are "hard working" (4:2). Their productivity, rather than their ability, is what determines whether or not they can keep their property. Tom's initial fervor has been diluted through his assimilation into the Crawley family and through his involvement with the management of the Downton estate.

In fact, on a number of occasions the series provides a kind of meta-commentary on the vanishing nature of Tom's socialism. In one episode, Tom jokes that his politics have vanished along with the chauffeur Branson (4:7). An interesting dichotomy arises between "Branson" and "Tom." When he worked as a chauffeur he was addressed as Branson and his socialist politics were intrinsic to who he was. When he became part of the family through marriage he was expected to be addressed as Tom. This transition is a slow and difficult task for Robert, as well as Violet, who celebrates the possibility of returning to addressing him as Branson once he accepts the landlord position, but with time the transition is complete. Tom's reservations about dressing in the proper attire dissipate, and fiery retorts such as when he scolds Robert for having "a narrow view of socialism" are isolated incidents following his exile from Ireland (3:7).

When Tom makes the joke about his vanishing socialism, he keenly observes how starkly different the socialist chauffeur Branson is from the aristocratic Tom. In another episode, Tom defends Robert's support of the farmers and explains, "I haven't abandoned all of my socialism, although, sometimes it feels like it" (4:5). Tom's self-examination operates as a reminder to the audience of just how drastically Tom has changed. A character once solely defined by his socialist politics had been transformed into one who still appreciates farmers and the pastoral lifestyle but has embraced an aristocratic lifestyle.

Who's the Real Socialist Here? The Case for Robert

Unlike Tom, Robert does not undergo a remarkable transformation of character. Rather, it is his intransigence which allows his values and politics to be so starkly contrasted with both Matthew and Tom. Robert finds Matthew's fixation on profitability to be crude and unscrupulous, ranting "profits, profits, profits" when advocating for a gradual change which does not disrupt the lives of the tenants (3:8). Matthew's position reappears in the form of the surveyor in season 4 who criticizes owners who "refuse to think about income" and demands owners "face up to the fact that farming is hard work or they don't deserve to keep what they have" (4:7).

This view, much like Matthew's, Robert finds entirely offensive. Robert also distances himself from Tom's rather routine shows of concerns for the farmers' fate. Tom's concerns are passive and demure compared to Robert's impassioned enthusiasm. When Matthew proposes that Branson work a large portion of the land, Robert implores, "It is not how we do things. Many of the farmers' families have been at Downton as long as we have" (4:5). In part, Robert is advocating for tradition for tradition's sake, but the constancy of his support for the farmers reveals a more genuine concern for their fates. When the topic emerged earlier Robert begged, "What about the tenants? What about the men and women who put their trust in us. Is it fair to them?" (4:5). This concern is made most apparent when Mary and Tom indicate their desire to foreclose the lease of one of their tenants, whose patriarch had recently died, and farm the land themselves. Mary justifies the decision by stating "the rent has not been paid in ages" but even then Robert is left saddened because the family had been farming the land for ages (4:5). He prevents the family from losing the farm by secretly paying the tenant's past rent from his private funds.

He treats ownership, what socialists like Marx and Fourier critique, as merely a civil duty. For Robert, caring for the land equates to ownership in which the true owner is at the service of the tenant. This cannot be mistaken for advocating for a system without ownership, but Robert's narrow interpretation of ownership nearly amounts to the same thing. If caring for the land is tantamount to ownership, and profits are of little importance, then Robert's conservative aristocratic politics is hardly representative of an oppressive system.

Marx and Fourier would likely include Robert in their criticism of society but it is Matthew's capitalist agenda that is truly their concern. In fact, Tom's passivity would be akin to "capitalist pacification," a concept developed by contemporary Marxist scholar David Harvey among others. Essentially, Tom's radicalism is doomed to be pacified by capitalism which infiltrates all facets of society. Tom actually eloquently celebrates Robert's concern for the people above his own. Tom identifies himself as a hard worker knowledgeable about the land, Matthew as a man of law and business, and Robert as understanding the responsibility owed to the people around Downton, those who work for the estate and those who don't. In this confession, Tom limits his usefulness to agricultural knowledge, whereas he accredits Robert for his empathy and duty. Robert's own behavior repeatedly corroborates this assessment as he works towards fulfilling an idealized—dare I say, socialized—version of noblesse oblige and towards a society based on cooperation and reasonable contributions much like that imagined by Fourier and Owen.

So, Is Robert the Real Socialist?

Robert's socialism shouldn't be overstated. He certainly would reject the radicalism of Fourier and Marx. What should not be overlooked, however, is how Robert's concern for the poor, his tenants, and his community has far more in common with the ideals of socialism than Tom's self-confessed politics. The series frequently has its fun with Robert's anachronistic views. For instance, when he suggests that they invest with Charles Ponzi, a notorious criminal who developed a fraudulent investment scheme, the series attempts to show how misguided Robert's politics are and how poor his financial management skills (3:8). Robert is willing to attempt any other course of action which avoids the blatant act of attempting to profit off of the tenants. Probably not coincidentally, as Robert's politics are revealed to be pastoral and compassionate, he becomes a character offered for ridicule.

Yet, the series undeniably romanticizes Robert's conservatism. His concern for his tenants, the village, his employees, and his strict idealized adherence to his obligation of nobility is unquestionably historically suspect. Accuracy is unimportant here. So much of how we come to understand our history is derived from mediated forms, which frequently take creative license. Moreover, our task is not to interpret *Downton Abbey* as a piece of history but as a work of television imbued with myriad philosophical issues.

Tom's quick transformation reveals socialism as a fad for those without means. It was untenable for Tom to remain a socialist once he was granted a position of power. He became a new man with a new identity, shedding the socialist chauffeur Branson. Matthew's capitalist interests are eventually accepted as inevitable if the family wishes to maintain Downton as a source of employment. In this, capitalism is treated as a means for approaching the future while maintaining the past. It is also frequently characterized as cruel for prioritizing profit over people. Finally, Robert's conservatism proves to have the most in common with socialist ideals. By treating ownership as a duty not a privilege, Robert's obligation to his estate cannot be severed from the utopian ideals of our responsibility to both the land and one another. Certainly, the series romanticizes the past but it does not romanticize the vanishing of one's ideals.

3
Matthew's Dark Side

JAMES WILLS

The truth is that lots of people on this planet would love to be rich; and stinking rich if at all possible. From the moment we are old enough to understand, and whether we like it not, money is ultimately what drives us. But can having too much money actually have a negative effect on us as individuals, causing us to lose sight of our previous selves?

At first glance, the rich man's world is blissful when it comes to *Downton Abbey*. The rich love being rich, and the poor seem content (and ultimately grateful) to be working for their masters. On top of all that, it's where two good-looking, young people fall in love, and it's where, on Christmas Day, those two people get engaged. You cannot get more blissful than that. But what if I were to tell you that Matthew Crawley didn't really love Lady Mary? Even worse than that: what if I were to tell you one of Downton's most loved and decent characters was in fact corrupted and manipulated by all the riches that appear to fall from the heavens into his lap?

Ludicrous, right? I don't think so. One of the central plots of *Downton Abbey*'s first two seasons—those that see Mary and Matthew meet, fall in love, and get engaged—is so much more than that of an archetypal Period Drama. This is because Julian Fellowes is using the character of Matthew Crawley to suggest altogether darker ideas than usually seen in the straightforward "Will they–won't they" love story, and that darkness is because the backdrop to this courtship is money, and lots of it.

Matthew is introduced in the first season as a principled middle-class lawyer, but quickly seems to embrace the dreamy lifestyle of the aristocracy, taking on many rituals that he himself deemed "foreign." He appears, towards the end of that first season, to fall for the eldest daughter of the man he is set to inherit his unlikely fortune from, but, simply put, is he just greedy? And does this greed actually erode his once strong and individual values?

The Philosophy of (Having Too Much) Money

I'm not the only one who thinks that money has the ability to corrupt individuals. German thinker Georg Simmel (1858–1918) thinks so too in *The Philosophy of Money*. Here's the basic idea: Simmel argues that, if money increases in a person's life, their individuality will equally decrease. So if someone becomes rich, they effectively lose sight of who they are; their urge to make more money squashes the personal or emotional ties they might once have had.

With this in mind, let's look more closely at *Downton Abbey*'s Matthew Crawley, the middle-class lawyer and son of a middle-class doctor who discovers at the end of the very first episode that he has become the unlikely heir to the Crawley family fortune. He certainly appears very much the individual when arriving in Downton in the second episode of that first season, and like anyone who is principled and without huge sums of money, Matthew immediately claims he won't let it "change" him. So within seconds (of screen time), Matthew shows he is clearly not a man for turning; he is an individual in control of his own feelings.

This self-awareness continues as Matthew knows full well that Lord Grantham will want to "limit the damage by turning [him] into one of his own kind" (1:2), a view which initially makes him both hostile towards the idea of (unnecessary) servants, as well as rendering him incapable of allowing a submission to this new way of living. In an awkward early scene with Molesley, Matthew claims he'll "never get used to being dressed up like a doll" (1:2). The audience likes him for this, even if it is difficult to watch Molesley's livelihood being crushed, because Matthew is refusing to budge; he is behaving like a true individual, and that should be admired.

Set against these strong beliefs throughout the second episode of that first season however, are Matthew's initial forays into the rich man's world. The first dinner he attends is highly entertaining to watch, primarily because this new character's ideology is so clearly grounded and real when played against the (almost) comic and naïve members of the aristocracy:

> **Matthew**: I've got a job in Ripon. I've said I'll start tomorrow.
>
> **Lord Grantham**: A job?! You do know I mean to involve you in the running of the estate.
>
> **Matthew**: Oh, don't worry. There are plenty of hours in the day. And, of course, I'll have the weekend.
>
> **Dowager Countess**: What is a weekend?

The lines from both Lord Grantham and the Dowager Countess are comical to us as an audience because their sentiments are equally naïve: they aren't individuals; they have lived in that dreamy rich man's world all their lives. At this point then, we are firmly on Matthew's side: we are him and he is us; they are rich and we are not. His eyes are the ones through which we view this world of wealth, and if these opening exchanges are anything to go on, Matthew doesn't seem to see Downton Abbey as all that pleasant.

Later in the second episode of the first season though, we see the first indications that Matthew will have to change in order to fit in with the world he now finds himself. When he attempts to dispose of Molesley's services, Lord Grantham quickly rebukes the request:

> Is that quite fair? To deprive a man of his livelihood when he's done nothing wrong. . . . And when you are master here, is the butler to be dismissed, or the footman? How many maids and kitchen staff will be allowed to stay? Or must everyone be driven out? We all have different parts to play Matthew, and we must all be allowed to play them.

It is not long before, like the puppet he will soon become, Matthew is allowing himself to be dressed by his new valet. Already then, money is changing Matthew; suddenly, his individual need to be his own man and dress himself is taking second place to Downton's economic structure. The philosophy of money (according to Simmel at least) is ensuring that Matthew quickly learns how to "play" his part, and that is obviously the part of a rich man.

And so, as the first season progresses, Matthew continues down this inevitable path. In the fourth episode, he seems reluctant to examine the entail when the Dowager Countess visits him at his law firm. In response to this request, Matthew speaks in all the right ways and with an appropriately emotional register; "I don't wish to benefit . . . from an ignorance of the law" (1:4). However, it is not in his words, but his face that Matthew's true feelings are revealed. His sullen and almost frightened look at the prospect of examining the entail on the Dowager Countess's behalf tells you that he'd rather keep the ignorant law exactly that. It is no real surprise that when Matthew tells Lord Grantham later in the episode that he "cannot find one reason on which to base a challenge," it is said with a certain degree of relish. Whether the law backs him or not, Matthew is pleased enough to break the news that there is little that can be done. And because it is the law, everyone seems to believe in both his motives and his words.

Shocking though it may be, it is clear that Matthew has become enchanted by Downton's money; he loves his "new life" as well as the future one he will inherit. His once principled and highly moral character is being corrupted by greed and self-interest before our very eyes.

All You Need Is Love

What am I saying? Surely Matthew becomes accustomed to Downton's world, and ingratiates himself into the Crawley family because he falls madly in love with Lady Mary. It makes for perfect viewing in a period drama: it's what audiences know, what they expect. Across the rest of the first season, Mary and Matthew become increasingly close. It is clear he is very jealous of her flirtations with Mr. Pamuk (1:3) and, in the fifth episode, Mary and Matthew flirt like school-children when Sir Anthony Strallan accidently eats salt on his strawberries rather than sugar. Even though Mary spoils things by trying to "out-do" her sister Edith, causing Matthew to flee the Abbey with his tail between his legs, by the sixth episode, the pair are kissing over sandwiches and wine in the dining room. The romantic tropes are all there: they are both young; they are both attractive; their first kiss takes place at a candlelit dinner (of sorts). As if the audience was expecting it, Matthew then asks Mary to marry him, appearing to solve the romantic and political problems created at the start of the series as neatly as you might expect at the end of a Shakespearean comedy.

But I don't think for one moment that this central romantic plot, designed to ensure the audience will "root evermore" for Matthew, is in fact romantic at all. As the first season reaches its final episodes, Julian Fellowes pits Mary and Matthew's apparently burgeoning romance against the "downstairs" relationship between Anna and Mr. Bates, and the audience can quite clearly see which is meant to be the loving courtship. Without money, Anna and Mr. Bates have nothing but their emotional longing for one another; throughout the first season, their relationship builds through ever more romantic moments, such as when Mr. Bates brings Anna food when she isn't well (1:4) and when Anna declares her love for Mr. Bates on the way to the Downton Flower Show (1:5). Without all the pomp and circumstance; without any of the frills or materialistic desires, theirs is a relationship based solely on love.

When Mary and Matthew's relationship is juxtaposed against the individual, emotional, and romantic relationship between Anna and Mr. Bates then, I find that I don't think Mary and Matthew are actually in love (there: I've said it). Theirs appears as a relationship of convenience, and one ultimately driven by money. In a rich man's world, where marriage is largely an economic transaction (or, in *Downton Abbey's* case, a way of solving the problem of the entail), the kiss between our two romantic heroes is just a little too predictable (1:6). But I think that simply suggesting they are not in love is far too straightforward; it is why Matthew appears to love Mary that has a far darker meaning for audiences.

Money is the main topic of conversation in the first season, and virtually every scene that takes place in the "upstairs" rooms of the Abbey in some way references it (such as early scenes in the fifth episode). For a young man who has spent most of his life as a bachelor, having dinner with his mother and working in a local solicitors' firm, it would certainly be an enchanting and bewitching world to find himself in. Because of this, I believe that Matthew becomes enchanted by Mary, too. But does she just further symbolize Downton's wealth? Would marrying her just make things easier for Matthew's desire for money?

Funnily enough, Lord Grantham tells Cora that Mary can be "such a child sometimes" (1:5), suggesting that she sees men as "toys" to be played with. However, I would argue that it is in fact money which is the toy, and it is the rich who play with it so gleefully in *Downton Abbey*; for example, when Mr. Carson's reputation is at stake because an old friend from his performing days appears at the Abbey, Lord Grantham simply pays twenty pounds to keep him quiet (1:2). There it is: money is a toy; a mere trifle for people of the aristocracy. By the end of the first season, I think that Mary becomes a transaction too; just like Mr. Carson's past being dealt with by means of a bribe, marriage between Mary and Matthew becomes the perfect financial solution to Downton's problem of succession. But there are ultimately no emotions at work, and their love can be measured out as easily as the fortune Matthew is due to inherit can be counted.

Matthew: The "Romantic Hero"

But all this convenience is thrown into turmoil quite brilliantly in the finale of the first season (episode 7), as Cora shockingly falls pregnant, which could disinherit Matthew from the title of heir, should the child be a boy. Manipulated far too easily by Aunt Rosamund, Mary decides to hold off the marriage to Matthew until the child is born, and his initial reaction to this news is fascinating:

> **Matthew:** Shall I tell you what I think has altered you? My prospects. Because nothing else has changed . . . if your mother's child is a boy, then he is the heir and I go back to living on my wits. And you'd rather not follow me.
>
> **Mary:** Oh Matthew, you always make things so black and white.
>
> **Matthew:** I think this is black and white. Do you love me enough to spend your life with me?

Audiences are encouraged to think Matthew is being a perfectly wonderful romantic hero; he is making an individual stand against the aristocratic dependence on money, whilst

Mary has obviously "taken advice from someone with false and greedy values" (1:7). But as I have been asking all along: is it really as simple as all that? Remember that Mary has only ever lived in a rich man's world, whilst Matthew is only just getting used to it. Those "false and greedy values" that Mary is being guided by will in fact only serve to darkly foreshadow Matthew's own decisions as *Downton Abbey* enters its second season.

After Cora loses the baby (which turns out to be a boy, of course), Mary suddenly changes her mind, and that fickleness leads Matthew to reject her desire to marry him now that he is the heir again. In doing so, he also makes perhaps his most important statement ever:

> **Mary**: You can't leave Downton.
>
> **Matthew**: I can't stay . . . the experiment is at an end. I'm not a puppet, and I must take charge of my own life again. (1:7)

Shocking the audience and Mary herself, Matthew decides to leave; to leave behind his "new life" and all that money he is due to inherit. There is a real sense in these words of Matthew possessing his own life again, and of taking control; the way he speaks reminds audiences of the highly individual and principled man whom they first met at the beginning of the series.

Whose "False and Greedy Values"?

With all this in mind then, the next question to ask is why does Matthew return to Downton in the second season? He was so adamant that he wanted to "take charge" of his life and be an individual again. What is more, in the first episode of that second season, the audience discovers that he has proposed to a young middle-class woman by the name of Lavinia Swire. Now this woman clearly loves Matthew, shown when she says that she wouldn't know what to do "if anything happened to him [during the War]" (2:2). Lavinia, although not aristocratic, comes from a decent background and has a house in London; she proves countless times during the second season that she is a caring and thoughtful woman, who will do anything to please her fiancé (such as being willing to leave London and live at Downton for him—episode 1). She appears to be the perfect match for Matthew Crawley and, without exorbitant amounts of money, their love could flourish in similar ways to that of Anna and Mr. Bates.

I know what the audience wants: they want Mary and Matthew to get together, not Lavinia and Matthew; they need it to happen. But Matthew said he wasn't a puppet; at the start of the first season, he said that Downton wouldn't change him. Despite those resolute final words he says to Mary at the garden party (1:7), Matthew comes back to Downton. Despite the fact that Lavinia is a wonderful fiancée (I know she dies of Spanish flu, but Matthew doesn't know that), he returns time and time again throughout the second season, before inevitably asking for Mary's hand in the subsequent Christmas episode. This appears to neatly tie up many of the loose ends in the two-season narrative arc for the "upstairs" characters: it appears to ensure the legitimacy of Downton's estate stays very much in the family (with Mary set to at least have some say in its future); it means Matthew returns to his new home a hero (now a war hero as well as a romantic one); it means that the audience gets what it craves, and their romantic urges are satisfied.

But it's not as simple as that, because I think Julian Fellowes is exploring far more than what an audience *needs* to happen. Yes, Mary and Matthew get engaged. Yes, it's all very romantic. Yes, the family politics appear to be resolved. But (and there are no bigger uses of that word in this chapter), *Downton Abbey* is actually more interested in exploring what makes the middle-class Matthews of this world tick, and whether we like it or not, it really does seem to be money. He comes back for the same reason that we do: because we are addicted to having lots of money; because we are ultimately powerless in its presence; because, just like Georg Simmel suggested when philosophizing about such things, it can corrupt and destroy who we—as individuals—truly are.

Like Simmel before him then, Julian Fellowes is really getting to the core of the negative effect too much money can have on individual and decent people; basically, people like Matthew Crawley. I don't for a moment think that *Downton Abbey* is suggesting that Matthew is a terrible and vile human being for not being able to love Mary (or Lavinia) as much as he loves his money. I actually think that *Downton Abbey* is saying something far darker, because Matthew's character arc in the first two seasons in fact tells us as much about our own philosophy regarding money as it does his own.

Don't forget that, at the beginning of the first season, we are encouraged to side with him: we are him and he is us; we laugh at the comical naivety of the aristocracy because Matthew does. But once he is introduced to the idea of having too much of it, money means everything to Matthew, so he naturally changes his attitude; and so do we, rooting evermore for that perfect marriage of economic bliss as the second season reaches its conclusion. Therefore, money corrupts and manipulates us in just the same way. Firstly, it wants us all to be middle-class Matthews: at our core, frightfully principled and highly moral, but when it comes to it, powerless to wealth's charm and ultimately greedy for wanting too much of it. But money also wants us to believe in Mary and Matthew: not because they are truly in love with each other, but because the economic structure of Downton Abbey would benefit from such a union and become a perfect working institution and oppressor of individuals for countless generations to come.

Wealth and riches may be a seductive and potent force, but Matthew's changing relationship with his inherited fortune in *Downton Abbey*—and Georg Simmel's words before him— should serve as stark warnings; what is most worrying though is that they are ultimately warnings that too many will too easily ignore, such is the corruptive power and manipulative strength that money has over us all.

4

Finding One's Place and Being Useful

JOHN V. KARAVITIS

The first four seasons of *Downton Abbey* follow the events surrounding the Crawleys, an upper-class British family, from 1912 and the sinking of the *Titanic* up to 1923. This was a period of rapidly changing social norms in the Western world, and it included a devastating world war. As we observe the lives of the Crawleys, the members of their household staff, their close acquaintances, and others, it becomes immediately apparent that, in one way or another, the issue of work is foremost on everyone's mind. This can be seen in the attitudes expressed by the characters with regard to the place that work has in their lives. People talk about their work, or their rejection of it, and how it affects their lives, constantly. Despite the fact that the series appears on the surface to be about class distinctions in a rapidly changing world, work is the true central theme of *Downton Abbey*, and not social class. In this respect, we'll see that we're not all that different from these characters.

Obviously, work does not affect people's lives in a vacuum. No one is denying that social class is an issue in the lives of the characters. We can clearly see in *Downton Abbey* that work is tied directly to the issue of social class. In general, the upper class and the working class each view work differently. The upper class has disdain for any form of work, especially the manual labor on which they depend to maintain their lifestyle. The upper class feels that they have no obligation to work, and are unashamed to express their disdain. The rest of society has no choice. The rest of society *must* work, regardless of anyone's personal view of work.

Regardless of social class, the characters in *Downton Abbey* either accept the existing social order and its consequences for one's place and one's obligation to work, or else they challenge and reject them. To reject existing social norms regarding work is to want to change one's place in society. The two social classes, and whether one chooses to accept one's place in society, provide us with a simple two-by-two matrix that we can use to understand the opposing views regarding the idea of having to work to live. This matrix of class membership versus acceptance or rejection of the existing social order will allow us to explore the philosophy of work, and the consequences for accepting or rejecting one's place in society with regard to it. Looking at the opposing views of work in *Downton Abbey* will give us a better understanding and appreciation for work and what it does, can—and perhaps should—mean in our own lives today.

Advances in automation and information technology will without any doubt whatsoever bring forth a world where no one will ever again have to work for a living. Say what you will about what the future will hold—everyone's opinion is as accurate as anyone else's when it comes to predicting the future (my apologies to Nate Silver). But given advances in automation and information technology, there is one compelling prediction regarding what our world will eventually look like: *There will be no jobs in the future—for anyone.* I believe that this prediction about the future of our world is inescapable. And as we've never had a period of time in human history where people haven't had to work to live, we'll also try to leverage our understanding of the philosophy of work to figure out what it could mean to live in such a world.

For those of you who are die-hard *Downton Abbey* fans, and who consider yourselves to be both astute observers of human nature and good with details, I have a small challenge for you. One of the conclusions that we will arrive at regarding what work means to us can be found in the opening credits of each episode. Another conclusion can be found in the final minutes of the final episode of season 4. They are both subtle hints, and many of you might argue that I'm stretching the facts a bit—that I'm forcing an innocent, unintentional detail in the opening credits, and the ending of the final episode of season 4, to fit our conclusions. So be it. But before you continue reading this chapter, at the very least, please go back and take a look at the opening credits of *Downton Abbey* if nothing else. A very close look. *Look closely.*

Gentlemen Don't Work—Not *Real* Gentlemen

Let's start at the top, with the most conservative position. The first cell of our matrix of class membership versus acceptance or rejection of existing social norms has the members of the upper class standing firm and defending the existing social norms. The characters who best represent this position are Violet Crawley, Dowager Countess of Grantham, and her son, Robert Crawley, Earl of Grantham. The Dowager Countess presents the position of her class in no uncertain terms: "We don't work." In discussing Matthew Crawley, a distant heir who will inevitably inherit Downton Abbey, and the fact that he not only works as a lawyer but that he enjoys doing so, we are informed that "Gentlemen don't work—not *real* gentlemen." And in what one might fear was, and perhaps still is, an accurate representation of the attitude of the British upper class, and not just a moment of creative screenwriting, the Dowager Countess even asks with a straight face, "What is a 'weekend'?"

But to say that no one in the upper class works is only to look at extreme examples like those of the Dowager Countess. Indeed, as a *female* member of the upper class, her duties would be limited to marrying appropriately within one's class, having children (preferably male heirs apparent), managing the household by fiat, and maintaining social contacts. As for male members of the upper class, they don't really work—they "manage." They manage their ancestral estates, their families, and their investments. (Although as we saw, the Earl of Grantham mismanaged his family's assets by investing almost exclusively in a Canadian railroad company that eventually went bankrupt. This talent for mismanagement must be hereditary, as it was the Earl's father who created the "entail" that specified that only a *male* heir could inherit the ancestral estate.) The Earl of Grantham informs us of his personal point of view regarding his duties: "I am a custodian, not an owner." Downton Abbey is likened to a company, but we are told that it exists "to protect tradition." There is some small indication, however, that even the Earl of Grantham is aware that the way of life that he has always known may not be working: "Before the war, I felt my life had value. How much more I want from life now than I did then."

Those members of the upper class who see work as being beneath them accept and defend the existing social order. However, the result of this attitude is that nothing of any substance ever gets done. As we saw with the Earl of Grantham, his steadfast adherence to the way things are done, and demanding that everyone know his place in the social order, results in an inability to change when change is required to survive. Avoiding real work and maintaining an insular mindset, especially in a time period when the pace of change in all facets of life is accelerating, can only lead to disaster. It also leads to a numbness to the realities of the world, and eventually, for those who can become aware of it, a sense of dissatisfaction.

But I Just Want to Be *Useful*

Given the inflexible attitude of the vast majority of the British upper class, it is interesting to observe examples of those who go against the existing social order and actively seek out work. This is the second cell of our class membership versus acceptance or rejection of existing social norms matrix. The best examples of this are Isobel Crawley (Matthew Crawley's mother) and all three of the Earl's daughters. (Although Cora Crawley, the Countess of Grantham, does state at one time that she wants to be "useful," this single instance is not enough to include her in this cell of our matrix. She definitely belongs in the first cell.)

For Isobel Crawley, the desire to be "useful" appears to be *the* major theme of her life. (For die-hard fans of *Downton Abbey* who enjoy drinking, one may have a splendid time watching every episode in a marathon session with close friends, with everyone having a drink every time she states that she wants to be "useful." Congratulate yourself if you manage to reach the end of season 4 in a non-comatose state.) Her position is understandable, though. Taking a step back, one would see that with her only child, Matthew, now an adult and working as a lawyer, and without an estate of her own to manage, she really has very little to do. Her desire to be of use is understandable *to us*. But not to her peers in the upper class. To be useful also implies that one "fits in," whereas her efforts frequently have her at odds with her peers, most notably with the Dowager Countess. Her desire to be useful is so intense that she applies it to situations for which she has no real responsibility. In a discussion with Cora Crawley, the Countess of Grantham, and the Dowager Countess, about the eventual end of Downton Abbey as a hospital for wounded soldiers, Isobel Crawley rejects the idea of returning the estate to its former status as private property. She asks "Wouldn't you rather Downton was useful?" The third season finds Isobel volunteering at a center in York to help prostitutes. (Although when she nurses the Dowager Countess back to health in season 4, I'm sure that her time and efforts are appreciated.) Paradoxically, we find Isobel Crawley all over the place, as she goes from one personal project to the next. But to her credit, she does do a lot of good for a lot of people as she pursues her personal projects.

The Earl's daughters also provide examples of the desire to find meaning in one's life through work. They reject the existing social norms and yearn to find some form of work that will occupy and satisfy them.

Lady Sybil "wants to do something," and ends up taking a job as a nurse: "I feel useful for the first time in my life, and that must be a good thing." Her future husband, former Irish chauffeur Tom Branson, observes, "So you wouldn't go back—to your life before the war?" She replies "No. No. I can never go back to that again."

Lady Edith stands firm in her desire to find work. At a family dinner, she offers to drive a tractor to help John Drake, a local farmer. Upon hearing this, the Dowager Countess exclaims "Edith! You are a lady!" Lady Edith retorts, "Well, I'm doing it!" Lady Edith also helps to care for wounded soldiers, and eventually finds herself writing articles for a newspaper.

After Lavinia Swire falls ill with Spanish flu, Dr. Clarkson is called. He counsels that she only needs some nursing for a day or two. The Earl notes, "Oh, don't worry about that. All our daughters are professionals." At this point, even the Earl knows that his daughters have minds of their own regarding work.

Lady Mary, the most aloof of the Earl's three daughters, eventually ends up taking a more active role in managing the estate. She completes her move from the first cell of our matrix to this cell after the death of her husband Matthew. To her credit, the Dowager Countess, seeing how despondent Lady Mary is over Matthew's death, suggests to her that she has to "choose death or life." In an uncharacteristic move, the Dowager Countess wants Lady Mary to have an active role in running Downton Abbey. In a later episode, we even see Lady Mary roll up her sleeves and prepare breakfast in an abandoned farmhouse!

Those members of the upper class who reject existing social norms regarding work do so because they see work as providing meaning to their lives. It is interesting that all of these examples are of women. However, this may simply be a nod by the screenwriters to the fact that women's rights were expanding during this time period. Nevertheless, in this cell of our matrix, work is seen not only positively, but as a necessary part of life. Work, mostly in the form of personal projects, gives the Crawley women recognition, personal satisfaction, meaning, and direction to their lives. Rejecting the existing social norms *works* for these women.

There's No Shame in Hard Work

The third cell of our class membership versus acceptance or rejection of existing social norms matrix has members of the working class accepting the existing social order. The best example of this is habitually unemployed butler Joseph Molesley, but we'll also take a quick look at Anna May Bates (née Smith).

Molesley is clearly the most pathetic character in the series. Getting on in years, with no family or friends, and socially inept, he has one misfortune after another in terms of finding and keeping work. And given his lack of social and monetary resources, he needs work desperately. It's not that Molesley isn't grateful. Far from it. "I'm glad of my job, m'lady," he says. Eventually out of the Crawley households, he ends up doing manual labor, and then working as a delivery boy. But Molesley believes in the system, and sticks with it, through thick and thin. For him, "There's no shame in hard work." Mr. Carson eventually offers Molesley a job as a footman, which Molesley initially rejects. He considers being a footman "a permanent inferior place." But he eventually reconsiders, rationalizing to himself about "the power to do good that all employment brings without loss of dignity." Desperate for work, Molesley finally convinces Mr. Carson to re-extend his prior offer and hire him at Downton Abbey as a footman. More than anything, Molesley needs to work.

The most poignant and compelling example of how much the working class identifies with its work is the sexual assault of Anna Bates. Shortly after having been attacked, Anna re-dresses herself and steps out into the hallway. There she bumps into her husband, John Bates. While in the middle of a conversation with him, suddenly, at the far end of the hallway, her attacker, Mr. Green, Anthony Gillingham's valet, appears. She responds to his cavalier verbal greeting automatically, as if nothing had happened between them. Anna Bates is so ingrained in the mechanics of her job that even at that moment she responds to her attacker's greeting in the way that she has been trained: directly, and with courtesy. Work changes people in subtle ways, without their being consciously aware of it. The ways we are taught to behave at work affect our attitudes, behaviors, and cognition outside of the workplace. We may vehemently refuse to admit it, but it's true: we *become* our work. We *are* our work.

In the third cell of our matrix, the working class is found to be ironically in the same position as the upper class is in the first cell. With "our kind of people" one has to know "one's place." Indeed, we must never forget that "We're servants, you and me." The members of the working class who accept the existing social norms are destined to live rigid and unchanging lives, just as those of the upper class do.

I Can Do Better than "My Place"

The fourth and final cell of our class membership versus accep-tance or rejection of existing social norms matrix consists of members of the working class who reject the existing social order.

In the first season we see Gwen Dawson, a housemaid, who has purchased a typewriter that she tries to keep hidden from her co-workers. She wants to work in an office, and to do so she has to learn how to type. Upon discovering this, her co-workers are offended that she would want to "leave service." However, she perseveres; and with Lady Sybil's help, she succeeds.

Tom Branson is the Irish chauffeur who marries Lady Sybil. He eventually returns to Ireland to be a journalist, saying, "I have to go where I am useful." Later he becomes the estate manager of Downton Abbey.

Kitchen maid Daisy Mason (née Robinson) has her sights on becoming an assistant cook. Beryl Patmore, Downton Abbey's cook, notes that "Daisy is the future, and we are stuck in the past."

Alfred Nugent, Mrs. O'Brien's nephew, was a waiter before coming to Downton Abbey as a footman. He wants to train to be a chef at the Ritz. He deeply desires to advance and improve his position beyond just being a footman at Downton Abbey. "I can do better than 'my place,'" he says. And so he enters the training program at the Ritz, and eventually gets a job there.

The reality for people living in Britain at this time was that those without social status or wealth were forced to work as servants or in manual labor. Young women in particular were encouraged to find a "table" (in other words, a wealthy household) they could "put their feet under." Their only other real option was to work in a factory. Opportunities to break out of the social class of one's birth sometimes arose, but doing so required gumption and effort on the part of the individual. We see this happening in *Downton Abbey*, and the result is that those members of the working class that reject the existing social order have more fulfilling lives.

It's Doing Nothing That's the Enemy

So let's see what we've discovered by applying our two-by-two matrix to the characters of *Downton Abbey*:

UPPER CLASS/ACCEPTS SOCIAL ORDER

"Work" keeps one busy, and although important, the type of work is based on the demands of one's social class. Life is stagnant. In a sense, members are trapped. [Lord Grantham, the Dowager Countess]

UPPER CLASS/REJECTS SOCIAL ORDER

Personal projects lead to a sense of purpose and fulfillment, greater satisfaction with life, personal growth, and recognition. Efforts positively affect other people. [Isobel Crawley, Lady Mary (eventually), Lady Sybil, Lady Edith]

WORKING CLASS/ACCEPTS SOCIAL ORDER
"Work" keeps one busy, and although important, the type of work is based on the demands of one's social class. Life is stagnant. In a sense, members are trapped. [Mr. Molesley, Anna Bates]

WORKING CLASS/REJECTS SOCIAL ORDER
Choice of a new career path provides opportunities for personal growth and social advancement, recognition, a more active engagement with the world, and a sense of direction in life. [Tom Branson, Gwen, Daisy, Alfred]

I think that the results speak for themselves. Rejecting the existing social order and forging one's own path in life, although fraught with danger and the possibility of failure, nevertheless provide opportunities for a richer, more satisfying life. One's social class doesn't matter. It's working at what one finds enjoyable and personally fulfilling that does. "It's doing nothing that's the enemy."

By the way, now would be a good time to ask: Have you figured out the first of my two claims regarding the conclusions that we would reach? At the beginning of this chapter, I claimed that the opening credits held a clue that would reflect one of the conclusions that we would reach regarding the meaning of work in our lives. The more astute observers would have latched onto the fact that, while reading the opening credits, *the surnames of the actors are all in alphabetical order— regardless of the social class of the character each actor plays.* Although in itself not unusual, if one were to look at the actors as they are listed in the Internet Movie Database, one would see that the actors playing the "more important" characters are listed first, followed by those actors whose characters either have less screen time in terms of number of episodes, or length of time on-screen. But we've seen that with regard to work and the effect it has on the lives of the characters of *Downton Abbey*, family name and social class don't matter. Working at something that one finds fulfilling does. Just as with the actors in this series. They act because it's what they want to do with their lives. It's what they find fulfilling, or they wouldn't be doing it. And so it makes sense to list them in the opening credits in alphabetical order by surname, and not by how "important" their characters are.

Within the social fabric that we find ourselves in, we're all affected in the same way by life and our attitudes toward work. We're really all cut from the same cloth.

Is It "Work" If You Are Enjoying Yourself?

We've scoured the first four seasons of *Downton Abbey* in order to discover the underlying philosophy of work that's presented. What we've found is that there are two types of work. The first is work that one must do because of one's circumstances. It's the kind of work that comes to mind when most people speak of having to work. But the second type of work is one where people decide what new career paths or personal projects they want to pursue. And we've seen that what we get out of work—whether it's drudgery or pleasure—does not depend on one's social class.

Philosophers have been of two minds regarding work—one negative, the other positive. And each view of work parallels what we found in our two-by-two matrix. Jean-Jacques Rousseau (1712–1778) believed that it was the need for work that led to our downfall. The invention of agriculture led to a division of labor, which in turn exacerbated the natural inequalities that are found among any group of people. This in turn led to private property and class differences. (Sound familiar?) Ironically, the steps that people took to improve their lives and safeguard themselves against starvation led to social stratification and inequality. So it seems as though we escaped one hardship—the threat of starvation—but ended up creating another in its place—social inequality.

Adam Smith (1723–1790) believed that the economic wealth of a nation was the result of individuals blindly pursuing their own self-interests, and that a division of labor was necessary in order to maximize the efficiency of labor. His example of how a pin is manufactured, with each person working at only one of the sequence of steps that go into making a pin, supports the factory model of the Industrial Revolution. One person performs the same task all day long in order to lead to the overall efficient production of goods. But the repetitive nature of this type of work has a negative effect on one's happiness and satisfaction in life. (Sound familiar?)

Karl Marx (1818–1883) believed many things that a lot of people now disagree with. However, he did have some insights that can help us understand the meaning of work. Marx believed that the factors of production, that is, the tools and machines that are available to produce goods and services, affect how society operates. That is, technological advances spur economic development, which in turn has a social impact, and thus an effect on people. Marx also felt that the wage earner was always taken advantage of, in that, for the owners of capital to make a profit, the wage earner could not, and would not, be paid fairly based on what he had produced with his own hands. This idea comes under what was known as the "labor theory of value," which stated that a good or service is worth the physical labor that went into it. This idea has since been discredited, since we know that a good or service is worth what someone is willing to pay for it in the free market, and not what it cost to make. But the idea that workers are never paid fairly for their work remains with us today. Finally, Marx felt that society operated under an ideology, which represents the unspoken rules of the social order. (Sound familiar?)

So some philosophers have seen work as at best a necessary evil to at worst one that we need to reform to make life more equitable. The definition of work here has one performing activities that one does not find fulfilling or enjoyable. Work has utility in that it allows us to survive, even if it comes with unpalatable side effects for our quality of life and potential for happiness.

The other view of work has philosophers who embrace work because they see it as a stepping stone to a more fulfilling life. In the *Nicomachean Ethics*, Aristotle (384–322 BCE) saw a life of happiness as needing not only friends, but also the opportunity to pursue activities chosen for their own sake. Work exists in order that we may have the opportunity for what Aristotle referred to as the "pleasures of play." This "play" refers to pursuing personal projects—what we would refer to as "leisure time."

In his essay "In Praise of Idleness," Bertrand Russell (1872–1970) supported the need for what he called "idleness" because he felt that "immense harm is caused by the belief that work is virtuous." Russell felt that we would all be happier if there were less work, and that the notions that people had about work were derived from people's experiences in the pre-industrial world. The modern world, with access to "modern technique," makes it possible to reduce the labor required for society to produce the necessities of life and thus insure everyone's survival. The modern world could now make leisure available to everyone. It made no sense to hold onto ideas that were expressed when most men lacked freedom, and the product of their labor could be claimed by a small number of warriors, priests, or rulers: "The morality of work is the morality of slaves, and the modern world has no need of slavery." Russell notes that, in nineteenth-century England, proposals that the fifteen-hour workday be reduced were met with resistance. A long workday "kept adults from drink and children from mischief." (One wonders what a full "weekend" would have led to!)

Contemporary philosopher Josef Pieper, in writing about what philosophy is, acknowledges that we work to survive, but then asks, what is it that we survive for? For him, as it was for Aristotle, the answer is leisure. Leisure is the basis of culture, and it transcends the utilitarian nature of work. For Pieper, leisure allows us to pursue activities like poetry, prayer, love, and to be able to appreciate the fine arts.

Looking closely at those examples in *Downton Abbey* where individuals pursue personal projects that do not simply satisfy the utilitarian aspect of work, like Isobel Crawley, we find that people lose themselves in what they are doing. American psychologist Mihaly Csikszentmihalyi has noted that people who are focused intently on the activity at hand, where time loses any meaning, are in what he terms a state of "flow." Contemporary philosopher Loren Lomasky, writing in *Persons, Rights, and the Moral Community*, notes that people by nature want to pursue personal projects. By doing so, Lomasky claims that we enter into a virtuous circle of morality. By pursuing my own personal projects, I claim that what I do and, by extension, who I am both have value. But if I have value because I freely pursue my own personal projects, then so do others.

We Can Afford to Live a Little

Work has a central place in people's lives. We work to survive, but, if we're lucky, we can take more from our work than mere survival. We've seen in *Downton Abbey*, as we've surely seen in our own lives and the lives of others, that work can provide one with status, purpose, direction, recognition, and fulfillment. Work provides us with many of our close acquaintances, if not outright friends. People meet their life partners at or through work. At best, our work can afford us time for leisure. Leisure allows us to pursue personal projects, and to work at personal activities that transcend mere survival. We are more than just animals trying to survive. As Pieper noted, we lay claim to poetry, prayer, love, the fine arts—and even that activity that most represents leisure: philosophy. For Pieper, philosophy is the most leisurely of activities.

But work does a lot more for us. *With work, we find ourselves needing each other.* As Adam Smith noted in his famous example of manufacturing pins, by breaking a work process down into separate steps, we can produce, and thus achieve, more as a group—working together—than we ever could working alone. *Work maintains the social fabric. Our world is defined by the fact that most people have to get up in the morning and go to work.*

We will face a quite different problem in our future—the *end* of work. Advances in automation and information technology mean that the end of work in the future is inescapable. When we no longer need to work, what will our world look like? What will we do with all of our free time? Will we even need each other anymore?

It's now that I want to address the second conclusion about work that I referred to at the beginning of this chapter. Did you have a chance to review the ending of the last episode of season 4? It's the scene where the household staff of Downton Abbey are given a day at the beach. They are conversing, playing with each other, or just relaxing and enjoying the day. But we know that this will only be for that day. And it can't be for any longer. To have been able to afford that day of leisure, they had to work. And their leisure will only be pleasurable until boredom sets in. As much as the household staff, or we, complain about our work, and our desire to have unlimited time to play, without being involved in an activity where we can make a difference, whether it's in work or leisure, we'll all end up alone and in a state of boredom. And few things could be worse.

Minding Manners
and Making Do

5
The Morality of Manners

Kathleen Poorman Dougherty

The sense of decorum and dignity that *Downton Abbey* conveys is part of its immediate appeal, harkening back to an earlier age where manners and etiquette reigned, and life, at least for the privileged, was beautiful and genteel. Decorum at Downton, however, is not reserved for the Grantham family; even the servants at Downton, or at least the most appealing of them, show a significant sense of propriety and respectfulness of demeanor that many feel is missing in modern life. In a society where people shop in sweatpants and running shoes, and family dinners take place in front of the television, an image of dressing for dinner every evening and welcoming callers with tea has a certain appeal. The measuring of the table settings in the opening montage is surely set in the minds of most viewers as a testament to the fact that everything at Downton is done precisely as it ought to be. We admire Carson's maintaining everything to the utmost standards, something that appears dignified and refined, even if a bit stuffy.

The manners displayed in *Downton* are much more than just a representation of an elaborate system of etiquette or the civility of a bygone era—they are taken as an indicator of character and moral dignity. The moral status of the most sympathetic characters, such as Lord and Lady Grantham and Anna Bates, is represented by their impeccable manners. This connection between manners and morality carries through in the myriad instances throughout *Downton Abbey* where the traditional manners and customs of the Crawley family are challenged by those perceived as outsiders. The outsiders initially seem coarse, presumptuous, and ill-mannered in their dealings with the Crawley family. In many cases, those who challenge tradition come from a different class or have a different social status. Numerous examples are readily at hand, but perhaps the most obvious are Matthew Crawley, Isobel Crawley, Tom Branson, Sir Richard, and a bevy of household servants. These characters may be morally justified in challenging the preferred customs of Downton, and the aristocracy more generally, but they still come across as ill-mannered for doing so. Notably, as characters gain more respect for the Crawley family, they tend also to comply with the manners deemed appropriate in the household.

Through these many characters, *Downton* suggests that manners are not incidental to morality; on the contrary, manners are a central means through which we demonstrate moral character. Manners are employed to demonstrate respect for another; likewise, feeling respect motivates the desire to behave in a mannerly way. However, manners should not be thought of as a sure-fire marker of virtue: used in a disingenuous way, "manners" can illustrate a lack of respect. Manners, then, can demonstrate something distinctly positive about a person's character, but can also serve as a mask for lack of virtue.

Matthew's Mistakes

The first Downton "victim" who temporarily falls prey to a lapse of manners is Matthew Crawley. We are introduced to Matthew in the opening scenes of season 1, episode 2, as he arrives at his home, where he is promptly greeted by his new butler, Mr. Molesley. Matthew has already been expressing to his mother his displeasure at their new circumstances, and clearly has no idea how to handle Molesley. Matthew—a man used to doing things for himself—is well aware that he will be a disappointment to his butler, and wants to make it known that he will do things his own way. Mrs. Crawley recognizes the challenges facing them, saying, "What they expect, Matthew, is that we won't know how to behave. So, if you don't mind, I would rather not confirm their expectations."

Throughout the entirety of the episode, Matthew blunders over and over again. Matthew's desire to live a simpler lifestyle is admirable, yet he surely is unaware of how his beliefs and commitments appear to others. Even the servants are unhappy about his arrival, stating openly that he is not a suitable heir, and noting that he is not a proper gentleman. The Matthew we learn to know and love would be mortified to know what offense he has created with his habits. Matthew's sense that he doesn't need Molesley leaves Molesley feeling useless and invaluable; Matthew's greatest and most profound error is telling Molesley that being a valet seems "a very silly occupation for a grown man."

However, Matthew is a quick study. Upon explaining to Lord Grantham that he finds Molesley superfluous, Matthew obviously takes in very carefully Lord Grantham's explanation that it would be unfair to deny Molesley his livelihood when he has done nothing wrong. Perhaps Matthew is moved by the comparison to his own mother's satisfaction from her work or by the recognition that everyone has a part to play. Regardless of what motivates him, Matthew's demeanor towards Molesley and the other staff shifts readily and noticeably, as he allows Molesley to take a much greater role in his dressing and shows a new respect for Molesley's role.

In showing greater respect for the role of the servants, most notably Molesley, Matthew Crawley shows more respect for the individuals themselves. In learning to see Molesley as needing to feel that his career and position are valuable, Matthew learns to see Molesley's need for life satisfaction in the same way he sees his own or his mother's need to work and to feel useful. Matthew quickly learns that he underestimated the significance of the ways in which servants are perceived and the pride they take in their work. It is a marker of Matthew's decency and good character that this recognition quickly carries over into a change in behavior. His manners and demeanor shift along with his understanding. Decorum becomes the outward sign of respect.

Branson Becomes One of the Family

Tom Branson's shift is surely slower, but perhaps more significant. We first meet Branson in episode 4 of the first season when he arrives at Downton as the new chauffeur. His forwardness is readily apparent when he begins a conversation with Lady Sybil in the car, and unsolicited, shares with her some political pamphlets he expects she will enjoy. His admiration of Lady Sybil is immediately evident, and he brazenly seeks her attention and her favor, knowing that doing so could cost him his job should she reject him. Though she is somewhat slow to warm to him, Sybil's rebellious and free-spirited nature are compatible with Branson's political ideals and Sybil eventually agrees to marry him, much to the dismay of the Crawleys. Upon the announcement of their engagement, even the servants find it inappropriate. Mr. Carson admonishes Branson for being so brazen, "Have you no shame?" Branson's seeming lack of respect for the Crawley family more generally does not prevent him from seeing Sybil for who she is and loving her deeply. In getting married, both Branson and Sybil have broken the rules, both of etiquette and class.

Though Branson truly loves Sybil, it's difficult for him to find his place in the Crawley family. This is most apparent at Mary and Matthew's wedding when he resists dressing according to custom, continuing to wear his tweed suit even for white tie dinners. His challenge is made even more difficult by a cruel joke played by a houseguest that leaves Branson appearing drunk and belligerent. Prior to Branson and Sybil's arrival the Dowager Countess insists that prurient interest in Branson would subside if he could learn to behave "normally." Presumably by "normally" she means as a traditional member of an aristocratic family, which is altogether contrary to Branson's political views and his views regarding the aristocracy. Branson is insistent in his refusal to comply saying, "I cannot change into someone else just to please you." He even remarks to the Dowager Countess and Mrs. Crawley that he finds the formal "costumes" that the family wears to be "uniforms of oppression." Both Sybil and Matthew point out to Branson, in different moments, that he isn't making it very easy for anyone. Branson certainly feels patronized, but perhaps what he does not notice is that he is failing to show the same kind of respect for the Crawleys that he wishes them to show him. Good manners would seem to require that he comply with tradition, but morality might too.

Certainly it is not always wrong to offend, for there are instances in which offending someone else's sense of propriety is exactly what morality demands. When genuine wrong has occurred or someone's honor has been challenged, propriety can easily be dispensed with, especially if there is no way to right the wrong or stand up to injustice without impropriety. But Branson is not in this situation. Branson is in a situation of his own choosing. It is impolite, disrespectful, and thus wrong, even if not grievously wrong, for Branson to make a scene of his politics when it is unnecessary. He's demonstrating a lack of respect for the Crawleys by insisting on flaunting their customs when he has chosen to be present at their table. Imagine if Branson had truly refused to wear a morning coat to Mary and Matthew's wedding: Branson would have made his own politics the center of attention rather than the happy couple.

Branson's position regarding the Crawley family changes considerably after the family protects him from prosecution for participating in the burning of an aristocratic home in Ireland. It seems to be only when he sees the Irish family fleeing their home that he makes the connection between his political convictions and the actual people that might be impacted by them. Though the relationship between the family and Branson had thawed considerably leading up to Matthew and Mary's wedding, Sybil's death is a real turning point. As the family welcomes him more and more, Branson's respect and fondness for them grow. Moreover, as Branson begins to feel greater and greater respect for the family, his willingness to accede to their manners increases as well. He reprimands his own brother for failing to show sufficient respect for the family, and by season 4 we find Branson concerned that the Dowager Countess is coming for dinner and he is in merely a tuxedo. Moreover, the rather forward and nosy approach from Sarah Bunting makes him especially uncomfortable. No doubt he sees his own earlier behavior in her, and is thus sympathetic to her at the same time that he recognizes the moral error. Nothing in all this is to suggest that Branson's political convictions are wrong, even if his aims in raising them at the dinner table are less than courteous.

Looking Virtuous

Both Matthew Crawley and Tom Branson confirm the philosophical claim that manners are morally significant, more specifically, that respect for others is demonstrated and manifested through mannerly behavior. Both Matthew and Branson behave in ways more akin to the family's manners as they gain more respect for the family and their servants. Branson may not have changed his views regarding the aristocracy more generally, but he has gained respect for the individuals with whom he lives and works. Respecting the Crawleys as individuals and for the distinct human beings that they are is consistent with still objecting to aristocracy more generally. He may not want harm to come to the Crawley family even if he doesn't think aristocracy is a sustainable political system. The respect he has gained for them is even more substantial than the respect he might show to all people more generally; it is rooted in knowledge of them in all their particularity. As Branson tells Sarah Bunting in season 4, episode 8 when she dismisses the Crawleys' type, "I don't believe in types, I believe in people."

Philosopher Nancy Sherman describes manners as providing the "look and feel of virtue" or the "aesthetic of character." Sherman argues that manners are more than just inconsequential adornments, and that manners can make up part of the substance of virtue. Sherman makes her case in the context of the virtue of kindness, but her ideals can extend beyond this. Many of the manners that we see Matthew and Branson eventually express are more importantly ways of showing kindness and respect. The point in thinking of manners as having a significant place in morality is not to show concern for trivial class distinctions or social conventions, but to demonstrate the ways in which courtesy and kindness for another person show themselves through our behavior, and our manners more specifically.

Extraordinary Virtue

Sherman's claim that manners are the "aesthetic of character" also helps to explain what makes certain characters in *Downton* appealing: part of what makes us like Lady and Lord Grantham is not just their manners, but that their manners reflect a genuine sense of respect and decency for those around them. Though they are part of an aristocratic class, they are genuinely interested in the well-being of their guests, their staff, and those whom their estate must serve.

An emphasis on the appearance of moral virtue goes back at least as far as the Ancient philosopher Aristotle (384–322 BCE). Aristotle's theory of virtue was presented to aristocratic young men in Athens expecting to become statesmen. The virtues Aristotle espoused were those most necessary for one who was going to take an aristocratic role in society: generosity, courage, good temper, and temperance, just to name a few. Though Aristotle never talks about manners directly, he is very clear that the morally good person would appear in particular sorts of ways. Not a lot of focus is given to Aristotle's notion of the person of extraordinary virtue, but it is an early description of how the ideal statesman might appear and gives us the sense that good character should also carry with it a certain aesthetic. Without that aesthetic, it's a little hard to imagine how a person's virtue is to be received. Moral virtue needs with it the trappings of the aesthetic; a good person who cannot function socially to make that virtue appealing lacks effectiveness in action.

A Complicated Case

Matthew's mother, Mrs. Crawley, is an altogether contrary study in manners and respect. Mrs. Crawley often finds herself violating the manners and decorum of the Crawley household because she has so much respect for *everyone*. She quietly cheers Branson's democratic values and encourages his individualism. Though she does not necessarily endorse his socialist politics, she carries on her own version of democratizing Downton. This makes her often a bit tedious and a thorn in the Dowager Countess's side, but good and decent nonetheless. Mrs. Crawley's methods of flaunting Downton's formal manners are somewhat more restrained and focused on the welfare of others rather than on her own political views. Her weaknesses in decorum are usually the result of trying to help someone. For example, she allows Ethel, the fallen maid, to work in her home, causing a stir. Similarly, she pressures the family to abandon their aristocratic ways and open up Downton for use as a convalescent home for wounded soldiers during the war.

All these ways of caring for others challenge traditional manners, and they even make Mrs. Crawley something of a handful, but it is hard to see her as anything but a good and decent person. Mrs. Crawley shows so much respect for everyone, that she often pushes the limits of conventional manners; however, she always wants the best for everyone concerned. In many ways, she prompts people to a more moral position. In a moment of rare honesty in season 4, episode 4, even the Dowager Countess must admit, albeit begrudgingly, that Mrs. Crawley is a good woman, saying, "there are moments when her virtue demands admiration."

A Study in Boorishness

Sir Richard Carlisle provides a significant contrast to Matthew, Branson, and Mrs. Crawley. Sir Richard's lack of manners demonstrates an utter and complete lack of respect for the Crawleys, their values, and their ways. In all the time he spends with the Crawley family, he never acquires respect for them or the accompanying manners. When Sir Richard complains that the family is not served at Christmas lunch or on New Year's Eve, he claims that the reason the family finds this acceptable is that they haven't had to fight for what they have. Mary points out rightly that such comments make him sound "angry." In his approach to the Crawley family, he shows a consistent lack of respect for their ways; he shows the same kind of disdain that Branson showed in his early days, but from an entirely different perspective. Sir Richard is so focused on the ways in which he has built his own fortune that rather than show respect to anyone else, he looks down his nose at nearly everyone.

Sir Richard's lack of respect readily shows itself in his boorish comments and unkind approach. His failing in both manners and morality is most obvious as he is leaving Downton for the last time, thoroughly insulted to finally be rejected by Lady Mary. He demonstrates not only his disdain for Lord Grantham, but also his disdain for manners themselves, saying: "How smooth you are. What a model of manners and elegance. I wonder if you'll be quite so serene when the papers are full of your eldest daughter's exploits." His lack of respect, even for a woman he intended to marry, makes it impossible for him to be civil. And thus, his lack of civility also betrays a lack of moral character.

Perhaps Sir Richard might have benefitted from some insights from philosopher Sarah Buss. Buss argues that rather than simply demonstrating respect for others, manners are a constant reminder that someone is worthy of respect. Reminding ourselves consistently to show good manners can reinforce our recognition of the respect others deserve. As manners are often more binding and constantly present than morality they can support our moral outlook and behavior, even when we are not thinking morally. According to Buss, appearing respectful is morally significant because it provides myriad and constant little reminders about the moral status of others. Focusing on good manners ought to help bring about respect for others. Thinking about how we ought to treat others with civility should eventually prompt us to see others as deserving of civility. Perhaps if Sir Richard had made good manners a priority, good character might have followed.

Manners as a Cover

None of this is to suggest that formally good manners always indicate good character, for manners might be used for ill or to hide a lack of respect. Surely it is possible to be socially savvy or to have cultivated good manners without the accompanying good character. We can see this in the Dowager Countess's thinly-veiled barbs that keep us laughing through most of the show. The Dowager Countess's manners seem not so much to indicate good character, but rather merely the pretense of it. She is frequently interested in appearances simply for the sake of appearances, noting that the family must not be a matter of discussion in town. Often, we think that she is concerned more with how things look than with what is right. It is partly her caustic comments, delivered ever so politely, that make us love her. Shortly after Sybil's death, the Dowager Countess reminds Lord Grantham that people in their position are not unhappily married. Though she goes to great effort to repair the relationship between Lord and Lady Grantham, we remain unconvinced that it is really their happiness that matters to her.

Consider, similarly, scenes in which the Dowager Countess is concerned to minimize gossip regarding Ethel. Though she claims that leaving Downton would be good for Ethel, the Dowager Countess is also all too well aware that Ethel's leaving would be good for the Crawleys, too. And she takes steps to ensure Ethel's departure, saying that "happily it was not needed" to send Ethel's son Charlie to the butcher to make it happen. Here we are sure that her dark humor is partly just to spite Mrs. Crawley, but we also suspect that the Dowager

Countess would have been willing to take far more radical steps to get rid of Ethel if necessary. In many instances where we think she might have done something genuinely good, it is often just to maintain the good name of the family. This doesn't suggest that she is a bad person, but that her manners are often used to bring about her own self-interest or the interest of her family rather than to demonstrate her good character.

Thus, the characters in *Downton Abbey* demonstrate that the relationship between manners and morality is complicated, but these same beloved characters also show that manners certainly cannot be dismissed as irrelevant to good character.

6
Keeping It under Control

Andrew P. Mills

Once upon a time, a man who was lame in one leg lived in one of the world's great empires and served a politically connected master. He taught those around him to endure misfortune, slander, ill-health, exile, and even the death of loved ones, all the while urging them to maintain honor and dignity no matter how they were treated.

I'm speaking of the Stoic philosopher Epictetus (50–135 CE), who lived and taught in ancient Rome, but *Downton Abbey* fans are excused if they thought I was speaking about John Bates. Bates is many things, but what is most admirable about him is his calm fortitude: he's content with the situation in which he finds himself and deals with misfortune and hardship, all the while remaining in control of his emotions. Mrs. Patmore is ever throwing a fit about the incompetence of Daisy, and, in one episode, panics at the thought of going blind and losing her job (1:7). Thomas the footman is never satisfied with his situation and is always scheming to move up. But, with rare exceptions, Bates is uncomplaining, in control of his emotions, and—though he engages in forgery and maybe even homicide—always does what he takes to be in the best interest of those he serves and loves. In this way he exhibits the Stoic philosophy of that other servant with an injured leg, Epictetus.

The benefit of maintaining control of one's emotions and as a result finding contentment even in the midst of great suffering—this is the major insight of Stoicism. By looking at the character and behavior of Bates and some of the other residents of Downton, we can understand how the Stoics urge us to live our lives and how, if we practice Stoicism, we can live good lives no matter what happens to us.

Stoicism

Stoicism is a school of thought that began in Athens in the third century BCE. Its founder, Zeno of Citium, gathered with his disciples on the *stoa poikile* or "painted porch," a public building in the main marketplace of Athens. This "stoa" gave the philosophical movement Zeno founded its name. Stoicism came into full flower a few centuries later in the Roman Empire, and it wouldn't be wrong to call Stoicism the dominant philosophical outlook of classical Rome. In addition to Epictetus, prominent Stoic philosophers included Cicero (a Roman Senator during the time of Julius Caesar and Marc Antony), Seneca (one-time tutor to the future emperor Nero), and even the Roman Emperor Marcus Aurelius himself.

Epictetus, who shall be our guide to Stoicism, was a slave as a young man, a servant to an influential figure in the court of Roman Emperors Nero and Domitian. He studied philosophy while a slave and, after being freed, set himself up as a teacher. He injured his leg at some point in his life, and is often depicted with a crutch. He never wrote anything himself, though, thanks to one of his note-taking students, his teachings have come down to us today. His most popular and accessible work, *The Enchiridion*, has served generations as a concise and clear introduction to Stoic thought. Through it we learn about what is truly valuable, the importance of paying attention to what we can and cannot control, how to deal with death and other misfortunes, and how to treat other people.

Control

The very first lines of Epictetus's *Enchiridion* implore us to pay attention to what is in our control and, more importantly, what is not. Like the residents of Downton, many of the things we want are things we don't have control over. Mary doesn't control whether she inherits her mother's money; Bates cannot keep himself from prison; and William Molesley doesn't have it in his power to win the Grantham Cup at the flower show. What do we control? We need only turn to the Dowager

Countess of Grantham—more of a Stoic than one would expect—for the answer: "I hope we're in control of something, if only ourselves" (1:3).

The Dowager Countess is thinking about the control we have over our behavior, but for the Stoics, controlling ourselves also means that we're in control of our desires, our opinions, and our values. And that's it. Our health, our wealth, our reputation, our jobs—these are all things that we don't, ultimately, control. Cora Crawley can control whether she *values* breaking the entail that would hand her money to unknown cousin Matthew, whether she *desires* to work against her husband on that matter, and what *action* she takes in pursuit of that goal. But the outcome itself—that's something she doesn't have power over.

Why does this matter to the Stoics?

First, if we recognize that we can control what we desire and value, we can eliminate stress and frustration. Moreover, we can achieve complete freedom by not desiring, or seeking to avoid, something that we can't control. We're enslaved, the Stoics think, when we place too much value in things out of our control. Our failure to get what we want, or to hold onto it if we do, precludes any chance for remaining calm and content. Consider Thomas, who's miserable because he isn't given the job of valet he so desperately wants (1:1). Or Mary, whose anxiety about the possible publication of the news of her affair with Kemal Pamuk leads her to consent to marry Richard Carlisle (2:5), a man she clearly doesn't love. Trying to control what they cannot—a job, a public scandal—enslaves Thomas and Mary and causes them stress.

Second, while we can't guarantee the success of our endeavors, recalling that we're in control of our actions means there's nothing stopping us from striving to achieve what we dream of. The Stoics counsel us to avoid the enslavement that comes from subjecting our happiness to the acquisition of something (like a job, an inheritance, or the cover-up of a scandal) that's out of our control. But they don't tell us to abandon all ambition or effort. The trick, of course, is to keep trying to achieve the goal without becoming enslaved to it. When, in season 1, episode 4, Gwen the housemaid begins to despair that her dream of becoming a secretary will never become a reality— "There will never be anyone less suited for the post or worse qualified than I am," she says—Lady Sybil offers sage Stoic advice: "No one hits the bull's-eye with the first arrow." We cannot guarantee success, but we can persist in trying. And this is because our persistence is within our control. We just have to remember that trying doesn't guarantee success, and it may cost us some trouble in the bargain.

Finally, by reminding ourselves that much of life is not in our power, we're much less distressed and disturbed when misfortune befalls us. "Nothing in life is sure," says Mrs. Patmore in response to the sinking of the *Titanic*, which, in the very first episode, sets in motion much of the drama surrounding Mary, Matthew, and the future of Downton Abbey. Bates embodies this outlook as much as anyone. He deals with so much misfortune during his life—multiple spells in prison, the acquisition and loss (a couple times over!) of his job at Downton, the machinations of his wife Vera who stands in the way of his marriage to Anna, not to mention his lame leg that makes life in a big house without an elevator a serious challenge—yet seems so rarely distressed about it. "I can manage," he says over and over again in season 1, episode 1, when the staff and Lord Grantham question whether he can do his job with his injury. And manage he does. He doesn't rail at his imprisonment, or his separation from Anna. He doesn't pitch a fit when, in that same episode, Miss O'Brien kicks out his cane, forcing him to, embarrassingly, fall to the ground in front of Lord Grantham and the Duke of Crowborough. He picks himself up (with a little help from Anna), dusts himself off, and endures, recognizing, in good Stoic fashion, that all we can do is "manage" the fortune, both good and bad, that life throws in our path.

The Good, the Bad, and the Indifferent

The Stoics' view of what we can control—our values, desires, opinions, and behavior—connects closely to their theory of what is good, and what is bad. According to the Stoics there are only two good things: virtue and tranquility. The only truly good things in our lives are our own virtuous behavior and the calm peace of mind that comes when we're not agitated or anxious. Consequently, there are only two really bad things in life: vicious behavior and a disturbed, anxious state of mind. We're tempted, no doubt, to think that wealth, land, fine clothes, a duchess's coronet, and all the trappings of the aristocracy are valuable and essential components of the good life. And that a life filled with illness, poverty, death, long hours of work, and an uncertain future cannot possibly be a good one. But the Stoics say otherwise: since virtue and tranquility are the only "goods," and vice and disturbance are the only "bads," everything else—wealth, social status, health, love, even life itself—should be a matter of indifference to us. Whether we live upstairs or downstairs, whether we find ourselves being rejected by potential suitors, languishing in prison, or scrubbing pots as the kitchen maid, we live good lives if we are virtuous and tranquil, and we live bad lives if we're not.

These "indifferents" aren't part of the good life precisely because we lack complete control over them. Our health, wealth, and status are not really our possessions, say the Stoics. Bates gives voice to this outlook during his first day on the job in the very first episode of the series. Looking over Lord Grantham's collection of snuffboxes and cufflinks, he says to Thomas, "We live with all of this—a pirate's hoard—within our reach. But none of it's ours, is it?" Bates is remarking on the situation of servants amid the wealth and grandeur of the Crawleys, but the same could be said of even the Crawleys' relationship to their own possessions: a ship sinks, an investment goes belly-up, and all that the Crawleys have threatens to vanish. This goes for their lives, health, and social status, too. Since the Stoics maintain that whether we live good lives should be entirely in our power, the things that are not in the complete control of the people who possess them—Mrs. Patmore's eyesight, Lady Edith's marriage prospects, Lady Mary's reputation, William Mason's life, or the future ownership of Downton Abbey itself, for example—should not matter to whether we are living good lives or not.

If we cling to things not in our control, we run the twin risks of acting viciously in the pursuit of those "indifferents" and being disturbed because of our failure to acquire them. One need look no further than Thomas, who, discontent with his job as the first footman at Downton, is driven to theft, deceit, and potential blackmail in pursuit of a promotion to valet. Thomas is disturbed at not being given the position he wants; his frequent scheming partner, Miss O'Brien, is disturbed at the possibility of having hers taken away. Her distress leads her to behavior that is no less vicious; indeed it is likely worse. Believing (falsely) that she is about to be fired, she contrives, in season 1, episode 7, to have Lady Grantham slip on soap as she leaves the bath, leading to the miscarriage of the baby boy she was carrying. Or consider Lady Edith who, throughout season 1, is upset at her failure to secure a serious suitor. Due to factors entirely out of her control, Lady Edith faces the prospect of being the "old maid" who takes care of her parents in their declining years. Far from being tranquil, Edith's bitterness and spite leads her to spread all over London society the story about Mary's "indiscretion" with Pamuk (1:5). Many of us, when we can't get what we want, become upset and act in less than honorable ways as a result. The cause of this disturbance and vice is desiring the indifferents in the first place. The solution, the one Epictetus offers, is to cease desiring them.

Indifferent though they may be, keeping Downton "in the family," becoming a gentleman's valet, getting married, securing a job as a secretary, and even winning the Grantham Cup for the best bloom in the village are things that we would prefer to have, all other things being equal. Though we will never be disappointed if we never seek anything we don't have complete control over, it is surely better to find love than to fail, to hold on to a job rather than be sacked, to win the Grantham Cup rather than to lose it. The things that we would *prefer* to have, but to which we should be *indifferent*, are called by the Stoics, unsurprisingly, the "preferred indifferents."

There's no problem preferring these things, according to Epictetus, just so long as we remain indifferent to whether we get them. Epictetus explains this odd idea by saying that we should behave in life the way we do at a banquet (a frequent Downton event!): we can take our share of the food when it comes our way, but we shouldn't grasp for it or try to hold the dish back when the footman carries it on to the next guest. Having another slice of Mrs. Patmore's roast would be wonderful, but if it runs out before I have a chance, I should recognize how delicious that first slice was and how fortunate I was to be able to dine at Downton at all. And so we should be in life, Epictetus tells us. We should enjoy our possessions, our jobs, our family, and even our own lives—we can prefer to have these things—but we should, as good Stoics, try to remain undisturbed when they leave us. As certainly they will.

Death

Of all the things not in our control, death—our own, and that of those close to us—is the most significant. Unexpected death seems to be a regular visitor to Downton Abbey and its inhabitants. Beyond the death of the unfortunate Mr. Pamuk and Cora's miscarriage, there is the death of the presumptive heir to the Grantham title (and Mary's fiancé) on the *Titanic*, the influenza death of Lavinia Swire, Lady Sybil's death immediately after the birth of her daughter, and, equally tragic, Matthew's death just after he has met his newborn son. These deaths, of course, set in motion many of the plot twists of *Downton Abbey*, but the challenge for all of us, according to the Stoics, is to figure out how not to let the prospect of our own death, and the deaths of those close to us, entirely undo our tranquility.

Death is the great *rejected* indifferent: one of those things that are neither good nor bad but which most of us would reject if given the chance. Epictetus takes a hard line: it is not death itself that disturbs us, but rather our judgment that it is bad. To see this in action, recall the death of Pamuk in season 1, episode 3. When she first hears of his death, the Dowager Countess is not unduly disturbed by it: he was a foreigner, after all, she remarks! But once she learns the circumstances of his death and the risk that a scandal poses to Mary's marriage prospects, she becomes rather more disturbed: now, she judges, his death is something bad.

If what disturbs us about death is our judgment that it's bad, we're in luck. For, say the Stoics, that judgment is wrong: death *isn't* one of the truly bad things, only vice and disturbance are. Additionally, our judgments and opinions are in our control, so if we judge death to be bad, we can change that judgment, and regard death as an indifferent. Easier said than done, of course, but it does bring out a rather important aspect of Stoicism: that we can alter the way we feel by changing the way we think. A perfect example of thoughts that can calm our distress at our own mortality comes from Mrs. Hughes who, in season 3, episode 2, finds a lump on her breast. When Dr. Clarkson's tests don't definitively rule out cancer, it is Mrs. Patmore, Mrs. Hughes's confidante in this matter, who is distressed. Mrs. Hughes, like a good Stoic, recognizes the truth. "One day, I will die. And so will [Mr. Carson], and you, and every one of us under this roof," she sighs to the cook. "You must put these things in proportion, Mrs. Patmore." By having the thought that we all must die sometime, Mrs. Hughes helps to calm herself, and perhaps also Mrs. Patmore in the process.

Often harder to deal with, though, is the death of someone close to us. In season 4, episode 1, Isobel and Mary are utterly grief stricken at Matthew's death. Far from tranquil, their depression renders them unable to engage with the world. The Stoics don't say we can't grieve, but we need to find a way to return to life. We can think to ourselves the sorts of thoughts that comfort Mrs. Hughes, for example. Or, like Tom Branson, who, in season 3, episode 6, names his motherless daughter Sybil after his recently departed wife, we can find a way to recall the happy times we spent with those who are no longer with us.

How We Should Treat People

So far we've discussed tranquility and the importance of maintaining it in the face of misfortune. Let's finish by thinking a bit about what the Stoics say about virtue, and in particular, what they say about how we should treat other people. One of the most striking features of life at Downton is that everyone has a specific role which defines how they behave. From Lord and Lady Grantham all the way down to Daisy the kitchen maid, everyone knows how to address each other, whose opinions are to be deferred to, and how much of their personal life it is appropriate to share, and with whom. Life at Downton is strictly stratified: its inhabitants—and not just the downstairs staff—are confined to their roles. In his *Enchiridion*, Epictetus endorses an approach to how we should behave based on our social relationships. There is the way we should treat our father, mother, daughter, servant, master, and so on, and we act virtuously when we fulfill those socially established obligations.

Another, lesser-known, Stoic called Hierocles offers a more intriguing (and frankly more attractive) approach to our actions toward other people—an approach which seems to upset the social roles that are so important at Downton. Not much is known about Hierocles, but his most famous surviving fragment uses the image of concentric circles to help us understand our relationships to those around us.

We are to imagine ourselves in the center of this set of circles, with the second circle containing our nuclear family members. Each successive circle contains people more distant to us: closer relatives, distant relatives, people in our local community, our city, our country, and on and on until the largest circle, which contains everyone in the entire world. What we are to do, Hierocles urges, is to draw all these circles together. We should treat the people in the outer circles as if they were members of the inner circles, and we should treat the people in the inner circles as if they were in the first circle: as if they were us. Continually working to treat strangers like friends, our friends like family, and our family like we would treat ourselves—this is Stoic virtue, at least in regards to our treatment of others.

Some of the most moving and touching moments at Downton take place when the social roles are put aside and forgotten, and in this way (some of) the residents display their Stoic virtue. Think of Sybil helping Gwen get the secretary job, or Mr. Carson comforting Mary after the death of Matthew. The downstairs staff are as elated at Mary's marriage to Matthew as the upstairs residents are upset by the imprisonment of Mr. Bates and they expend every effort to get him released. In season 1, episode 7, the staff is thrilled at the news of Cora's pregnancy and Daisy and William mull over getting gifts for the new baby: they see their mistress as part of their "inner" circle. Yet Thomas mocks them, spitting out that the Crawleys can probably afford to outfit their new child. Nor can Thomas understand the sadness the staff feels at the news of Cora's miscarriage, remarking that he sees the Crawleys merely as his employers, not family. When, in that same episode, the servants' hall talk turns to the prospect of war, Anna, Bates, and William speak of the importance of national unity, but Thomas can think only of himself and how he might use the war as an opportunity to improve his own prospects.

Hierocles would say that we should not be like Thomas, who has room for no one else in his "inner circle." The Stoics were "cosmopolitans," and by that they meant that we should not let social, ethnic, national, racial, class, or other boundaries separate us from others. Virtuous behavior toward others requires that we see them—whoever they may be—like family, if not even closer.

We Can All Manage

It isn't just Mr. Bates, but many of the residents of Downton
Abbey who embody, to a greater or lesser extent, the central
principles of Stoicism. Remember what we can control and
what we can't. Work to avoid enslavement to things outside our
control. Never forget the inevitability of death. Treat everyone
as if they were family. When gathered together, these Stoic
principles set out a challenging path, more challenging, perhaps, than carrying out the duties of a valet with a busted leg.
But we're all capable of succeeding in the task. We can all, in
the words of Mr. Bates, "manage," and if we do, the Stoics
promise us complete freedom and the riches that come from
leading a calm and happy life—the sort of thing all of us imagine when we think about living like the Lord of Downton
Abbey.

7
Disabled at Downton

AARON RICHMOND

Downton Abbey introduces a number of persons with disabilities, though its portrayal of them is, morally speaking, mixed. According to Paul K. Longmore, "The scholarly task is to uncover the hidden history of disabled people and to raise awareness of the unconscious attitudes and values embedded in media images. The political task is to liberate disabled people from the paternalistic prejudice expressed in those images and to forge a new social identity." Longmore goes on to argue that disabled individuals often feel unjustly excluded from society until individuals like themselves are seen in the popular media and are represented realistically. Now in *Downton Abbey*, because Mr. Bates is a positive, realistic example of a person with a disability, disabled viewers can appreciate him. On the other hand, because Matthew Crawley is unrealistically portrayed, his character, or at least the portrayal of his character's disability, can harm disabled viewers by further contributing to their sense of societal isolation.

Bates

In the early twentieth century, individuals with disabilities faced widespread ability-based discrimination due to the unfounded societal belief that people with disabilities could not participate meaningfully within society. As a result, persons with disabilities had very few economic opportunities, were discouraged from seeking romantic relationships, and were frequently institutionalized. In Britain after World War I,

the government failed to provide adequate re-education programs; as Deborah Cohen explains in her essay "Will to Work,"
"While the Ministry eventually re-trained 82,000 men (most of
whom were not severely disabled), it is doubtful that more than
half of these found work in their trades . . . [Finally] the
Ministry of Labour closed the list for training in September
1921, with an estimated 100,000 disabled ex-servicemen unemployed." In the world of *Downton Abbey*, Mr. Bates, a veteran of
the Second Boer War (1899–1902), also experienced some of
these challenges; indeed, in the DVD comments on season 2,
episode 2 Brendan Coyle remarks, "Someone with such an
injury would rarely, if ever, be employed in service in a house,
so it's of huge import to him that he's given this chance."
Coyle's statement serves to demonstrate one of the ways that
Downton Abbey seeks to be historically accurate by clearly representing the obstacles that persons with disabilities faced in
their attempt to become contributing members of society.

When viewers are first introduced to Mr. Bates, we are
introduced to a man who has been hired by Lord Grantham to
serve as his valet. During his service in the Boer War, Mr. Bates
was Lord Grantham's batman (military servant in the British
army), and it is because of this that he was hired. Throughout
the first season, Thomas Barrow and Miss O'Brien try to get
Mr. Bates fired, seemingly because of his disability. O'Brien's
ability-based discrimination is made clear after her first meeting with Mr. Bates when she says to Mr. Carson, "Well I cannot
see that lasting long" (1:1). After numerous attempts to get Mr.
Bates removed from his position, Barrow and O'Brien nearly
succeed in getting him dismissed. However, Lord Grantham
changes his mind about removing Mr. Bates at the last minute
when he decides that it would be wrong of him to dismiss Mr.
Bates because of his disability; indeed, Lord Grantham informs
Mr. Carson that "It wouldn't be right" (1:1).

However, even after Lord Grantham's decision to keep Mr.
Bates, Barrow and O'Brien continue to try to get him sacked.
One of Barrow's attempts takes place after he has been caught
stealing wine by Mr. Bates. In retaliation Barrow tries to get
Mr. Bates fired for stealing one of Lord Grantham's antique
snuffboxes, and, just as significantly, O'Brien kicks Mr. Bates's
cane out from under him in front of an honored guest, which
causes Mr. Bates to be publically humiliated.

Despite these ongoing acts of disability-based discrimination, Mr. Bates becomes a trusted employee at Downton Abbey. We see evidence of this when Mr. Carson welcomes him back after Mr. Bates was released from prison, saying, "Welcome back Mr. Bates. I have waited a long time to say that" (3:7). Mr. Carson's statement reveals that he has come to value the contributions Mr. Bates makes to Downton Abbey. At the same time Mr. Carson's statement is tacit acknowledgment that people with disabilities are capable of being highly valued employees.

Another important aspect of Mr. Bates's character is his self-confidence, including his ability to face the obstacles that others have placed in his way. However, there is one occasion when his optimistic outlook wavers, as a result of which, he gives into the pressure that others have placed on him. This occurs when Mr. Bates purchases a leg brace, which is designed to correct his limp (1:3). However, the leg brace causes him significant pain, which is noticed by Mrs. Hughes who persuades him to tell her what is wrong. Afterwards, Mrs. Hughes convinces him to get rid of it:

Mr. Bates: Well here goes.

Mrs. Hughes: Do you not think we ought to say a few words?

Mr. Bates: What? Good riddance?

Mrs. Hughes: That, and your promise.

Mr. Bates: Very well. I promise I will never again try to cure myself. I will spend my life happily as the butt of others' jokes, and I will never mind them.

Mrs. Hughes: We all carry scars, Mr. Bates—inside or out. You're no different to the rest of us, remember that.

Mr. Bates: I will try to. That I will promise.

Here, Mrs. Hughes helps Mr. Bates deal with his temporary self-doubt as well as his desire to hide his physical disability, the result of which is that Mr. Bates has personally and permanently rejected the idea that a disability requires, above all, a simple medical solution. Instead, Mrs. Hughes helps re-establish Mr. Bates's sense of self-worth as an individual who is really no different than anyone else. And in case we are tempted to imagine that Mr. Bates's brief period of self-doubt somehow distinguishes him as a disabled person, we should note that this is actually the opposite of the case. Otherwise, Mr. Bates would be a "super-crip," in other words, a person with a disability who is able to so completely adapt to his or her environment through the use of technological or other means that the disability no longer impacts him or her in any appreciable way. By permitting Mr. Bates to experience these emotions, and embrace his disability as part of his identity, he is more able to reflect the ways that persons with disabilities— like myself—honestly feel about themselves. People with disabilities are not super-human overachievers, nor are they especially weak and pitiable individuals who wallow in self-doubt and pity.

Finally, Mr. Bates challenges the socially constructed norms for individuals with disabilities by falling in love and having his love returned. From the first episode of *Downton Abbey*, Anna treats Mr. Bates respectfully which in part leads to their eventual romance. Mr. Bates tells Anna, "Go to sleep, and dream of a better man"—to which Anna responds, "I can't, because there isn't one" (1:6). This is an important, culturally challenging moment because during the early twentieth century most people with disabilities were discouraged from marrying, and were not believed to be romantically desirable. In contrast to this wrongly believed stereotype, Mr. Bates falls in love with Anna and they eventually get married (2:8).

So, Mr. Bates views his disability more as a socially constructed event than as something especially medical; he self-confidently, persistently disproves the socially held belief that persons with disabilities can be neither effective employees nor romantic partners. And by challenging both of these societally held ableist beliefs, Mr. Bates is a positive figure for disabled persons in society.

Matthew Crawley

In addition to Mr. Bates, several other *Downton Abbey* characters, including Matthew Crawley, acquire disabilities while serving in the armed forces. Matthew's disability occurs when he attempts to rescue William Mason during the Battle of the

Somme. This attempt leads to his being hit with a shell, resulting in his becoming a temporary paraplegic (2:5).

Matthew's new status as an individual with a disability radically alters his self-image as well as how he chooses to relate to others. As part of his re-envisioning of himself, Matthew decides to end his engagement to Lavinia because he does not want to be a burden to her nor does he want to prevent her from having children. Matthew makes his beliefs about himself known to Lavinia when he tells her, "We cannot be properly married . . . That is why I have to let you go" (2:5). Then later on in their conversation Matthew continues, "I couldn't possibly be responsible for stealing away the life you ought to have."

Matthew believes that his disability would prevent him from having children and would be a huge burden on Lavinia. But she rejects both of these arguments, saying, "But that side of things, it's not important to me, I promise . . . I won't leave you. I know you think I'm weak, and I don't know what I'm taking on. I'm not saying it'll be easy for either of us. But just because a life isn't easy doesn't mean it isn't right" (2:5). However, even after Lavinia's assurances that she loves him regardless of what the future holds, Matthew harshly rebukes her in that same episode, saying, "Go home. Think of me as dead. Remember me as I was." By making this statement, it is clear that Matthew is not able to accept himself as a person with a disability; he also fails to realize that aquiring a disability does not prevent someone from living a fulfilling life. As a result Matthew decides to end their engagement.

A second character who demonstrates her ongoing devotion to Matthew after he becomes a paraplegic is Lady Mary. Lady Mary's devotion to Matthew is witnessed when she takes him for a walk outside in his wheelchair. While they are outside Matthew also expresses his desire that Mary not devote herself to him because she is engaged and he does not want to become an obstacle in her relationship:

Mary: I don't have to marry him, you know.

Matthew: Yes, you do. If I thought for a moment that I was an argument against your marriage, I should jump into the nearest river.

Mary: And how would you manage that without my help?

Matthew: I'd get you to push me. Seriously, I can only relax because I know that you have a real life coming. If I ever thought I was putting that in jeopardy, I'd go away and never see you again.

Mary: You don't mean that.

Matthew: But I do. (2:6)

Even though Matthew expresses the desire to be left alone, it is clear that Lady Mary, like Lavinia, is willing to remain in his life and to support him during this difficult period of transition.

Matthew's life as a person with a disability is only temporary, which is not the case for the vast majority of individuals with a spinal-cord injury. This is because Matthew receives a "miracle cure" or, as Dr. Clarkson explains, he had misdiagnosed Matthew in the first place (2:7):

There is only one possible explanation. It starts with my own mistake. Every indication told me that the spine was transected, which would have been incurable. . . . He [Sir John Coates] thought that it could conceivably be a case of spinal shock. That is intense bruising. Which was significantly severe to impede the leg mechanisms.

Later, Dr. Clarkson and Matthew have the following conversation:

Dr. Clarkson: You must take it slowly. Rome wasn't built in a day.

Matthew: I know.

Dr. Clarkson: And I'm afraid you will carry a bruise on your spine for the rest of your life.

Matthew: But I will have a life?

Dr. Clarkson: Yes. I think we can say that. You will have a normal life, and it won't be long in coming.

It is clear from the way that both Dr. Clarkson and Matthew Crawley use the word "normal" to describe Matthew's life that both men hold to the medical model of disability, which assumes that persons with disabilities are abnormal and are not able to have "normal" lives. As a result, they are creatures to be pitied and their lives are "over" when a disability arises. Truth be told, it is a little surprising that both men have this belief about persons with disabilities in light of the fact that Mr. Bates has clearly demonstrated throughout the series that persons with disabilities do have "normal" lives. However, the personal opinions expressed by Dr. Clarkson and Matthew are historically accurate and serve to establish their discussion within *Downton Abbey*'s early twentieth-century context.

But this is also harmful. It is harmful to real-life disabled persons for characters in TV shows with disabilities to experience "miracle cures," because by representing disability in this way people with disabilities are wrongly led to believe that they are seriously defective and that their lives are over. This may lead a person with disabilities to believe that he or she needs a miracle healing or new advances in medical treatments to become happy. Instead, I'd like to see characters who acquire disabilities learn about their new level of physical functioning and then find personally meaningful activities that their disability permits. I want more Bateses, and fewer Matthews; more "I can thrive in society," and less "Will I have a life?"

The Ability of Disability

Thus, *Downton Abbey* offers both positive and negative representations of persons with disabilities. As a result, the series presents clear examples of both the historically believed stereotypes about people with disabilities alongside the contemporary societal beliefs about them, thereby showing viewers the historical ability-based discrimination that persons with disabilities faced, while also affirming the value they have in society.

What Can We Know?

8

Lie Is So Unmusical a Word

COURTNEY NEAL

The aristocracy has always thrived on controlled truths, often aided by the veil of courtesy to maintain order and relationships. Politeness is taken to extremes and what may seem like a slight at Downton is more like a modern-day burn. Life at Downton revolves around who does (and can) know what, with upstairs life being less secret than the Crawleys hope it to be, and the servants downstairs trying to hide their own, with much the same success rate. While reputation and appearances are the most important things when regulating the truth (remember the aftermath of Mr. Pamuk's death?), truth, and the manipulation of it through lying, is a matter of self-preservation for the entire family.

Relationships are maintained as much through genuine affection as they are through the concealment of unpleasant information. In the wake of Lady Sybil's death, the division between Cora and Robert seems overwhelming, as Cora blames Robert and his pride for the death of their daughter. Violet, the Dowager Countess, realizes that Cora will not forgive Robert anytime soon, if at all, and intervenes by asking Dr. Clarkson to review the research and tell Lord and Lady Grantham that the surgery he advocated for to save her would not have worked. Clarkson, though he doesn't seem to think the research supports this conclusion, follows Violet's wishes and tells the Crawleys that his surgery would not have saved Sybil. This revelation causes the couple to cry in each other's arms, reunited in grief. The success of Clarkson's lie is unmistakable, but the question remains, was it the moral thing to do?

You Kant Do That

Lying for Immanuel Kant (1724–1804) is black and white, and the rule behind his philosophy, including his famous Categorical Imperative, is simple: you should never lie, not ever. In his work *The Metaphysics of Morals* he outlines his view, stressing that if rules are broken once, faith in those rules is lost; therefore, the truth must always be told so it has strength and value. Kant rejects the concept of lying for a good reason: he believes that lying to other people is a violation of the liar's duty to others, and that to lie is to lose one's dignity. Kant focuses on the relation between the liar and the person being lied to, and stresses that lying violates the rights of each person involved. Lying for Kant can never be a positive thing because lying itself is absolutely wrong, and shows a lack of conscientiousness. In a Kantian world, there is absolute necessity, meaning that everyone has to follow the same rules, because if one person doesn't (for example, one person lies), then everyone can break the rules. It's all or nothing for Kant, and therefore lying cannot be allowed.

This black and white world, though, has long been disputed for its inability to permit exceptions, the most famous of which is the "lying to the murderer at the door" scenario, in which a murderer comes looking for his victim, and you have this choice: tell the truth and reveal the victim, or lie and save the person. The answer for many is to lie, because it results in saving a person's life, whereas Kant asserts that no one can lie ever, because faith in honesty would be lost. Lying is still absolutely wrong and is the greatest violation of one's duty to oneself. The content of the lie is not important or relevant in the face of the Categorical Imperative because lying itself is an absolute wrong and does harm; therefore, it can't result in good deeds, no matter the motive. For Kant, there is no such thing as lying for a good reason. The Dowager Countess, however, would care to disagree.

Have We Nothing in Common?

Violet is troubled by the strain Sybil's death has put on Cora and Robert's marriage, especially because she can see that

Cora will not forgive Robert his arrogance that apparently led to Sybil's lack of treatment and death (3:5). When Robert seeks counsel on how to deal with his newfound unhappy marriage, Violet approaches Dr. Clarkson with a proposition that he revisit the research regarding pre-eclampsia and determine that even with surgery, Sybil would still have died. In episode 6 of season 3, Violet pushes Clarkson to reveal the exact number of cases in which this course of treatment worked, resulting in the follow exchange:

> **Clarkson:** Not many, I admit, I'd need to do some research.
>
> **Violet:** I want you to tell Lord and Lady Grantham what you have almost admitted to me.
>
> **Clarkson:** But there was a chance.
>
> **Violet:** Dr. Clarkson, you've created a division between my son and his wife, when the only way they can conceivably bear their grief, is if they face it together.
>
> **Clarkson:** So you want me to lie to them and say there was no chance at all?
>
> **Violet:** Lie is so unmusical a word. I want you to review the evidence, honestly and without bias.
>
> **Clarkson:** Even to ease suffering I could never justify telling an outright lie.
>
> **Violet:** Have we nothing in common?

Violet's goal is quite clear despite her attempt to hide behind courtesy: she wants Clarkson to lie for a very specific reason about a very specific circumstance. Clarkson, through a combination of professional pride and personal ethics, reveals almost immediately that he realizes Violet wants him to lie but that he is not comfortable with this, much to Violet's exasperation. At the end of the episode, however, Violet brings Cora and Robert to an impromptu meeting, in which Clarkson, clearly prompted forward by Violet (and accentuated with camera cuts that show Violet encouraging him at every point he appears to weaken), reveals findings that are quite in line with the Dowager Countess's wishes:

Clarkson: On that awful night, I'm afraid I may have given you the impression that my recommended course of treatment offered a real chance for Lady Sybil's survival. The truth, and I've done a great deal of research since as you can imagine, is that the chance was a small one, a tiny one really. I've read that early delivery was the only way to avoid the trauma—and it is—

Cora: As you tried so hard to tell us.

Clarkson: But, what I did not quite realize was that eclampsia is almost invariably fatal, with or without a Caesarean. Had you agreed we would have subjected Lady Sybil to the fear and pain of a hurried operation when in all likelihood, she would have died anyway.

Cora: But there was a chance.

Clarkson: An infinitesimal one. But the discomfort and the terror would have been all too certain.

Robert: So you think Tapsell was right?

Clarkson: Oh I cannot go that far. Sir Philip Tapsell ignored all the evidence in a most unhelpful and may I say arrogant manner—

Robert: But Sybil was going to die.

Clarkson: When everything is weighed in the balance, I believe that Lady Sybil was going to die.

Cora and Robert are overcome with emotion and are reunited, as they are able to grieve together without blaming each other for their loss. Violet's plan is a success; however the question remains, was Clarkson right to lie to Lord and Lady Grantham?

Weighed in the Balance

The traditional Kantian answer, as explained above, would be a firm no, that lying is never justified. However, the disadvantages for not only Cora and Robert, but the whole Crawley family and estate would be drastic. Throughout the show Cora and Robert are regarded as a practical match that became a love match, and despite Robert's dalliance with a maid, their union was strong. With the prospect of Cora and Robert living in separate houses, Violet takes what little action she can, and effectively conscripts Clarkson into solving the problem. Clarkson is loyal to the Crawleys and is even friendly with them; however, lying to them clearly troubles him.

The crux of the moral debate over Clarkson's lie for many involves weighing the good (saving the Crawley's marriage) versus the bad (it's unethical for a doctor to lie). There is no obvious further harm to be done by Clarkson if he lies; Sybil has died and her condition was rare, therefore the likelihood that another Crawley lady would fall to pre-eclampsia is incredibly low, and a repeat scenario is not a worry to the family. Clarkson's reputation is also secured; Cora has always viewed him highly and his ability to spot the pre-eclampsia is acknowledged by all. His advocacy for surgery after the fact is not as important as it was during Sybil's labor, so the state of the research describing whether or not it would have been successful (or even had a higher chance of success then Sir Philip's course of treatment) only holds importance in Cora's mind regarding what-if. If Clarkson agrees to lie, it will have one central effect: to state that Lady Sybil would have died regardless of any action taken, and that it is not Robert's pride that resulted in her death, but natural causes. Therefore, the question becomes did Clarkson actually lie? We see Clarkson deliberating during the actual scene when the camera angles switch back and forth between him and Dowager Countess Violet, indicating that he did, especially when his earlier reservations are taken into account. Clarkson's change of heart (and change in moral wiggle room) saves Downton.

Absolute Morality

Clarkson may very well hurt himself by lying: as he previously told Violet, he has trouble justifying this very beneficial lie, but he does so anyway. Clarkson is well aware of his failings with the Crawley family (his failures with Matthew's spinal condition and Lavinia's death from flu are mentioned early in season 3, episode 5), and he takes his position as the family's main doctor and director of the hospital very seriously. As Kant worries, lying can sour interpersonal relationships, and Clarkson can internally worry that he can no longer say he's always been honest with the family. For Kant, the imperative against lying aims to protect rationality and your highest duty to yourself in

maintaining dignity, and lying for Kant is a simple way to
throw this away. What we can consider then is if there can be
an exception of motive behind the absolute morality—that is, is
lying generally wrong, or always wrong?

It is arguable that there are exceptions, and clearly this is
what Violet is aiming to convince Clarkson of. She is asking
him to sacrifice a small part of his dignity in order to save
Robert and Cora's marriage (and therefore preserve Downton
itself). Repeatedly in the show the concept of stewardship is
discussed, especially the idea that Downton isn't owned by
Robert, but is in his care for his lifetime, and that he must protect it (even though his attempts are more often failed ventures
than not). Other characters feel this duty to a certain extent
despite the repeated chorus that times are changing and large
estates can't go on forever. Clarkson's duty is here directly
framed by Violet to be one of preservation and healing: Cora
and Robert can only successfully mourn and grieve if they can
do so together. She indirectly states that it is Clarkson's duty
to remove the division he himself has placed there by dis-
agreeing with Tapsell by telling Cora and Robert that Sybil's
death was inevitable (whether or not it truly was). She frames
the lie in such a way that it becomes a manipulation of facts (as
Clarkson states, the chance was admittedly small), but one
designed to save the Crawleys.

Clarkson still maintains a duty to himself by refusing to
admit that Tapsell was right ("Oh I cannot go that far. Sir
Philip Tapsell ignored all the evidence in a most unhelpful and
may I say arrogant manner—"), but he concedes that the
extremely small chance of a successful surgery was not worth
it. Clarkson is operating within the parameters of Kant's
morality, as he clearly has limits to what he will say and especially why, but good reasons alone are not enough for Kant.

Duty to Downton

In his famous essay "On a Supposed Right to Lie Because of
Philanthropic Concerns," Kant discusses the famous "murderer
at the door" scenario, but there is wiggle room in his absolute
morality. Kant discusses this case in the legal sense and deals
a lot with responsibility and legal implications, especially the
condition that you have no right to lie (especially in the legal

sense). Clarkson's actions are outside this realm of legal action, but his duty to Downton remains, as does his intention. As a doctor Clarkson is sworn to do no harm, and his refusal to lie would have a clear negative effect on Lord and Lady Grantham, whereas telling the lie would remove their grievance. Two important factors—the respect for both rationality and human life—provide an avenue for exception for Clarkson.

First we can evaluate rationality. Violet has carefully thought out her plan of action and knows exactly how her plan will impact her family. This is not an improvised plan or an off-the-cuff decision, and therefore it meets the criteria for a rational thought.

Second, although no lives are in danger, Violet is intimately concerned with the welfare of her family. Her plan seeks to alleviate Robert and Cora's pain; therefore, it, too, meets the criteria for respecting human life. An exception could then be made on the grounds that Clarkson is not betraying the dignity of the Crawleys, and can lie with a moral approval. He is also performing a duty to Downton by lying because he is preserving order.

Kant's morality, though often absolute (or "always"), allows little wiggle room. Lying for personal gain is clearly out of the question, but lying regardless of motive can be damaging to dignity. Possibly Violet's purpose in asking Clarkson to lie is because she sees the greater moral duty being to preserve a marriage, and even Downton itself. Cora and Robert are respected as people, but they are at an impasse, one that is severely hurting not only their happiness, but their family as well. Clarkson in agreeing to lie helps Cora and Robert in a way that only he can, and uses evidence—rationality—to do so.

This is important because (especially in Violet's opinion) Cora has begun to act irrationally towards Robert, blaming him for Sybil's death. Violet succeeds in her plan to reunite Cora and Robert because she understands Cora's thought process, and employs a plan to rectify the situation. Perhaps Kant would agree that if this thought-out plan is the only path that could help reunite the couple, then an exception could be permitted on the basis of preserving human dignity.

The Rule Still Holds

Kant is famous for his hard stand on lying and it is easy to view his beliefs in an absolute manner. His edict against lying strives to ensure that interpersonal communication is reliable and meaningful, without damaging either party. Cora and Robert's relationship is damaged, however, and Clarkson's lie brings them together again. Clarkson avoids many of the pitfalls of Kant's prohibition because he does not attempt to lie for personal gain, but his reluctance shows he struggles with his own moral view, which seems to be fairly in line with Kant's. Clarkson's off camera deliberation we can only assume leads him to believe he can lie, and that his conscience doesn't have to suffer for it.

Violet is careful in her selection of agents as well as in the reasoning behind her choice. She acts critically and carefully to save her son's marriage, and her success rests squarely on Dr. Clarkson's shoulders and his agreement to lie for her. Although Kant is firm, Clarkson meets the two criteria for a possible exemption to Kant's ban on lying: it is a rational lie and he values human life. Clarkson knows what the result of his inaction will be, and does so because it is the only way to help Robert and Cora. Clarkson shows great care in his deliberation, and although lying should generally be avoided, an exception can be made for the good doctor in *this* particular case for *this* particular moral reason.

9
Why Did Lady Sybil Die?

MATTHIAS EGG

The variety of goals we can pursue by asking the simple question "why?" is quite amazing. When Mrs. Patmore asks why the oven isn't working, she is mostly interested in what could be done about it. When Lady Grantham asks why Mary is so downcast, she seeks to understand what troubles her daughter's heart. And when Carson asks why the soup is being served too late, he wants to know who is to blame for this unacceptable state of affairs.

Despite this variety, there are some similarities among why-questions in wildly different contexts. The common feature that interests us here is a process that kicks in whenever a why-question doesn't immediately get a satisfactory answer. What happens then is a kind of contest between the various hypotheses that would, if true, answer the why-question. Some of these hypotheses might be so implausible that we dismiss them immediately. We then compare the remaining options, assessing how good a job they do at answering our question. Finally, we conclude (tentatively, perhaps) that the winner that emerges from this process is the correct answer to the why-question. This kind of reasoning is called *inference to the best explanation*. It doesn't only apply to everyday affairs like malfunctioning ovens, girls' moods, or delayed soups, but can also become a matter of life and death.

Different Types of Inference

Inference to the best explanation plays a role in some of the dramatic events at Downton, so let's first look at how it differs from other forms of inference. What an inference does is produce some new piece of knowledge (the *conclusion*) on the basis of some already existing pieces of knowledge (the *premises*). The premises can be connected to the conclusion in different ways, and this yields a distinction between two fundamentally different kinds of inference, called *deduction* and *induction*.

In a deductive inference, the premises logically imply the conclusion, which is to say that the truth of the premises guarantees the truth of the conclusion. Here's an example: in the third episode of the fourth season, Mrs. Hughes asks Carson if he doesn't think that Dame Nellie should dine with the house party, to which he replies, "An Australian singer? Eating with her Ladyship? Never mind the Duchess! No, I do not!" The underlying reasoning seems to be that

- No Australian singer eats with her Ladyship (1st premise),

- Dame Nellie is an Australian singer (2nd premise), and therefore

- Dame Nellie does not eat with her Ladyship (conclusion).

The argument is valid, which means that everyone who accepts the premises must (as a matter of logic) accept the conclusion as well. But the example also shows that the validity of an argument is quite a different thing from the truth of its conclusion. In fact, Lady Grantham herself finds the conclusion preposterous, but this has nothing to do with the logic of Carson's argument. What she disputes is the truth of his first premise, prompting her to ask "Am I the only member of this family who lives in the twentieth century?" It is characteristic of deductive inference that any disagreement about the conclusion must involve a disagreement about the premises, because once the premises are accepted, deduction leaves no room for disagreement about the conclusion.

Induction is a bit different than deduction. While deduction takes us (with certainty) from true premises to a true conclusion, induction can at most make the truth of the conclusion highly probable, but never certain. To illustrate induction, consider the case of Lady Edith's hope of ever getting married after she's been jilted at the altar by Sir Anthony Strallan (3:3). Her desperate conclusion that she is just "a useful spinster, good at helping out" is not only based on this particularly devastating experience, but also on her earlier failures to catch the interest of marriageable men such as Patrick Crawley (1:5; 2:6) and Matthew (1:3). It's inductive reasoning that takes her from this unfortunate series of particular facts to a general statement about her lot in life. The difference between this case and the case of deduction is that if we disagree with Edith's pessimistic self-description (and we all sincerely disagree with that, don't we?), we don't need to reject any of her premises. Everything about these previous disappointments may be perfectly factual; yet, still, probable truth isn't certain truth, and there is still hope, even if slim hope, for Edith finding a marriageable man.

How does inference to the best explanation fit into this picture? Inference to the best explanation looks like an inductive argument, but it starts with just a single fact (often a surprising one) for which an explanation is sought. The first philosopher to emphasize this difference was Charles Peirce (1839–1914), who used the term "abduction" to refer to a third form of inference (besides deduction and induction) which corresponds more or less to what we now call inference to the best explanation. Other philosophers called into question the distinction between induction and inference to the best explanation, arguing that they are really the same thing in different guises or that one of the two should be seen as a sub-type of the other. We don't need to go into that here. What I am concerned with is demonstrating how inference to the best explanation functions in *Downton Abbey*.

Simply the Best: How to Evaluate Competing Explanations

Before discussing the problems that come with inference to the best explanation, let's look at an example where it works in all its glory. In one of their conversations in prison, Anna Bates explains to her husband why she's sure that his ex-wife killed herself, rather than being murdered, "Well, I know you didn't kill her. Then what's the alternative? A thief broke in, cooked an arsenic pie and forced her to eat it? It's not a very likely scenario" (3:1). Anna doesn't for one second buy into the (legally accepted) hypothesis that Bates killed Vera, because she's absolutely convinced that her husband couldn't possibly be a murderer. (As we know, this conviction will be dramatically shaken in season 4, but that's another story.) This leaves her with two remaining hypotheses: suicide or some far-fetched scenario involving a nameless burglar-murderer. No prizes for guessing which one of the two is the best explanation for Vera Bates's death.

But what exactly is it that makes one explanation better than another? Even though we readily identify the best explanation in cases like the one just discussed, describing in general terms what it is to be "the best" turns out to be surprisingly difficult. An important clue comes from the philosopher of science Peter Lipton who, in his book *Inference to the Best Explanation* suggests that the quality of an explanation is evaluated along two dimensions, which he calls *likeliness* and *loveliness*. A *likely* explanation is one we can justifiably believe to be true, given the available evidence. An explanation counts as *lovely* to the extent that it would, if correct, provide understanding of the fact that it explains. Applying these criteria to our example makes it plain why the burglar story can't be the best explanation for Vera's death: It isn't likely, because there is no evidence that anyone broke into her house that day (quite apart from the fact that cooking pies and feeding them to their victims is not what burglars usually do). Nor is this explanation lovely, because even if it were true, a story involving such a mysterious murderer wouldn't provide much understanding of the crime. Now one might try to remedy this defect by adding to the story some details about the identity and the motives of the murderer. This would indeed raise the loveliness of the explanation. But at the same time, adding details for which there is no independent evidence whatsoever would make the explanation even less likely than it already was. Taking account of likeliness *and* loveliness together shows that there's no way to get a good (let alone the best) explanation out of such a story.

To get a firmer grasp on the respective roles of likeliness and loveliness, let's look at two more examples. The first one concerns a suspicion expressed by Daisy in the fifth episode of the first season: "I was thinking, first we had the *Titanic* . . . I think of how we laid the fires for Mr. Patrick, but he drowned in them icy waters . . . And then there's the Turkish gentleman.

It just seems there's been too much death in the house." In her search for a connection between these two cases of death, Daisy implicitly appeals to explanatory loveliness: wouldn't it be comforting if we could account for these two troubling events by means of some overarching explanation? On the other hand, it isn't at all likely that there is any significant causal connection between the two tragedies. Anyone who looks at the facts a little more soberly than Daisy will conclude that their joint occurrence was just a coincidence and that Daisy's desire for a lovely explanation has compromised rather than enhanced her understanding of what's really going on.

One might thus think that loveliness is much too entangled with our subjective preferences and our (possibly hopeless) longing to understand a complicated world to count as a reliable guide to true hypotheses about objective reality. And this in turn would imply that inference to the best explanation doesn't really have that much to do with explanation after all. For if loveliness is neglected and explanations are only evaluated along the "likeliness" dimension, then "inference to the best explanation" is just a different name for "inference to the most likely hypothesis," and the question of whether or not this hypothesis *explains* anything has simply dropped out of the picture. Some philosophers have indeed followed this line of thought and argued that explanation is of little use in the quest for truth.

A second example shows, however, that this is too quick and that loveliness sometimes *does* point the way to hypotheses that then turn out to be true. In the eighth episode of the fourth season, Edith surprises the family with her announcement that she and Rosamund are going on a sabbatical to Switzerland to improve their French. In the following discussion at dinner, two possible explanations for this unexpected project are mentioned: Edith herself states that she fancies getting away for a bit, while Mary suspects that this is an incognito search for the missing Mr. Gregson. Both these explanations have a reasonable degree of likeliness, but as we know, the real reason for the trip to the continent is Edith's secret pregnancy, which she has confided to no one but to Rosamund. The only other family member who smells a rat is Violet, and this is not because she thinks that the explanations offered at the dinner table aren't likely enough, but because they aren't lovely enough: even if true, they wouldn't quite relieve the puzzlement about Edith's plans, let alone Rosamund's involvement in them. By contrast, Edith's dark secret would perfectly explain not only her desire to leave the country for a while but also two otherwise inexplicable pronouncements of Rosamund: first, her telling Violet that Edith is to be cherished, and second, her sudden awareness that her French needs improving, on which Violet sardonically comments, "Rosamund has no interest in French. If she wishes to be understood by a foreigner, she shouts." Violet is convinced that a hypothesis which explains so many different facts at once must be true, and she's right. This shows that loveliness of explanations must not be disparaged in the search for true hypotheses.

Not So Simple: Dr. Clarkson vs. Sir Philip Tapsell

Unfortunately, people often disagree about which hypothesis best explains a given set of phenomena. This usually doesn't make for a lot of drama. But if the hypotheses concern such a delicate matter as the state of health of an earl's daughter and if the disagreement about them occurs between two doctors who are trusted to varying degrees by different members of the family, then inference to the best explanation can take center stage in some dramatic developments. This is what happens in the fifth episode of the third season, to which we now turn.

At first, only Dr. Clarkson, who has known Lady Sybil from childhood on, notices that there is something unusual about her condition when she goes into labor. He interprets her swollen ankles, her muddled state of mind, and the smallness of the baby as possible symptoms of pre-eclampsia, whereas his antagonist, Sir Philip Tapsell, prefers a less ominous explanation of all this, "It means she's having a baby." Now which one of these two explanations is better? As far as likeliness is concerned, Sir Philip's hypothesis fares pretty well; no one would doubt its truth. What Clarkson contests is therefore not the truth of Sir Philip's hypothesis, but its ability to explain the relevant phenomena. To use Lipton's term introduced above, it's the *loveliness* of the explanation that is at stake: do we really understand what's going on by merely alluding to the fact that Sybil is having a baby? After all, many women give birth without suffering from swollen ankles or mental confusion. By contrast, the pre-eclampsia hypothesis is lovely in this sense, because it would, if true, adequately account for these distinctive features of Sybil's condition. At the same time, the hypothesis is not very likely, because (as Tapsell is quick to point out) pre-eclampsia is a very rare condition. With likeliness and loveliness thus pulling in opposite directions, the contest between the two competing explanations is not easily decided.

The plot thickens if non-medical motivations for favoring one or the other explanation are taken into account. Throughout the episode, Sir Philip's concern to keep up the impression that everything is under control outweighs all other considerations. This is particularly obvious when he simply ignores what should (under normal circumstances) count as decisive evidence against the thesis that everything is as it should be: an excess of protein in Sybil's urine. On the other hand, we may also suspect Clarkson not to be guided by the quest for truth alone. At least that's what Robert does when he insinuates that it's just Clarkson's professional pride that has provoked the disagreement with Tapsell.

These kinds of considerations are characteristic of what happens when laypeople have to decide what to do in a situation where the experts disagree. They then engage in a kind of second-order inference to the best explanation, where the question is no longer why a patient displays certain symptoms but why a doctor reaches certain conclusions. This may sometimes help to settle the issue, but it doesn't in this particular situation. Instead, it only has the unfortunate effect of transforming the disagreement between the experts into a disagreement between the family members, culminating in Violet's characteristically crisp description of this desperate situation, "The decision lies with the chauffeur."

The dispute is finally settled—in a most tragic way—by the ensuing events. Sybil's death leaves no doubt that she had indeed been suffering from pre-eclampsia, which led to the more serious eclampsia. Clarkson had been right, Tapsell wrong. End of the story? Of course not. It would be the end if the explanation were just about the search for the truth about the facts of situation X, but, as mentioned at the beginning of this chapter, we also have other things in mind when we ask why. One of them is that we want to know the truth of who's to

blame, and for that purpose, eclampsia by itself is not a satisfactory explanation of Sybil's death. At least that's what ani-
mates the conflict between Cora and Robert in the sixth
episode of the third season.

Changing for the Best: The Dowager Countess and an Inconvenient Truth

We have already seen that an explanation can be accepted as true
by everyone and yet fail to be the *best* explanation because it
doesn't provide a sufficient amount of understanding. Something
similar happens when we consider possible explanations for
Sybil's death. Everyone will agree (at last) that Sybil died from
eclampsia. But is that explanation sufficient? Cora thinks it isn't:
she holds Robert responsible, because he failed to listen to
Clarkson's arguments. The underlying assumption is that
eclampsia isn't always fatal and that therefore Sybil's death could
have been prevented if Clarkson's advice had been followed.
Robert actually admits this, so what threatens the Crawley's
marital harmony here is not a disagreement about explanations,
but the fact that the agreed-upon explanation burdens one of the
spouses with a guilt that the other one can't forgive.

It seems, then, that inference to the best explanation in this
case leads to an impasse of quite a different sort than the one
discussed above. The problem here is not any kind of weakness
or ambiguity in the application of inference to the best explanation. To the contrary, the problem rather seems to be the
strength of inference to the best explanation, which produces
the disturbing conclusion that Robert is at least partly responsible for his daughter's death. And so it seems that there's nothing to be done but to face the facts, even if we don't like them.

Well, maybe that's how it works for common people, but not
for Violet Crawley, the Dowager Countess of Grantham. If the
facts aren't to her liking, then why shouldn't it be the facts that
have to change? And our above discussion suggests where to
apply the lever to achieve such a change: since the inconve-
nient truth resulted from an inference to the best explanation,
the competing explanations need to be reassessed. So the question is, once again, whether Robert's behavior is really needed
to explain Sybil's death or if eclampsia alone could legitimately
be seen as the best explanation for that dreadful event. The

main trouble with that question is that no one knows with any certainty whether Sybil would really have survived if Robert had given Clarkson's advice a fair hearing. The best one can come up with is some statistical statement about the survival rate of patients in similar circumstances.

And here lies Violet's chance to modify the outcome of our inference to the best explanation. She summons Clarkson and tries to make him retract his statement that he might have saved Sybil's life had he been allowed to. She wouldn't go so far as to force him to lie ("so unmusical a word"), but then, who needs lies when there are statistics? In the final scene of the episode, Clarkson says he's done a great deal of research, which led him to the conclusion that Sybil would most probably have died anyway. We're not told any details about that research, but here's a conjecture: When making statistical statements, much depends on how one defines the relevant set of events. For example, the chance of surviving eclampsia might be quite different if one only considers patients who suffer from it in a particular phase of pregnancy, as opposed to all patients. Now if one is interested in the chance of survival for one particular patient, the cases on which one's statistics are based should be relevantly similar to that particular case. And since there's quite some room for interpretation about what counts as "relevantly similar," we can imagine how Clarkson manages to revise his assessment without doing too much violence to his scientific standards.

As a consequence, the "eclampsia alone" hypothesis now becomes the best explanation for Sybil's death because its rival ("eclampsia plus Robert's misjudgment") includes an explanatorily irrelevant element (which in general makes explanations less likely and less lovely); and if Clarkson's revised statement is true, then whatever Robert thought or did had no impact on Sybil's fate. From a scientific point of view, we might be uncomfortable with that result because we can't get rid of the suspicion that Clarkson somehow had to twist the evidence in order to arrive at the statement that the countess urged him to make. But as we witness Cora and Robert crying in each other's arms again, we have to admit that what they have now settled on is at least in some sense the *best* explanation for their daughter's death.

10
Does Bates Know Who Raped Anna?

Clara Nisley and Thomas Nisley

In *Downton Abbey's* third episode of the fourth season, we watch as the Crawley family anticipates the arrival of the famous Australian opera singer, Nellie Melba. The guests start arriving and the downstairs servants scramble to make the proper accommodations for the guests and their servants. Earlier in the day, Lord Anthony Gillingham, Lady Mary's childhood friend and potential suitor is invited to attend the concert. He, of course, being an aristocrat brings along his valet, Mr. Green. Outside the servants' quarters, Lady Mary's maid, Anna, greets Mr. Green by helping him with his bags.

Let's look into what some would say is one of the most controversial story lines in *Downton Abbey*. Anna Bates's rape was distressing to those of us who have followed her love story with John Bates. In season 3, we watched as she saved him from life imprisonment when she brought evidence that cleared him from the charge of murdering his first wife. What makes this story line controversial, aside from the rape, is that the focus has been on Mr. Bates's beliefs about who attacked his wife. The issue that we will explore is whether Mr. Bates's belief about who raped Anna can be called "knowledge" or not. Just how good are Mr. Bates's beliefs in meeting the standard definition of knowledge? In the *Theaetetus*, Plato (424–348 BCE) claims that knowledge is justified, true belief. In the past, at least, philosophers working on the theory of knowledge have accepted this definition. The challenge, therefore, lies in being able to satisfactorily justify Mr. Bates's belief about who committed this horrendous act against Anna.

What Bates Sees

Let us revisit this wrenching story in episode 3 of season 4. We left off with Anna helping Mr. Green with his bags. Immediately, Mr. Green and Anna have several lighthearted teasing exchanges. Mr. Bates spots this bantering and acknowledges to Anna that Mr. Green "gets his goat." He expresses to Anna that he does not like the interest that Mr. Green seems to be taking in her. It seems that Mr. Green has a fondness for Anna, and she appears to enjoy their informal exchanges. Yet, Anna calls him by his Lord's name, Mr. Gillingham, and when he asks her to call him Mr. Green, Anna refuses, using the excuse that Mr. Carson would not approve. He responds by saying that "all work and no play makes Jack a dull boy and Jill a dull girl." She maintains a respectful distance by not allowing him to become too familiar, stating, "she believes in getting on with [her] work." Mr. Green states that he will organize a new card game, "Racing Demon." The servants, among them Anna, seem to enjoy playing the new card game. While they are playing, Mr. Bates walks in, calling on Anna. When she does not hear him the first time, he raises his voice to call to her attention that Mrs. Patmore "has been taken ill" and that they are "making a racket." This is the first time that we get to see any kind of disharmony between Mr. Bates and his wife. Until Mr. Green arrives on the scene, Bates and Anna have been living an undisturbed life in the cottage near Downton Abbey.

Meanwhile, the Crawley family is preparing to give a concert in their estate. We watch the family and their guests as they are entertained by the famous Australian opera singer, Nellie Melba. The staff, being invited to listen, sits in a nearby room, upstairs. While Nellie Melba sings Puccini's "O Mio Babbino Caro," Anna complains of a headache and goes downstairs for a headache powder. While she drinks the headache medicine, Mr. Green appears and asks if she "would care for something strong?" When she refuses and starts off upstairs, Mr. Green intercepts her. We watch in alarm, as Mr. Green punches and drags Anna into the kitchen. Although we never see the rape, we hear her screams and then a punch. After the attack, we watch horror-stricken as she emerges with her disheveled hair, torn clothes, and her face scratched and bruised. Meanwhile, upstairs where the servants are somewhat bored listening to Dame Nellie sing, we watch as Mr. Green walks into the room, buttoning his blazer.

After Dame Nellie's performance is over, Mrs. Hughes walks into a room off the kitchen where Anna is crouched down hiding behind a china cabinet. Immediately, Mrs. Hughes wants to inform someone of the crime and see whether the doctor is still in the home. She tells Anna that she must at least inform Mr. Bates. Anna refuses, afraid that "if he knew, he would murder the man who's done it, and then he'll be hanged." Anna reappears on the scene wearing a dress that Mrs. Hughes lends her. Mr. Bates, returning from the concert, runs into Anna in the hallway. He notices the cut and bruises on her face and that she has changed her dress. Anna tells him that while she was drinking the headache powder, she "suddenly felt dizzy and . . . must have fainted . . . and hit the edge of the sink." As Anna tells her lie in order to spare her husband of another murder charge, Mr. Green walks by wishing them both a goodnight and thanking them both for looking after him. Anna responds by saying goodnight, but we see her physically change as an effect of her rape. At the end of episode 3, we watch as Anna walks back to her cottage by herself, while Mr. Bates calls out her name.

At the start of episode 4 of the fourth season, Anna is left with no other place to sit at the breakfast table but next to Mr. Green. She has to explain, when asked, that "she fell and cut [her] lip." Mr. Bates asks Mrs. Hughes, "how was Anna, when you lent her that dress last night?" Mrs. Hughes dissimulates by stating that she doesn't know any more than Mr. Bates does.

In our story, we must take into account Mrs. Hughes's denial that she has any knowledge. We must come to ask how Mr. Bates is doing with regard to the pursuit of truth and his quest for knowledge. It seems that in order to have knowledge, Mr. Bates must have evidence, and he would have to rely on Mrs. Hughes's testimony. This is one of the answers that philosophers have used to answer the question—how can we be certain that our beliefs are an account of knowledge? The answer is that if your beliefs were based on sufficiently strong evidence, then you have knowledge. The evidence serves as a sufficient condition in which you would be justified in your belief. Mr. Bates must acquire knowledge through sufficient conditions that would provide the grounds for his belief. We know that Mrs. Hughes has denied any knowledge; therefore, we must continue with our story, so that we can analyze Mr. Bates's evidence or information (for example, Mrs. Hughes's testimony). Testimony serves as a sufficient condition on the grounds that Mr. Bates recognizes that Mrs. Hughes is a rational agent whose testimony is trustworthy. We are not claiming that Mrs. Hughes's testimony is an independent source for justification. What we are saying is that Mr. Bates's belief is partially dependent on accepting Mrs. Hughes's testimony but not wholly. For Mr. Bates being justified in holding a belief requires more than Mrs. Hughes's testimony.

Returning to episode 4, season 4, we see Anna flinching when her husband places his hand on her shoulder. Anna is to accompany Lady Mary to London for a day. Unbeknownst to Anna, Lord Gillingham is with his valet in London. On Anna's return, Mr. Bates asks her for a kiss. When she refuses to kiss him, he asks what has happened. Anna is clearly upset; he insists that he needs to find out why she is upset and will "at the end," he says, "find out."

So far, Mr. Bates does not know that Anna has been raped, and more importantly, he does not know that Mr. Green is the assailant. At the end of episode 4, Mr. Bates does not have a true belief. Anna has moved out of the cottage; she had asked Mrs. Hughes to allow her to move back upstairs into the servants' quarters. Mrs. Hughes urged her to go to the police. She refused, afraid that Mr. Bates would find out that she had been raped by Mr. Green. She would rather have him heartbroken than hanged: "Better a broken heart than a broken neck," she says to Mrs. Hughes. Mr. Bates confides in Lord Grantham, who expresses his opinion to "wait, until things become clear."

What Bates Suspects

In episode 5, we see Anna covering her bruise with makeup. As she walks downstairs, Mr. Bates is waiting to greet her. He demands an explanation of "what has gone wrong between [them]." While in the hallway, Mr. Bates heard Mrs. Hughes advising Anna that she should tell him the truth. He walks into Mrs. Hughes's sitting room and in his pursuit for the truth, threatens to hand in his resignation. When he stands up to leave, Mrs. Hughes tells him that Anna loves him. When we see them once again in her sitting room, Mrs. Hughes has conveyed that

Anna was raped. Immediately, Mr. Bates asks when the rape occurred: "Was it the last night of the house party, when she told me she fainted and hit her head? . . . Then, I know who it really was. . . . I think it was Lord Gillingham's valet who teased her and flirted with her from the moment he arrived." Mr. Bates believes that Mr. Green raped Anna and his belief is true.

Yet most epistemologists agree that a true belief is not sufficient for knowledge. Mr. Bates must have sufficient conditions for his true belief. The sufficient conditions require that Mr. Bates must have beliefs that are obtained by good reasoning and are coherently formed. Mr. Bates's true belief does not qualify as knowledge, unless he has a relation of reasons that are logically consistent with his belief.

We must take into consideration Mrs. Hughes's false testimony where her testimony conceals Anna's actual assailant from Mr. Bates. Mrs. Hughes swears that it was not Mr. Green who raped Anna. She tells him that a stranger raped Anna. If he discards her testimony, he may seek to verify Mrs. Hughes's testimony with another member of Downton Abbey. But, in our story, the fact that Mr. Bates ends up with a true belief is not through evidential testimony. When he confronts Anna, she adamantly denies it was Mr. Green and confirms that it was a stranger.

Let's consider whether Mr. Bates has reasons for his belief based on testimony. It would be an account of knowledge based on someone's statement that Mr. Green raped Anna. Through testimony, Mr. Bates would have acquired knowledge as to who raped Anna. He would come to know on the basis of someone's statement. Testimony would only count as a source of knowledge if and only if the testimony that Mr. Green raped Anna came from a reliable source. We have Mrs. Hughes's testimony that Anna was raped by a stranger who broke into the house. Mrs. Hughes is in fact a reliable source, since she is in charge of the female servants and so far as Mr. Bates is aware is an honest and credible woman. Mr. Bates has no reason to suppose that Mrs. Hughes's testimony is not true. However, Mr. Bates doubts Mrs. Hughes's testimony, even though there is no other statement that contradicts Mrs. Hughes's statement. His belief must be part of a mental process that would allow him to choose that a stranger raped Anna. If he were to choose a stranger raped Anna, instead of Mr. Green, his reasons would proceed from Mrs. Hughes's testimony. Because Mrs. Hughes is a reliable person, her statement that a stranger raped Anna counters Mr. Bates's belief that Mr. Green raped Anna. Mr. Bates would need someone such as a servant, one of the Crawley family members, or someone else to tell him that Mr. Green raped Anna. Their testimony, then, might provide him with sufficient reasons for his belief.

But, testimony cannot play the proper role in providing knowledge for Mr. Bates. Given the deceptiveness of Mrs. Hughes's testimony, he can't be said to know that Mr. Green raped Anna. As we have learned, Anna will not tell Mr. Bates the truth for fear that he will do something drastic, like kill Mr. Green. However, Mr. Bates is determined to find out the truth, as to who raped Anna. Truth is required for knowledge, but a true belief is not sufficient for knowledge. That Mr. Green raped Anna is true, but it may be the case that it is true, but not for the reasons that Mr. Bates thinks it's true. Given that Mrs. Hughes has given Mr. Bates misleading testimony about Anna's assailant, it could just be a matter of coincidence that Mr. Bates's belief that Mr. Green raped Anna is true.

Is Bates Justified in His Belief?

Justification requires that Mr. Bates's true belief follow from correct reasons. Believing that Mr. Green raped Anna, Mr. Bates has to have the right sorts of reasons to justify his belief. So, let's see whether his reasons for his true belief are justified, or if he has a faulty step in his reasoning. We think that an examination of the conditions under which Mr. Bates first encounters Mr. Green will show how Mr. Bates concludes that Mr. Green raped Anna. But, whether he is justified in his conclusion remains to be seen.

At least one of Mr. Bates's reasons for suspecting Mr. Green comes from his teasing and flirting with Anna. Mr. Bates is very confident in connecting the flirting to the rape. But he may have misunderstood Mr. Green's feelings about the desires he had for Anna. This is to say that it is certainly possible that Mr. Green could flirt (inappropriately) with Anna and still not be the rapist. It seems that something about Mr. Bates's true belief does not meet the standard account of knowledge. We need more than just the observed teasing and flirting.

At the start of episode 6, we see that Mr. Bates is preoccupied with his thoughts. While at dinner at an upscale restaurant, Mr. Bates reveals to his wife that he wants to kill the man who raped her. Lady Grantham, who accompanied them back to the house, tells Lady Mary that Mr. Bates "feels that he should have protected [Anna]." In episode 7, Lord Grantham is going to America and requires that his valet go with him. Mrs. Hughes reveals Anna's rape to Lady Mary. As a result, Lady Mary persuades her father to take Mr. Barrow, instead of Mr. Bates. When Lord Gillingham returns to Downton Abbey, his valet, Mr. Green, joins the servants while they are eating at the kitchen table. When Anna walks in, she sees him and stops mid-sentence. Mr. Bates observes her reaction. Later, as the servants are eating dinner, Miss Baxter says that she admires Dame Nellie and regrets that she was not working at Downton Abbey at the time. Mr. Green expresses that he "couldn't take [Dame Nellie singing] for one more moment." She sounded "as if her finger were caught in the door." When Miss Baxter asks, "so what did you do?" He replies, "Well, I came down here for a bit of peace and quiet." We see Anna staring at him, then turning; she gives her husband a sideways look and smiles. We're left with Mr. Bates gazing hatefully at Mr. Green. As he gazes at Mr. Green, he becomes convinced that Mr. Green raped Anna.

But is all this sufficient for justified true belief? Mr. Bates set out to inquire into Anna's rape. First, Mrs. Hughes denied that it was Mr. Green who raped Anna, but she confirmed that it was the *night of the house party*. Second, Mr. Bates's initial reason for suspecting Mr. Green is shameless *flirting and teasing*. Third, Green himself confirmed that on the night of Dame Nellie's concert that *he went downstairs*—where, as it happens, Anna was raped. Whereas there were true statements, there were false statements as well. Note, Mrs. Hughes made a calculated false statement in order to conceal that Mr. Green raped Anna. Could Mr. Bates have knowledge, if he based his belief on testimony solely? Justification requires that statements be true. But, Mr. Bates's reasons for his belief are not wholly based on testimony; the initial reason for his belief was based on his observing the interest that Mr. Green took in Anna; however, as we find out in the fifth season, Mr. Bates based his belief on Mr. Green's testimony. Although the statement is true, Mrs. Hughes's statement is false. Mr. Bates is not justified on the basis of his belief. He does not have knowledge, and Anna, a non-philosopher, tells him that he might have suspected, but he did not know.

11
What Mary Didn't Know

Tamás Demeter

One of the dominant themes in the first three seasons of *Downton Abbey* is Mary and Matthew's relationship. It begins with Matthew's rather obvious first-glance attraction to Mary, to which she initially responds in a rather cold manner. But gradually she becomes more open and friendly, and eventually falls in love with, and agrees to marry, him. But until this conclusion is reached, their relationship negotiates a complicated path.

But why did Mary hesitate to accept Matthew? According to the most obvious interpretation of Mary's behavior, her hesitation is due to the uncertainties surrounding the future of the estate: Is it going to belong to Matthew or the eventually unborn son of Lord Grantham? This unsettled question may be seen as a crucial element in the process of Mary's deliberation. But in the light of future developments her motivations might be interpreted in different ways, and the various interpretations shed different lights on her character. At times even she hints at her ignorance of her own motivations behind her wavering suggesting that the interpretation of her hesitation is certainly not a straightforward matter. And as some of her comments on the affair with the Turkish diplomat suggest, there may also be hidden psychological obstacles lurking behind her actions. Not surprising, then, there are various, and at least partly conflicting, interpretations, and the existence of these interpretations present us with some challenges.

Facts of the Matter

Most of the crucial events take place in the first season. In episode 3, Mary enters into a questionable love affair with Mr. Pamuk, a Turkish diplomat who suddenly dies in her arms. In episode 4, it is conclusively settled that Mary cannot be the heiress of Downton, and it is Matthew who is to be the next Earl of Grantham. Robert, Mary's father and the present earl, raises to Mary the idea of marrying Matthew, which she dismisses with the line, "I'd never marry any man that I was told to." In a later scene, Mary bursts into tears under the pressure caused in her by the constant mentioning of Matthew's name in an after-dinner conversation, because she perceives that as meaning it is only Matthew who matters to her father, and she accuses her mother, Cora, of giving up on her because of the Pamuk affair. Cora only comments on this, saying, "Don't quarrel with Matthew . . . because one day you may need him."

In episode 5, Cora, in another conversation with Mary about the prospects of her marrying Matthew, proclaims to her that due to the Pamuk affair "You're damaged goods," and Cora emphasizes that this circumstance should be considered seriously in the present context. Especially because word is getting around in London that Mary is "not virtuous"—a piece of information that apparently shocks Mary, yet she insists on managing her own affairs and resists the pressure coming from her mother. It is also in this episode that one can perceive Mary growing increasingly more sensitive to Matthew's affections and approach. Yet, Mary seems to be more interested in competing with her sister, Edith, for the attention of Sir Anthony. Mary's behavior obviously hurts Matthew, but she realizes this only when he leaves the house.

In episode 6, Cora finds out about a letter sent to the Turkish embassy describing the circumstances of Pamuk's death. Following Matthew's suggestion to see each other more often, he proposes to Mary as a conclusion to an intimate after-dinner conversation in which Mary half seriously warns Matthew, "You must pay no attention to the things I say." Later Mary tells Cora about the proposal who asks what answer she gave him, and Mary replies, "Only that I'd think about it." Then Cora comments, "That's an advance on what it would have been a year ago," and asks Mary whether she loves him. Mary responds, "Yes. I think I do. I think I may have loved him much longer than I knew," and then to Cora's disappointment she hints at the Pamuk affair: "I'll have to tell him, if I didn't I'd feel as if I caught him with a lie." Here, the conversation ends as Robert enters the room.

In episode 7, Mary finds out that it was Edith who sent the letter to the Turkish Embassy. It also turns out that Cora is expecting a child who may be a son, and in this case Matthew would be pushed out as the heir of the title and the estate. Through a series of conversations we come to know that Mary does not know if she wants Matthew without the title: the title is one thing, his personal qualities make him desirable on independent grounds. Nevertheless, Mary keeps postponing the answer to Matthew while she is under pressure from various family members. Matthew thinks that Mary is postponing because she wants to wait and see whether her mother is expecting a boy—but in the end Cora loses the child. Matthew feels that Mary's hesitation forces him to leave Downton, and even if Mary is still uncertain, she very much regrets her hesitation and says that she "ruined everything."

Season 2 covers the years of World War I, Matthew's engagement to Lavinia, and Mary's adventures with potential suitors. Throughout this second season their mutual affections are strengthened. After Lavinia's death, in the Christmas Special, Mary confesses to Matthew her affair with Pamuk, and identifies its spring as coming from "lust" or "need for excitement." She also points out that this affair changed her life and she was made different by it. Matthew eventually proposes again to her and she accepts him, putting a formal end to a long period of hesitation.

Some Possibilities of Interpretation

Before turning to lessons and literary parallels of philosophical significance, let me sketch some lines of potential interpretations that can be constructed by turning various elements from this pool of events into evidence.

First, the "emotional uncertainty" line: Mary does not know how she feels about Matthew; her emotions are changing and evolving under influences from family members and events taking space in her life. Nevertheless, her emotions have a more or less clear tendency to grow increasingly affectionate toward Matthew. This line of interpretation conflicts with certain character traits Mary exhibits, such as being highly self-conscious, stubborn, and decisive.

Second, the "greedy" line: Mary is hesitant because she wants to find out where the fortune goes eventually, and she camouflages her greed with emotional uncertainty—possibly deceiving even herself. This conflicts with Mary's emphasis on Matthew's personal qualities and her insistence on accepting only someone she is attracted to. Besides, if greed were her motivation, then the rational course of action would be indeed to accept Matthew in season 1, episode 7 with the hidden proviso that if Cora's child is a boy, then she would withdraw. But Mary does not take this route.

Third, the "social exclusion" line: Mary is worried about the social consequences of the Pamuk affair, which threatens with a scandal, and time is not on her side. But she is hesitant to accept Matthew until it is clear that no better candidate turns up in reasonable time, so she keeps postponing the decision. This conflicts with Mary's several outbursts against socially accepted norms and her willingness to act against them; it also conflicts with her increasingly affectionate feelings for Matthew, for these are reflected in her behavior as well as in her conversations with and regarding Matthew.

Fourth, the "bad conscience" line: Mary is tormented by the Pamuk affair and her being "damaged goods" not worthy for Matthew. This leads to her hesitation to say yes because that, by her moral standards, would require a confession. But a confession runs the risk that it may prompt Matthew to withdraw his proposal and that could spread the word of an embarrassing affair. This conflicts with Mary's determination to face and accept the consequences of the affair in season 1, episode 5.

Fifth, the "conflicting influences" line: Mary is exposed to pressures in various forms and directions from family members to marry Matthew. These pressures come from her mother and father, her grandmother and aunt, and sometimes they suggest different paths to follow as in season 1, episode 7, in which her grandmother suggests she accept Matthew tentatively and then see if Cora's child is a boy, while her aunt suggests she wait until the child is born. The first option is dishonest and so morally questionable, and the second option entails the consequence, as her grandmother rightly points out, that Matthew's emotional commitments will be shaken if Mary's response is openly conditional upon the sex of Cora's child. Now, one could argue that the conflicting influences drag Mary into different directions and she cannot decide which advice to follow. But this line can be opposed by pointing to Mary's independent personality.

All five lines of interpretation (and I'm sure quite a few more could still be found) are, of course, not altogether contradictory and can be combined to some extent. However, there is a good deal of conflict between them as they cannot all be true: they rely on several mutually exclusive motivations and character traits in Mary.

The choice from among them, or the way they are combined, depends to a great extent on how one perceives Mary's general character on the basis of her appearances in various situations. This introduces an essentially personal bias into one's interpretation of her hesitation, as interpretation consists in arranging the facts of the matter and assigning significance to them so as to produce a coherent narrative of Mary's adversities. This is not an arbitrary process in the sense that one can arrange narrative elements and their significance as one wishes. Instead, the interpretation is composed against the background of personal sensitivities that make us responsive to certain aspects of situations and of the agents' behavior, thereby inclining us in specific cases towards accepting some interpretations as opposed to others. Thus our interpretations are always and irredeemably personal. It is our personal sensitivity that is expressed through the stock of psychological concepts we are accustomed to deploying in representing an agent's behavior as coherent—but creating this coherence can proceed in various and mutually exclusive ways. In what follows I will explore two ways of drawing the philosophical consequences of this personal bias in psychological interpretation by linking Mary's case to philosophically significant literary examples.

Does Human Knowledge Limit What We Can Know about Mary's Motivations?

For some it may seem that the problem arises from our less than ideal access to the relevant evidence: should we know

Mary's motivation and character better, we could describe her psychology adequately. Unfortunately, in social interactions we are never granted ideal access to an agent's mind; therefore, we are stuck with a pool of behavioral evidence from which only partial accounts can be construed, which leaves ample space for conflicting accounts.

Michael Frayn's play *Copenhagen* is intended to be an illustration of this indeterminacy. The situation it portrays cries out for psychological interpretation: it is the infamous meeting of Heisenberg and Bohr in September 1941 in Copenhagen. The drama stages a fictional, otherworldly conversation between them by reconstructing what happened in the actual meeting (as remembered later by the different participants) and interpreting it in radically different ways. The primary aim is to reveal what Heisenberg's intentions were in visiting Bohr, and thus to review the prospects of a moral evaluation of Heisenberg's behavior, and indeed of Bohr's own. The characters' "spirits" reconstruct the meeting in several inconclusive versions, demonstrating, thereby, the indeterminacy of the possible interpretations. According to Frayn, the main point of his play is that reporting one's motivations and ascribing them to someone else are equally subject to question. Intentions and motivations cannot be "precisely established" as they "remain shifting and elusive."

For Frayn the basic philosophical idea of his play is that in understanding motivations we face indeterminacy similar to the kind we face in the quantum world according to the Copenhagen interpretation. On the Copenhagen interpretation micro-physical indeterminacy is due to our intervention through our measuring devices, which not only measure but also influence phenomena in the quantum region. Indeterminacy here arises from the way we can access phenomena, and is thus related to the methods and limits of human knowledge. This is the only way we can have knowledge of quantum phenomena; but what we have knowledge of in this case is not the phenomena in themselves, but it is them and the measuring devices together.

Something similar may be the case with psychological interpretations, too. We do not have direct access to intentions, motivations, and character traits; we can only infer them on the basis of behavior, and in accordance with the conceptual and inferential resources our psychology supplies us with. And due to our different psychological sensitivities we always do this with an unavoidable personal bias. Therefore our interpretation of Mary's behavior, Heisenberg's, or anyone else's is jointly made up of behavioral facts and a personal psychological toolkit of concepts and sensitivities. So motivations and intentions can only be accessed through their effects (behavior) *and* the observer's psychological apparatus.

Lurking behind this picture is a commitment to a philosophical position known as realism because it does not deny that motivations and intentions exist independently of our psychological apparatus. On this view our psychological concepts are external to our mental architecture, even if we are unable to gain access to the latter without relying on the former. Given that our psychological apparatus is personal, psychological interpretation is underdetermined by the facts of behavior—even in the case of first-person reports, as they are also conditioned by personal psychological sensitivities. There is no way to pick the true interpretation that maps onto the actual mental architecture of Mary that causes her hesitation, as we are never in a position to choose from among competing interpretations on the basis of independent evidence. But in principle, if we could take an impersonal, objective view, a view from nowhere that is not influenced by personal biases—a God's-eye view, so to speak—then independent evidence could be reached and the psychological background of Mary's hesitation could be revealed.

Can We Ever Get Out of Our Heads and into Mary's?

One could argue, however, that comparing the interpretation of Mary's motivations to scientists' attempts to understand the quantum world is inappropriate on the grounds that there is no distinction between the phenomena to be measured (Mary's mental architecture) and a measuring device (psychological concepts and sensitivities). One could argue that our psychological apparatus is composed of the mental architecture that it seemingly describes. In this case the indeterminacy of interpretation is of a *metaphysical* kind: concepts used in psychological interpretation contribute to the creation of mental phenomena themselves, and so psychological indeterminacy is a different kind than the one that the Copenhagen interpretation suggests.

According to this view, even if ideal access (a God's-eye view) is granted, it is still possible to give a coherent interpretation of a person's behavior with the ascription of radically different mental architectures in its background, and this is due to the lack of facts independent of the psychological apparatus. The case is not that there are potentially relevant but for some reason inaccessible facts (for example, because of the limits of human experience, irreducible personal bias, and so on); rather, it is that the relevant facts cannot be identified without psychological interpretation, so the former cannot be used for grounding the latter.

As Daniel Dennett argues in "Real Patterns," psychological interpretations organize facts of behavior into patterns, and consequently the patterns themselves cannot be identified without the interpretations creating them. There is no independent ground for identifying patterns because competing interpretations would not even agree on which facts are irrelevant, disturbing "noises" and which are evidence. Giving an alternative interpretation changes the evidence as well: some parts of the agent's behavior cease to be noise and turn into evidence, other parts become noisy—as we have seen in the competing interpretations of Mary's hesitation. The case is thus not that we have different interpretations organizing and weighing facts of behavior differently. Rather, it is that different facts of behavior are turned into evidence that support an interpretation of Mary's behavior depending on the psychological apparatus with which we approach the events.

Classifying behavior, that is, telling which bodily movement means what, is done through our psychological apparatus, so behavioral evidence counting in favor of an interpretation is itself a matter of interpretation. In order to use some bodily movement as evidence, one needs to specify its meaning and significance; and *vice versa*, by ascribing mental states to an agent, one gives meaning to some of his bodily movements. Thus, there are no independent facts in the business of psychological interpretation.

Some similar understanding of human psychology can be illustrated through Henry James's 1904 novel *The Golden Bowl*. The story goes like this. Adam Verver, a rich American businessman, travels around Europe with his daughter, Maggie. A friend introduces Maggie to an impoverished Italian prince, Amerigo, and eventually they get married. Before their engagement the prince had had a liaison with the beautiful but poor Charlotte, and they had parted because of their financial circumstances. Although Charlotte is a school-friend of Maggie's, she does not reveal this former relationship to Maggie, who urges her father to marry again. He eventually marries Charlotte. Maggie and her father spend most of their time together along with Maggie's recently born child, thereby bringing Amerigo and Charlotte closer together, leading to a resumption of their old relationship. Although Maggie discovers this, she tries to sort things out while keeping everything under the surface. She succeeds; Adam and Charlotte return to America; Maggie and Amerigo begin a new life.

The indeterminacy of psychological interpretation is clearly perceived in a key scene of the novel. Charlotte asks for Amerigo's help in choosing a suitable present for Maggie without letting her know. It is not entirely clear, not even for Charlotte herself, what her purpose is in so doing, apart from having the prince in her company and having something said between them. What does this scene mean? Charlotte may want to compromise Amerigo; or to get closer to him by this common secret; or to initiate the renewal of their relationship; or to manipulate him by pricking his conscience for he is about to get married for financial reasons; or to remind him with whom he is actually in love. Or the situation can be interpreted as a heroic attempt to gain some kind of recognition for their former liaison, or even as a symbolic act of closing the affair. And it can also be said that this scene has no special significance, that it is an empty conversation in an uneasy situation which may have arisen from a bad idea.

The problem is quite similar to the one we face in Mary's case. Which interpretation to choose? None corresponds to the facts better than the others, so the choice depends on one's previous interpretations of the characters' preceding behavior, and will emphasize different aspects of the situation and the preceding events. So the choice will be made on idiosyncratic grounds, depending on which interpretation provides a synoptic view of the events for the interpreter from his or her personal outlook; which one corresponds best to the purposes the interpreter ascribes to the characters; which one seems the most appropriate given the interpreter's sensitivity to the situations encountered; which one makes the interpreter feel that he or she understand the situation and the behavior of the characters in them; and which one fits best with the overarching interpretation of the events portrayed in the novel.

As Robert Pippin points out in his *Henry James and Modern Moral Life*, James's position in psychological matters is more radical than the limits-of-human-knowledge view discussed above. However refined our insight may become, our motivations are just not the sort of thing that may be said to be "there." Again, the problem is not that one must choose the true interpretation from among rival ones in the light of the best evidence at hand, but that the evidence is simply not there before the interpretation—not even for the people whose actions are being interpreted, even if they think that their intentions explain everything. Their meanings, just like the interpreter's, also always depend on their own and others' reactions, future expectations, intentions, their views on the supposedly appropriate behavior, and so on. That is, meaning depends on several interpretations and even future interpretations. And these are available only retrospectively, and are open to constant revision without the possibility of being conclusive—that is, without there being facts that could settle the matter between conflicting interpretations, just as in the case of Mary's hesitation.

What Mary Does Not Know . . .

Based on the first philosophical understanding of Mary's hesitation to accept Matthew that I've sketched, it is in principle possible for us to learn what Mary knows, but we are limited by contingencies. By contrast, the second philosophical understanding suggests that "knowledge" may not even be the proper term to describe the outcome of psychological interpretation, so if we are inclined to accept this latter account, then we may easily conclude that what Mary does not know, may not be known at all.

Change and
Memory

IV

12
Should We Really Care about the Crawleys?

Tim Jones

Right this moment we're living in a time when America's super-rich are gorging on "a bigger and bigger share" of the economic pie and not appearing particularly keen to share their portion with the rest of us, according to a *New York Times* piece by Annie Lowrey. It's fair to ask, then, whether ultra-privileged characters like the Crawleys really deserve as much sympathy and attention as *Downton*'s huge success in the US suggests we're readily throwing their way. Surely it's more reasonable for us to be jealous of the Crawleys for enjoying unearned wealth that the majority of us can only dream of, or even to switch off the TV in disgust at a show that glamorizes the inequality that still causes misery today, like *Game of Thrones* actor Kit Harington told *Rolling Stone* that he's done.

By watching and loving *Downton*, we might even become a bigger part of the problem ourselves. Through being welcomed into the Crawleys' home each time we hear the opening theme start up, there's the danger that we're not just settling down to enjoy an hour of TV, but are opening ourselves up to being seduced into admiration for the world of luxury and hierarchy that greets us there. The more we coo at the Crawleys' fancy furniture and pretty costumes, or the more we think "gosh, doesn't that look nice!" every time there's an establishing shot of the building and its beautiful grounds, the more we're in danger of developing a sense of awe at the fine living that the Crawleys enjoy. And so the more we're in danger, too, of taking on the opinion of men like Carson, that these people are just so damn wonderful and significant that they surely

119

deserve such a lifestyle at the expense of the people beneath them.

If we're a little conspiracy-minded for a moment, we might even reckon that it's more than an accident that a show encouraging us to admire wealth and luxury has become so popular in this particular historical moment, when poverty and inequality are never far from the news headlines. The worst charge that could be levelled at *Downton* is that through its encouraging us to sit back and admire people who have so much more than we ever will, it wants to make us see inequality itself as something pretty beautiful, so that once the closing credits have rolled and the episode has finished, we're that little bit less likely to want to do anything about the inequality around us today in the real world. The inequality *outside* the episode will seem more and more to us like a perfectly natural part of life that we're monsters for complaining about and wanting to change, just like the inequality *within* the episode seems to Carson.

But despite all these possible problems with the show, I'm still inclined to think that it makes a pretty good case for the Crawleys (and people like them today) absolutely being deserving of our time and energy, neither because of their privileged position nor in spite of it, but because they're human beings just like the rest of us—and pretty decent ones too, beneath all their wealth. And if we buy the show's message, then recognizing this about people who have more than us is the first step towards a form of social change that could see everyone a little better off.

The Ties That Bind Us

Everyone alive right now shares a common humanity that binds us all together, and in *Downton Abbey* we're continually reminded of this, through the experiences of its most privileged characters as much as those of its least. Throughout the show, the Crawleys clearly struggle as human beings with experiences faced by the rest of us. Viewers who've gone through bereavement might see their own journey reflected in Lady Mary's struggles to move on with her life after the death of Matthew. Viewers who've suffered a miscarriage might identify with Cora's feelings following her fall in the season 1 finale. And viewers who've been unexpectedly dumped by their lover will know how Edith feels after being left at the altar by

Anthony in season 3. Even viewers who're lucky enough never to have had any of these things happen to them will see that the people of *Downton* feel the pain just as strongly as we would ourselves. They're all facing the experiences that come from being human just as surely as we've done, or will do, in our own lives. And *Downton* constantly shows that their money doesn't buy them relief from the emotional pain these experiences deliver.

Watching the Crawleys experiencing and working through these problems gives us a reminder of stuff we all have in common, stuff that crosses the divide between rich and poor. Just by watching, then, we're drawn into moments of contact between different classes (assuming you're not a part of the British aristocracy yourself, of course!), which do more than simply lull us into admiring what the Crawleys have and that we lack. They also impress upon us what we *share*. And it's not entirely impossible that these moments might even help us get through such difficulties ourselves. Someone who's just lost a husband might see, through Lady Mary taking on the day-to-day business of running the estate in Matthew's stead, a great example of how death can open up new avenues for us to go down, which lead in turn to new opportunities for love that she'd have missed had she carried on determined only to mourn and hang around indoors all day. And so *we're* reminded in turn that life is never over, even when we're utterly convinced it is. Sure, we don't all have a handy estate to throw ourselves into managing like Mary does, but the lesson we can take from her example is pretty relevant anyway, no matter our circumstances. Don't get stuck in grief, her story teaches us, for you'll miss the chances for joy that life still has to offer you.

But this angle on its own isn't an entirely convincing argument against the timely reasons for disliking the Crawleys that I started this chapter with. Sure, they share many of our own problems and might even give us inspirational models for how we might work through them. But they're still stinking rich in a way that mirrors the inequality around us today, and what I've argued so far leaves the show doing very little to challenge this state of affairs. The sympathy *Downton* generates for the Crawleys might even make the show more dangerous, since by stressing our common humanity with them, it might only bury a little deeper our hold on the reasons we should be switching off instead because of what's very *different* between us.

We're not just left in awe of the Crawleys like we might be during the first few episodes; we're made to feel increasingly sorry for them too. And they're still rich, while we're still poor. Never mind about having a cry with Mary when she's lost Matthew. What, if anything, does this show propose be done about *that*?

Change, One Flower Contest at a Time

Here's another reason why we're right to care about the Crawleys. This one isn't so compromised by the problem of them remaining so rich, for it comes from what they actually *do* with their privilege whenever contact with people from different walks of life gives them the opportunity.

Anyone who'd criticize the Crawleys should take a moment to consider that none of them asked to be born into the position they enjoy, and so it'd be wrong to blame them for this position purely on its own. It's not like any of them had the opportunity, before birth, to take a look at the state of the world that they'd arrive in and choose to be a part of the aristocracy, and by doing so deliberately create a middle and lower class that can only look in at them from the outside and be content with their lot. If the Crawleys had deliberately made such a choice, then it'd be a little more reasonable to think them selfish purely for the fact of their having the money alone. But since their arriving in such a position is as much an accident of birth as arriving in the very poorest household, then it's only fair to judge them on what they actually *do* with it. If all they do is flaunt their status in the faces of the people who have less than them, then I'd agree it's perfectly understandable that we turn our backs on them, just like I mentioned Kit Harington has done.

But this isn't what the Crawleys do at all. Throughout the series, we see them brought into contact with a massive number of people from different walks of life. This includes members of the household, like the Irish chauffeur Tom and the cook Mrs. Patmore, and also the people they encounter outside Downton, like the soldiers Sybil meets at the makeshift hospital in season 2 and the villagers who take part in the flower competition alongside Lady Violet in the fifth episode of season 1. And these moments of contact see the Crawleys showing a pretty consistent willingness to use their advantages to help the less privileged with their problems. These people remind the Crawleys that a world exists beyond Downton's grounds and that people who live there need a helping hand. Look at Lord Grantham paying for Mrs. Patmore's eye surgery at Moorfields Eye Hospital in season 1, episode 7. A moment of contact between people from different classes allows the guy on the top to recognize the problems faced by those beneath him, and to demonstrate his goodness of character by using the available resources to help her out.

And this stays true even when offering this helping hand directly contravenes the Crawleys' pretty ingrained, instinctive responses to the situation. A light-hearted example of this happens when Lady Violet is persuaded by the resolutely middle-class Isobel to throw the flower contest and let someone else win for a change. It takes a lot of work on Isobel's part to get her to do this, since it's pretty clear that Lady Violet has long taken it for granted that winning every single year is her god-given right. To get to the point she's at by the end of the episode, she's had to listen to and reflect on Isobel's challenging of an extremely deep-rooted belief about how village life should naturally work. Thanks to her meeting Isobel and being willing to work through the difficulties coming from an argument that's almost certainly entirely unfamiliar to her, Lady Violet no longer thinks that just because she's at the top of the social ladder, she therefore deserves to have everything come her way as a matter of course. She places the advantage that comes from her privilege to one side so that someone with less than her can see what being a winner feels like for a change. Think how much easier it'd have been for her to stick with what she's used to instead.

For a bolder example of the Crawleys allowing their attitudes to shift and change as they encounter people from different walks of life, look at their developing treatment of Tom. When Lord and Lady Grantham first hear of Sybil's relationship with this guy in the season 2 finale, they're absolutely horrified at their daughter's transgression of the class boundaries and the social disgrace that this leaves the family open to. And though the Crawleys' acceptance of Tom is probably motivated at least a little by the threat of losing Sybil, he eventually becomes their warmly respected friend. They even okay his wishes for their granddaughter to be christened a Catholic, and bring him in alongside Matthew and Mary to help run the estate. This goes far beyond merely tolerating his presence for Sybil's sake.

So like with Lady Violet at the flower contest, a moment of contact between the Crawleys and someone from a very different background provokes a dilemma about long-held views, which the Crawleys absolutely don't take the easy way out of. Instead, the dilemma becomes the means for them to grow into more sympathetic, dare I say *nicer*, people. It's cases like these that make *Downton* a show that stresses the value of mutual contact between people from different backgrounds and walks of life, rather than preferring that they stay segregated, or turn their backs on one another. It's these moments of contact that provide opportunities for the show's most privileged characters to develop beyond the moral and philosophical confines of the positions into which they were born. And we're right to care about the Crawleys because whenever such opportunities emerge, they usually take them.

Be Nice to Rich Folk

This is where the two separate points I've made about why we're right to care about the Crawleys start to come together, in a way that suggests that *Downton* isn't a show intent on arguing in favor of the privilege that divides people remaining intact. The show's actually keen to demonstrate one potential route towards social change that's just as possible today as in the early twentieth-century. By the end of this bit, you might think that my argument makes *Downton* sound a bit naïve or even condescending for carrying this message, over pressing for the more radical route that people like Tom's compatriots back in Ireland would rather go down. But the *will* for change is most definitely there.

Like I said a bit earlier, this is a show that stresses the shared humanity between the viewer and the people at the very top of the ladder. When I first made this point a few pages back, I was a bit dismissive about these moments, since on their own they seem to do little to actually sort out any of the wider problems affecting society both then and now. But when we look at them in light of what *Downton* shows moments of sympathetic contact between different people giving the Crawleys the opportunity of doing, these moments start to look more like the first steps of a manifesto for a particular process of social change.

At the same time as the show makes us feel all sympathetic for people at the top by reminding us of the horrible experiences we share, it also shows the Crawleys using moments of contact between themselves and people with much less privilege to put their views about how the world should work to a deeper scrutiny than they've ever done before—and then to change for the better. The show wants to get us all "awww" for the Crawleys, so that by recognizing that the people at the top at any given time struggle just like we do and feeling moved by this, we're more likely to remember that at the end of the day, they *are* people too. And we're less likely to turn our backs on them for having what we don't. They'll become our friends, rather than our enemies. And they'll then have the same opportunities that *Downton* keeps showing the Crawleys benefitting from—to meet people who're different, to re-think the assumptions that see them keeping their privilege for themselves, and to take some baby steps towards sharing it out a little. Don't fight them, the show urges us, but meet them as friends, and their good nature will see them start to level the playing field.

So by the philosophy of the show, a refusal to care about the Crawleys because of their privilege wouldn't *only* fail to take into account the experiences we share with them, or their goodness as human beings. It would also deny them the kind of contact they need (and that people *like* them, out in the real world, need too) if they're to learn and grow in ways that might help make society a bit more equal. If this show's right about what it's saying, then the more open we are to contact with people who're different from us, whether we're on the rich side or the poor, the more a society might gradually emerge where we join together somewhere in the middle. By being willing to meet them as fellow human beings, rather than wanting to turn our backs on them as potential enemies, they, in turn, meet *us*, and discover how and why people need them to be a bit more open to sharing.

This philosophy is well meant and demonstrates a really optimistic view of humanity's potential to sort out its problems through sympathetic contact, rather than through violent struggle. But it's not exactly impossible to pick apart. It puts a lot of responsibility for changing things onto the people who currently have less privilege, rather than on those who have more. It requires the people nearer the bottom of the hierarchy to act in certain ways, meaning that if the situation pointed out by the *New York Times* doesn't change, it's as much the fault of poorer people for not behaving as they should, as it's the fault of the richest. It's always a bit off to blame oppressed people for not acting in the right ways to help their oppression to end, and this is as true when we're talking about economic oppression as it'd be for giving gay people the responsibility for ending homophobia, or women for ending sexism. We'd be totally wrong to blame Thomas for Carson's remark in the season 3 finale about his sexuality making him "foul," because it's Carson's own responsibility to examine the attitudes behind it, rather than Thomas's to act in certain ways that make Carson more willing to do so. Ending oppression shouldn't ever be the duty of the oppressed. And I'd not feel entirely comfortable arguing if you'd insist that this is just as true when we're talking about the divide between rich and poor today. *Downton* shows us a road map for change that at least partially makes it the responsibility of those on the lower rungs of the ladder to be nice to the folks above them, and while it's great that it clearly doesn't want economic and social divides to stay as they are, we shouldn't ignore this pretty big issue with its solution.

In an ideal world, the Crawleys of today might realize the need to split up their share of the pie all by themselves, without us taking any responsibility for helping kick-start the process. The *New York Times* piece I started by mentioning suggests they're probably not going to do that any time soon, so a move for change led by people nearer the bottom might be what's needed. But it's not like the type of change that I reckon is backed by *Downton* is the only option. We *could* push instead for the sort of activism that Tom's friends go for after he and Sybil have moved to Ireland between seasons 2 and 3. I'm not personally sure that burning rich people out of their homes is ever the best solution, but were such a movement to get properly going, then the change it'd lead to would likely be somewhat quicker and more radical than the change that's started by a different person winning a flower contest for once, or by one extra person from a different class being welcomed into the elite because he's got it on with their daughter.

A sympathetic contact with people richer than us, which shows them our needs and wants and encourages them to take a step towards levelling the playing field—or open revolution? *Downton* prefers one option over the other, but this is a choice that each person wanting change can only make for him- or herself.

13
Topophilia; or, How We Got Hooked on *Downton*

LUCY ELVIS

Nestled in the heart of the English countryside, the camera pans past Lord Grantham and his dog Isis strolling towards the big house. Next, we're below stairs. A softly pealing bell summons Mr. Bates or maybe one of Carson's fleet of footmen up to the drawing room . . . and so it continues. After so many seasons, these first glimpses of the Abbey and its business-as-usual posture are comforting. These images signal the start of a cozy session of bygone Britishness. The show's characters are so familiar that the family and their servants feel like old friends, and we feel just as at home in the house as they do. But why do we feel this way? What is it about the show that draws us in and makes us feel native?

Sweating the Small Stuff

In his book *The Poetics of Space*, French philosopher Gaston Bachelard (1884–1962) develops a theory for exploring the way we experience architectural spaces. His theory is based on phenomenology, which as a method, concerns "lived experiences." When looking at an experience or phenomenon (in this case architectural space), phenomenology seeks to understand the generally agreed upon elements of the experience from a collection of individual accounts of that experience. A phenomenological theory of architecture, and a particular piece of architecture like the Abbey at Downton, will use the collection of people's personal experiences to get to the heart of what it means to live that experience.

Traditionally, philosophers approaching architecture looked at its physicality in order to build (if you'll pardon the pun) theories about it. Georg Wilhelm Hegel (1770–1831) and Arthur Schopenhauer (1788–1860) both formulated theories of architecture in this way. Each of them saw architecture as limited because it required giving form to heavy materials like stone, whilst performing a function (architecture has to be lived in or used as well as have visual impact). Bachelard decided to go a different way. Instead of focusing on the visual impact of architecture, he focused on the experiences and ideas architecture could give its users. He decided to sweat the small, even minuscule stuff—looking at the way we experience, write about, or even imagine small spaces, such as the rooms of a house, drawers, corners, bird's nests, and even shells. He used the way we experience these small spaces to gain insight into the way our conscious and unconscious minds interact.

Bachelard saw the home as a place that could allow us to daydream. His interest in dreams and the imagination drew him to psychoanalysis, especially the work of Carl Jung (1875–1961), a pupil of Sigmund Freud (1856–1939). Psychoanalysis identifies two elements in the human mind: the conscious and the unconscious. Dreaming is governed by our unconscious mind. As the name suggests, it's that part of the mind that we aren't aware of when we make decisions. While our conscious mind focuses on immediate concerns and elements of experience, our unconscious soaks up other elements of experience. When we dream or daydream, the unconscious mind uses this bank of experienced, unnoticed "stuff" to flavor our reveries. Rather than focusing on the way their buildings appeared, Bachelard argued architects should worry about the kinds of conscious and unconscious experiences they would give rise to. Better design could, in his eyes, lead to more chances to daydream productively and more chances to feel authentically at home.

Bachelard uses topoanalysis—a fancy term for an exploration of how we experience space—to reveal incidences of topophilia, an even fancier term for an intense love of place (from the Greek *topos* meaning "place" and *philia* meaning "love of"). Because he was trying to get at the unconscious mind, his tour of small, intimate spaces was not an account of physical experience, but a series of reflections about intimate spaces and incidents of hominess in. These fictionalized spaces are a jumping-off point for the imagination, a place for our minds to begin a search for an ideal home-space through a combination of recollection, lived experience, and shared notions of "home." All the small elements in our unconscious mind gather together, and we find seductive invitations to daydream in the close spaces of the opening sequence to *Downton*.

Downton's Intimate Spaces

So how does *Downton Abbey* reveal our penchant for intimate spaces? Gilles Deleuze (1925–1995) developed the idea of the *haptic*—a concept that describes a reaction by one sense, for example, the sense of touch, to something conveyed by another sense, such as vision. In television and film, the potential for the creation of haptic space is enormous since viewers are already using their senses of hearing and sight. So, it's not such a big leap to get a response from our sense of touch as well. Have you ever been so enthralled by an episode of *Downton* that you've felt the hairs on the back of your neck stand on end? Or been so engrossed in a shot sensuous enough that you could almost feel the texture of Lady Mary's gown? When we sit down to watch *Downton* and the opening credits start to roll, these techniques immediately draw us into the Abbey, making us a part of the action. Perhaps this is a hint as to why the series has enjoyed such enduring success.

Let's Start at the Very Beginning

In the case of *Downton*, the beginning is the very best place to start. Keeping Bachelard's topophilia concept in mind, we're going to wander scene by scene through the brief opening credits of the show. These have been used in seasons 1 through 4, although some of the most evocative shots (the opening shutters and the ringing bell) have even survived in the re-vamped opening of season 5. In this brief, thirty-five-second introduction we get nine snippets of Downton life. As viewers we're presented with opportunities to daydream in Bachelard's sense. The filming capitalizes on intimate spaces, and by appealing to our senses, closes the gap between the twenty-first century and the historic Grantham family and their staff. These haptic spaces make sure we begin each episode immersed in the rich environment of *Downton,* and feel at home there. Each of these haptic moments is a jumping-off point for the imagination; each is also a chance to daydream:

1) **Lord Grantham and Isis:** Crossing a green lawn, a figure strolls toward the house, a dog walking at his side. After an episode or two we assume its Lord Grantham and Isis, based purely on the trouser leg in the left of shot. Partly obscured by trees, Yorkshire's Highclere Castle (the location used for exterior shots of Downton) lies ahead of them. Strains of "Did I Make the Most of Loving You"—the *Downton Abbey* theme music—opens with urgent strings.

2) **The Shutter:** The second shot is our first glimpse inside Downton. The heavy shutters of a window open as the camera approaches. There is a sense of immediacy here. Light floods in to create a feeling of the house awakening. The shock of light is not softened by the camera at all, closing down the space between us as viewers and the fictional environment of the house. The view through the window gradually comes into a focus in a way that mirrors our eyes growing accustomed to sudden changes of light—a little like coming out of the movie theatre after a matinee screening.

   This direct appeal to our senses is a haptic moment. We're given a chance to recollect and escape. We might remember the shock of light on our first snow day—as the sun bounced off a blanket of white, or awakening at a honeymoon beach house pleasurably blinded for a moment by the morning salute of the sun. Of course, remembering is never just a case of recalling a place we were. We have a tendency to blend what we think we *know* to have been true at the time with elements we imagined or details that our unconscious mind noted behind the scenes. These are more than just simple rose-tinted-glass moments: they are interplay between our conscious and unconscious minds.

   Back inside Downton, the sharp contrast between the heavy curtains that surround the window and the brightness of the view through the window emphasizes the fact that we're inside. Our love of intimate space—the topophilia we talked about—is played upon to help us feel at home. Just as the filming here makes it feel as though we have emerged into the sunlight, a different haptic space is opened up in what comes next.

3) **The Bell:** Downstairs a bell is jerking to life. With this shot, at seven seconds into the opening sequence, we get the first sound that is not a part of John Lunn's theme music. The ringing of the drawing room bell below the stairs. The camera zooms in on the downstairs bell-panel as we take it in: the moving bell, its worn brassy color, the embossed rosette detailing at the center, the snail's shell curl of metal the bell is attached to, and the smart font on the plaque beside it. The high-pitched bell cuts through the buttery strings of the opening track—it demands attention as if we should be the ones to answer it. We feel for a moment as if we might be *in* the narrow service corridor. In this moment there's a number of sharp contrasts: the sudden movement of one bell amongst its dormant colleagues, and the sharp urgent sounds against the gradually building soundscape of the title track.

   The focus on the small details capitalizes on our tendency toward topophilia. Just like the spiral of the bellpull, Bachelard writes about the charm of the shell. It's a seductive shape—according to him—because not only is it a microscopic kind of home, but it invites us to imagine ourselves occupying its interior, mentally shrinking our bodies down to an infinitesimally small size in order to explore its geometry. We almost cannot resist imagining the internal dimensions of the bell, and how the sounds reverberate inside it.

4) **The Mail:** In soft focus, on the extreme right side of the frame, we see the fuzzy figure of a maid walking quickly upstairs, perhaps answering the call of the bellpull, or else going about the routine of the house. The camera tracks past her, placing sharp focus on the letter rack. A bundle of texture standing proudly out against the hazy

bustle of the maid's movements in the background. This focus on an inanimate object is the opposite of our human-centered expectations. Ordinarily, it's people that get the full focus of the camera. The cluster of correspondence here is reminiscent of Edward Collier's famous *Trompe L'oeil* letter rack (a painting so real-looking you'd be forgiven for trying to pop a stray envelope into the canvas in error).

Among the four letters in the shot, it's the one on an angle that catches our eye; we clearly see the franking and the sloping cursive of the address. Just like with Collier's painting, it seems as though we could reach forward and take the envelope and rip it open to read Grigg's blackmail to Carson, or the shocking news of injuries from the front. Our memories of previous excitement at receiving letters—perhaps a childhood birthday card or the thrill of a long-distance college love letter—help us to flavor this scene. What's more, there's something comforting about the low lighting in these two downstairs shots. Images of life above appear formal and flooded with light whereas downstairs we find cozy, muted light, corners to retreat into, and steaming pots on the stove.

5) **The Watched Pot:** We progress further into the downstairs world as a gleaming copper pot issues steam from its partially opened lid. The obscured reflection of (we assume) Mrs. Patmore approaches and she reaches out for the lid, ragged potholder in hand. This might seem a fairly mundane image, but our imagination is invited to have a field day. We might be reminded of our grandmother's cooking or the excitement of waiting for a holiday feast. These might be overlaid with our own impressions of what a kitchen ought to be like—the kind of delicious smells we would expect to find there. In this one fragmentary image lies a world of possibility. We construct a composite image of the rest of the kitchen. But where does this come from? With nothing else to base this on, fond memories, aspirations, and vague ideas get grouped together in our imagination to form a mental image.

6) **The Set Square**: And so to the dining room. We're back upstairs watching the regimented table-setting ritual. Warm copper is replaced by the cold gleam of silverware and cut-crystal glasses. Again the delight is in the detail. The place setting itself is being measured out judiciously. There's great textural contrast between the well-used wooden ruler and the various sparkling knives and forks. The hands of one of the footman, Thomas perhaps, appear at the bottom and the right of shot, carefully flanking the gold-rimmed, crested plates with sparkling cutlery.

7) **The Rose Petal:** Keeping with the cool brightness of upstairs, the camera pans across again towards the window. This time it takes in a sideboard complete with decanters and a cigar box. Can we assume that this is the drawing room? Lying to the rear of the polished table top is a vase of lush white roses. As the camera tracks past, a single petal falls from one of the blooms. Like the wonky letter in the rack it is this small detail that catches our eye and draws us in. The sense of time here is strange too. Although the petal's descent is not really slowed down at all, the contrast between the stationary items and the graceful arc of the falling petal implies the house has its own sense of time. It's almost like we see it in slow motion. In Bachelard's theory, time is an important feature. Since he focuses on the imagination and daydreaming, time has much more elasticity than we might expect. Just as *Downton* spans generations of the Crawley family, our daydreams have the capacity to combine the seeds of inspiration we find in fiction or lived experience as well as recent memories and our distant past, to form a fleeting picture.

8) **The Lamplight:** The location of the next shot is unclear: we pan across a desk—is this Carson or Mrs. Hughes sitting down to work on the staff duties or a footman lighting the lamps in Lord Grantham's study? The light takes on a different character here than in the second shot of the credits with the shutter. Unlike the way light floods in as the shutters open, this lamp light

flickers to life suddenly as the oil or gas is turned on. This acts as a focal point here; it seems to draw the surrounding objects to it, creating the same intimacy that we saw in the downstairs shots of the letters and the ringing bell. Just like the haptic moment in the shot of the opening shutters, the light emerging slowly from the lamp gives the feeling of the rest of the desk unfolding for us, producing for us another haptic effect.

9) **The Feather Duster**: The final shot shows more minutiae of the house as two textures collide. A soft feather duster tickles the hard edges of a crystal chandelier. As with all the other figures in the opening sequence, we can only speculate as to who is dusting here. From a cynical point of view this allows the writers the flexibility in a long-running series like *Downton* of writing characters in and out of the story. But, maybe there's a bit more to it? Presented with these fragments of images, we're able to infuse our impressions of what an ideal home-life is with our own recollections. Shifting the focus from the few people in the shot to the small objects causes us to focus intently, and draw on our imagination from the onset.

Downton Dreaming

In each glimpse, as with the thirty-five-second opening credits, *Downton Abbey* invites us to imagine. The sequence cleverly capitalizes on our love of small intimate spaces: our topophilia as Bachelard puts it. Even at the first viewing, when we don't know any of the characters of *Downton*, we still get a homey sense from the images before us. We don't know about Lady Mary's turbulent relationship with Matthew Crawley or of his tragic death. We can't envisage the austere demeanor of Maggie Smith as the Dowager Countess. So where do we get the building blocks for our imagination from? Our tour of the opening sequence is a hint at how Bachelard's idea of topophilia relates to the imagination at work. A single carefully formed image gives us a chance to combine homey aspirations with remembered moments, and crystallize them for a second. These partial images provide inspiration for our daydreaming.

It seems like the journey we've been on has been simply subjective or personal recollections so far. So what is it that can unite them all? What stops us spinning off into rootless reverie? Aside from the fictional house that inspires daydreaming and the recollected homes of our past, Bachelard presents us with a third idea (or ideal) of home. He calls this a future house. This is not because it's a house waiting to be built or discovered, but precisely because it *always* remains elusive. It's similar to waking up from a dream: we know that we've been dreaming and have a sense of the feelings the dream we had evoked in us, but we couldn't, if asked, give a full account of our antics. This is just like the experience of watching the *Downton Abbey* opening sequence. When we break it down into small particles as we have done here, we can see the moments when our imagination comes into play, but when watched at normal speed what we experience is a vague, if comforting sense of home.

When we think about the improbable global popularity of a more English-than-a-cup-of-tea story like *Downton*, Bachelard may have a point. Perhaps it's not the pompous grandeur we are attracted to, but the small intimate moments, combined with our tendency toward topophilia, that give the show its universal appeal. Perhaps it's not just a chance to keep up with the Crawleys, but a way of bringing ourselves home.

14

Things Can Happen That Nobody Could Imagine Only a Few Years Ago

DONNA MARIE SMITH

> I feel a shaking of the ground I stand on. The nature of life is not permanent but flux. Things are changing.
>
> — MR. CARSON (5:1)

An "unsinkable" ship sank. A Great War was fought in which millions died. A global influenza pandemic killed many more millions. An array of technological innovations changed the way people communicated, traveled, and worked. During the period from 1912 to 1919, the world fell apart, and life would never be the same, especially in Europe where monarchies fell, country boundaries were re-drawn, and financial hardships altered the structures of economies and social classes. The modernist ideas, culture, and technology that dawned in the late nineteenth century took hold in the aftermath of World War I, ushering the world into the dazzling daylight of the 1920s. Set amidst this sweeping historical backdrop, the British drama *Downton Abbey* has captivated audiences with its engrossing story about the lives of the Crawleys and the hard-working servants who help run their grand Yorkshire estate in the north of England.

If German philosopher Georg Hegel (1770–1831) were following the daily lives of the Crawleys, he would find woven into the narrative tapestry the opposing forces of tradition and progress, conservatism and liberalism, and Victorian and Edwardian morés and modern Jazz-Age values. He would see Lord Grantham and his daughter Mary struggling as they forgo some of their aristocratic ways in order to maintain Downton as a working estate and fulfill their duty as employers for their county. He would take note as Carson the butler, Mrs. Patmore the cook, and the Dowager Countess overcome their anxieties brought about by using the new-fangled technologies that have invaded their world. Meanwhile, he would observe that Matthew Crawley, Lady Sybil, and Tom Branson have learned to embrace new ways of thinking in order to find their self-worth and help build a better world. Hegel's philosophy—as grand and intricate as the fictional world of *Downton Abbey* created by Julian Fellowes—reveals that it is this conflict, this struggle between the old ways and new ideas, that has led people like those in *Downton Abbey* to improve themselves and the world in which they live.

Change Is Coming, but I Still Want My Cup of Tea

In his *Philosophy of History*, Hegel writes, "The history of the world is none other than the progress of the consciousness of freedom." At the heart of the tension between tradition and progress in *Downton Abbey* is the survival of the way of life of the Crawley family and the estate on which they live. Tradition has kept the estate going for many generations, but it is progress that keeps it going through the transformative years of the early twentieth century. The ideas of tradition and progress are more than age-old customs and laws and new-fangled ideas and technology.

When we first enter the world of *Downton Abbey*, we step into a place that seems both distant and familiar to us. It is 1912, and we think wistfully of the Edwardian Era with its abundant wealth, stately homes, and high society. We picture gentlemen in crisp linens playing cricket and ladies wearing colorful hats and sipping tea at an afternoon garden party. Touches of modernity are interlaced into the scenes, reminding us that the political philosophies, social upheaval, and technological innovations during that time were largely responsible for eroding the lifestyles and traditions of the nobility and the estate-based agrarian economy.

Series creator Julian Fellowes deliberately set *Downton Abbey* in the decades leading up to and after World War I, since this time was defined by unimagined conflict, destruction, and technological change. Yet, it was also a period of unparalleled innovation, creativity, and social awareness that transformed the world into what we know it as today. Fellowes drew inspiration for the drama from having grown up hearing stories about times past and roaming the halls of the great estates of his relatives and neighbors. His stories reflect this tension between tradition and progress and the resulting effects it has on individuals, both upstairs and down, and on society at large.

Like the era in which Fellowes set *Downton*, Hegel lived during the Age of Enlightenment, a time of social awakening, scientific and intellectual progress, and devastating wars and political revolutions. Hegel's sweeping philosophical system, which boldly tackles ethical concepts and includes an innovative philosophy of history that traces history in terms of humanity's intellectual and moral progress, came during an era when new ideas were percolating in the world. He was inspired by the idealism of those fighting for "liberty, equality, and fraternity" in the French Revolution. He and his friends saw the revolution as a symbol of progress toward a more open society, one that would allow for its citizens to find self-actualization and to work together for the common good.

Saving Downton Is an Estate of Mind

Downton Abbey depicts the life of a family estate, which for generations has provided a livelihood for the people who work in the village of Downton and who farm the lands that offer sustenance for the community. Owned by Robert Crawley, the Earl of Grantham, the estate has been in his family for many generations. Like other aristocratic families in Britain, the Crawleys are the stewards of the estate and village, a traditional duty to which many landowners proudly dedicate their lives. As Violet, the Dowager Countess and Robert's mother, points out in the first episode of the first season, the estate represents "everything Robert has given his life to." Hegel would agree with Violet. He, too, believes that estates like Downton play an important part in the thriving of both the community and the individuals who live within that community.

In Hegel's time, he saw the German estates, and the villages that developed around them, as being a critical component to society and its development. The tradition of aristocratic landowners providing a livelihood for people of the working classes has been a part of European history for many centuries. The land that the Crawley family owns is crucial to the rural community in which they live. Agriculture was the primary source of subsistence for towns and villages like Downton. The "cultivation of the natural products of the soil," as Hegel points out in *Elements of the Philosophy of Right*, is critical to the "security and satisfaction of needs" of people like the Crawleys and the people they employ.

The farming of the land is also important to the traditional way of life of the aristocracy. Hegel explains that aristocratic families were custodians of the land and did not need to work in a profession or trade. Their estates were self-sustaining, providing for their food, clothes, and shelter. The people who worked the land were in turn able to provide for their families.

Hegel's description of how greatly the aristocracy valued this economic system mirrors the Crawley family philosophy. Violet would agree with Hegel's statement in *Elements* that "the old nobility lives in the faith and confidence that the goodness of the land will continue to sustain them, and what they consume will be replenished." That is why, as we see in season 3, Robert is adamant about not wanting to sell any part of the land, nor the estate itself, after he lost all his money and the bulk of Cora's fortune in a bad financial investment. As custodian of his ancestors' lands, the earl believes that he "has a duty beyond saving his own skin, and that the estate must be a major employer and support the house, or there's no point to it" (3:1). We also see the importance of farming the land and of duty to the family in season 4 when Mary, the eldest Crawley daughter, braves toil and mud to save the pigs the family has acquired in order to diversify the way the land is used and to provide another means of sustenance and income.

But Why Can't Lady Mary Inherit Downton?

When we first meet the Crawley family, they are at a crossroads. The future of the estate becomes uncertain after they learn that James Crawley, Robert's first cousin and heir to the estate, and his son Patrick have died on the R.M.S. *Titanic*. Because of complex British inheritance rights known as primogeniture and property laws known as entails, the inheritance has to go to a male heir. Hegel explains in *Elements* that "the institution of the law of inheritance which, in order to preserve the family and to enhance its renown by means of substitutions [for example, Matthew Crawley is a substitute heir] and family testamentary trusts [such as the entail which keeps all the Crawley real estate with the title of nobility], either favors the sons by excluding the daughters from inheritance or favors the eldest son by excluding the remaining children."

Since Robert and Cora only have daughters, Robert's closest male relatives would be next in line to take over the estate and the title. With James and Patrick dead, the estate and title will go to Matthew Crawley, a distant cousin and middle-class lawyer whom the family hardly knows. Tradition, in this circumstance, is embedded in law.

Mary, as eldest child, believes that she is entitled to the inheritance, even though she is not the eldest male, the child to whom these estates would traditionally be passed down. Cora, as an American woman who inherited her father's fortune, doesn't think these inheritance laws are fair, especially when she learns that her fortune is tied up with the estate. Even Violet, who is a staunch traditionalist, campaigns on Mary's behalf. "The entail must be smashed in its entirety," she tells Cora in the first episode of the first season, "and Mary recognized as heiress of all." Love of her granddaughter and loyalty to family lead Violet to investigate options on how the entail could be dissolved, such as asking Matthew to research any possible legal recourse the family could take.

Mary, a smart and capable woman, can't become, as Robert described himself in the fourth episode of the first season, "the custodian of the great Crawley dynasty." Matthew, a virtual stranger, will take over the estate. As much as Robert would like to see his daughter be the one to succeed him, he puts duty, or what he thinks is morally right, over his personal wishes. To him, duty to the estate and the people who subsist off its land is of utmost importance. He considers this duty a tradition that he must uphold.

In terms of doing one's duty, Hegel would agree with Robert's choice. In *The Philosophy of History*, he points out that the "individual's morality consists in fulfilling the duties imposed by his social standing." He discussed how duty to the greater good is more important than an individual's personal desires, expanding on ethical concepts developed by fellow German and philosopher Immanuel Kant (1724–1804). To Hegel, as *Elements* translator H.B. Nisbet explains, "individual conscience, responsibility, and decency are paramount values." Despite the pleas of Mary, Cora, and Violet to challenge the law, Robert adheres to his strong sense of duty in not questioning this traditional law.

Hegel would view this traditional inheritance law and its exclusion of the Crawley women as arbitrary, because it depended on Cora and Robert having a son. Since he views marriage and family as an important social and legal institution necessary for meeting the needs of the individuals within a family, he argues in *Elements* that the law excludes those members of the immediate family who "have no right to recognition." The property that the family owns is tied into the marriage contract and should remain a part of that family. By giving the estate to a male Crawley, Hegel sees that as "an infringement of the principle of the freedom of property." The law gives more importance to keeping the legacy of the ancestral family and its home together, or as Hegel notes, the intent of the law is to "preserve intact the 'clan' or 'house' and not the immediate family."

To us modern viewers, Robert seems stubborn and old-fashioned. Although the entail was abolished in Great Britain in 1925—too late to benefit Mary—the law of succession that gives the title to a male heir is still being challenged. In fact, there is an "Equality Titles Bill" up in front of Parliament. The bill, nicknamed the "Downton Law," would allow females to inherit titles of nobility. Still, in terms of the Crawley family, the fact that Mary ends up marrying Matthew and giving birth to a male heir makes for a happy marriage between duty and desire and between Robert's heir and daughter.

War: The March toward Freedom

Remember, it's not just the end of the war but the dawn of a new age.

— LORD GRANTHAM (2:6)

The very first episode of *Downton Abbey* opens with the urgent tat-a-tat-tat of a telegraph machine and then cuts to a steam train as its blaring horn pierces the quiet of the scenic English countryside. It is April 1912. We are jarred by this contrast between the franticness of the machines and the calmness of nature. Perhaps, we even feel a sense of foreboding. Something is not quite right.

At the end of the first season, we finally get to see one of those famous Edwardian garden parties, replete with colorful concoctions worn on the heads of the female guests. Despite the recent loss of their unborn son, Robert and Cora insist that their annual summer garden party must go on. The gracious hosts preside over an idyllic afternoon of sunshine, tea, and frivolity.

The pleasant gathering is interrupted when Carson the butler brings a telegram to Robert. Like the telegram that opened the series with its news of the Crawley heirs drowning on the *Titanic*, this one closed the season with equally bad news. Robert shares this news with his guests: "My lords, ladies, and gentlemen. Can I ask for silence? Because I very much regret to announce . . . that we are at war with Germany" (1:7).

The war that Robert announced on that peaceful day in July 1914 is what we now know as World War I, the Great War, or the War to End All Wars. Millions of people died or were wounded and maimed. Social unrest resulting from low wages and unsafe working conditions caused many poor and working-class people to revolt against the powerful and elite class ruling many European nations, including that of Great Britain. The war also took its toll on many families from all social classes, leading them to suffer from the economic strain and the scarcity of food and other resources.

Although Hegel lived a few centuries before the Crawleys, he, too, experienced war firsthand. The French military leader and ruler Napoleon Bonaparte (1769–1821) swept through France and into Hegel's hometown of Jena after the French Revolution with the intent of conquering Germany. Hegel and his fellow students considered the occupation of their homeland a time of great hope. Germany was being liberated from an oppressive monarchy. Napoleon started out with good intentions. He wanted to carry out the ideals of the French Revolution by bringing freedom and equality to the people of France and beyond. Instead, his quest to expand the French empire left a trail of blood and horror in its wake.

Hegel, who lectured extensively on his philosophical ideas, was a part of a group of thinkers known as the German Idealists. They believed that through reason and intellectual achievement, individuals could lead better lives and humankind in general could aspire to greatness. Hegel and his followers saw the development of the mind (or what Germans call *Geist*) as the pathway to freedom. If war was sometimes necessary to free people in order to allow them to achieve self-fulfillment, then so be it. Having traced the rise and fall of the great civilizations like Greece, Rome, and China in *The Philosophy of History*, he showed how war could bring about positive change to society, with each subsequent stage of human history progressing toward greater knowledge and understanding of the world.

Ironically, young men like Matthew Crawley and Downton footman William Mason marched off to war against Hegel's Germany. The German Empire had not flourished in the name of freedom and reason as the Idealists had hoped. People remained oppressed under an authoritarian rule. Britain, France, and Russia held "the Huns" at bay for the most part, due to men like Matthew and William who braved the horrors of trench warfare. The generation of men who fought "for King and country" was much like Hegel and the German Idealists. They saw war as a noble cause and led the fight against the spreading evil. The war even broke down the rigid barriers of the British social class system, with the nobility, middle class, and working class all fighting side by side to survive the decidedly unromantic ordeal of war.

World War I was unlike any war before it. The nature of warfare changed with the implementation of new military vehicles and weapons of mass destruction, such as tanks, machine guns, and poison gas. While advances in technology and science were usually considered benchmarks of human achievement, here we see progress as destructive and not transformative. No one could have imagined anything more devastating than the traditional warfare of guns, bayonets, and swords, until whole companies of infantrymen were wiped out with the toss of one canister of mustard gas. Edith sums up the effects this so-called progress had on her fellow countrymen in the second episode of the third season: "almost every man we grew up with is dead."

The Upstairs and Downstairs of Social Change

Only that which is really new, which has no counterpart in antiquity, is modern. Thus, our mechanical civilization, with the conditions of life and the ideas begotten by it, are modern.

>—ALDOUS HUXLEY, "What, Exactly, Is Modern?" (*Vanity Fair*, May 1925)

The Modern Era, roughly from Hegel's time until World War II, was characterized by significant advances in scientific knowledge, exploration and conquest, and the Industrial Revolution. Hegel, while he upholds tradition and is conservative in many aspects of social life, is mostly a champion of progress, upholding the ideals of the revolutionary movements during his time. He sees progress as a necessary means to achieving enlightenment and understanding of the self and the world. Although he doesn't speak directly about technology or the philosophy of technology, he points out in *Elements* that the products of industry and the work of tradesmen are an important part of civil society.

When Violet was young, railroads and telegraph machines connected the world in previously unimaginable ways. Ever the traditionalist, she saw these innovations as practical means of transportation and communication. Yet, the newfangled inventions that are introduced on the estate later on in her life are vexing and unnecessary to her. She tells Robert in the first episode of the series that she doesn't want electricity at her home: "I couldn't have electricity in the house. I wouldn't sleep a wink with all those vapors seeping about." In the same episode, we learn that Daisy the kitchen maid is an impressionable, naïve girl who has no use for electricity.

More change is signaled when Robert asks Carson to have telephones installed at Downton. Carson, who values tradition as much as Violet and Robert, asks, "Why would we want a telephone at Downton?" (1:7). Mrs. Patmore, the cook, also is wary of the telephone, complaining in the same episode that its ring is "like the cry of a banshee." Over the next few years, household tools like electric mixers and toasters, and technological developments like refrigeration, change the work of the servant class, making some tasks less grueling and time consuming. Some people in service also saw this era as an opportunity to learn new skills, as Gwen the housemaid does when she takes a correspondence course in typewriting and learns, in the seventh episode of the first season, that she got the job she applied for with the help of Lady Sybil.

Sybil, and her younger cousin Rose, represent the spirit of the modern world. A new era emerged in the aftermath of the war and during the 1920s, and these girls embrace change wholeheartedly. Sybil symbolizes the more serious aspects of change, questioning class divisions and advocating for women's rights. She marries the family chauffeur, Tom Branson, an Irish-Catholic socialist, much to the despair of her Anglican, traditionalist father. Cousin Rose is equally as daring, wearing the shocking styles of the Flappers and flouting racial prejudice by dating a black jazz-band leader.

The tension between tradition and progress that we have seen in the matters of the inheritance and entail continues to be present as Matthew Crawley assists Robert in the stewardship of the estate. Matthew, along with Tom, who is now the estate agent, wants to bring Downton into the twentieth century. They argue with Robert about new ideas for increasing crop yield by using farm machinery. Throughout the series, Robert struggles with the changes he has seen. During the war, he felt as if he lost his sense of purpose. With Matthew and Tom now attending to the estate, he at first thinks that there is no use for him at Downton. Only after experiencing a devastating war and the unfortunate deaths of Sybil, Matthew, and his unborn child, does Robert gradually come around to accepting the changes in his family and in society. When he finally agrees to implement the ideas Matthew and Tom have for the estate in the eighth episode of season 3, he is summarizing his own personal growth: "Let's give it a go and see what the future brings."

Taking Tea with Hegel

Isobel Crawley could have been taking tea with Hegel as she explains to an acquaintance why she decides to go to Rose's coming-out ball for the 1923 London Season, something the forward-thinking, no-nonsense, middle-class woman would have previously thought frivolous. In the ten years since she and her son Matthew have joined their noble relatives, she has had a chance to see the positive aspects of tradition. "I suppose it came to me," she says, "that these balls and presentations and comings-out are not just aristocratic folderol but traditions by which members of this family measure their progress through life" (4: Christmas Special). The Crawleys have each in his or her own way learned that by embracing change they can also keep alive those traditions important to the nurturing and survival of their beloved family and estate.

15
Memories. In the End, Is That All There Is?

DAVID LaROCCA

Memory is commonly understood to be about the past. One cannot, for example, speak of having memories of the present much less the future. In a particularly moving and intimate scene that takes place in his office in the company of Mrs. Hughes, Mr. Carson offers the rueful summary in the fourth episode of season 4 that "The business of life is the acquisition of memories. In the end, that's all there is." Mr. Carson's sentiment—and it is a thought full of genuine feeling—might suggest that a principal endeavor of life is to, as it were, live in the past, that is, with a consciousness of, or attunement to, what has already happened, what is no longer present. One's life, then—what constitutes the phenomenon that we understand as personal identity—would, according to Mr. Carson, be devoted to the "collection" of past impressions.

First, Mr. Carson's model introduces a paradox: if the present is spent dwelling on the past (as known in or through memories) then the present is strangely altered—becoming either a mere period of contemplation about the past, or the site of new memory creation comprised entirely of remembering old memories. Secondly, based on contemporary neuroscientific research there is evidence to suggest that memories are not akin to things that can be collected (for instance, as we might photographs), but rather are more like drawings on an Etch A Sketch where memories can be *re-written*: conjured, augmented, erased, re-created anew, and even introduced.

If memory does in fact behave in this plastic fashion, allowing us to alter it in perhaps surprising ways, then the past (at least seen from a human level) is never past *per se*, and memories are not—or are no longer—the sorts of things we can consult as if found in an encyclopedia or a curio cabinet, but instead are more akin to a living activity exercised in the present. Mr. Carson might be shocked, and perhaps relieved, to learn that memories can't be acquired in the way he thinks, and far from being "all there is," memories are but a portion of a larger network of factors that constitute individual experience and thus personal identity.

Where Did I Put My Memory? Of Palaces, Cabinets, and Abbeys

Downton Abbey is a haunted house. Those who live there endlessly refer to the history of the place—the people who lived and died there, the legacy that has been handed down to them, their responsibility for "keeping" Downton alive, readying it for passage to the next generation. There is a very real sense in which these characters—meant to invoke or reflect on the actual English aristocracy (and their servants) from the early part of the twentieth century—are themselves not alive, but haunt the place (the palace), since they are forever deferring to the past, tradition, the way things were, the way things are done (and anticipating how these traditions will be bestowed on the next generation, and generations beyond that). In brief, there is very little time to be present, to be in the moment of one's own life, to have a clear appreciation for what one's individual life is *for* (aside from fulfilling some pre-assigned role, whether it be Lord or valet, Lady or Lady's maid, footman or cook). Yet as we think further about Mr. Carson's late-night confession to Mrs. Hughes that "the business of life is the acquisition of memories" and "In the end, that's all there is," we have to wonder what it even means to *acquire* a memory. Is such collection possible? In what sense? And does it genuinely constitute "all there is," especially as we think about life's ultimate value, and our own sense of the nature of personal identity?

Perhaps more than anyone else at Downton Abbey, Mr. Carson is aware of *where* everything is. He is not only charged with accounting for every last piece of silverware, but also for the amount of wine consumed (noting levels as he tidily returns decanted wines to their home bottles through a net). So it may not be surprising that Mr. Carson would be conscientious about the nature of property as such, even though none of it beyond the confines of his chambers belongs to him; along these lines, in the very first episode, Mr. Bates admires Lord Grantham's snuff boxes and comments to Thomas: "a pirate's hoard within our reach and none of it's ours." Mr. Carson's attunement to memory as a kind of thing one can acquire—and therefore have, as a possession—seems in keeping with a broader trend in the history of Western economics, art, and architecture, namely, that the aspiration of life becomes the collection of things: property, art works, homes and buildings, and also, one presumes, the fortunes to fund the pursuit of acquisitions. Mr. Carson reflects the general spirit of his age in several conspicuous ways.

Of the many metaphors for memory that seem to uncannily anticipate *Downton Abbey* and its chief butler's outlook on the "business of life," consider the *memory palace*. From antiquity, including prominent mention in illustrious works by Cicero (106–43 BCE) and Quintillian (35–100 CE), the memory palace was a mnemonic technique in which a person would imagine a familiar space and then populate it with lines of text, names, images, sounds, and the like that one could then later on recall by means of retracing this internal landscape. The conventional scenario finds a memorizer calling to mind an intimately well-known place (such as one's childhood home), or perhaps even walking a physical, empirical, three-dimensional location that could then be creatively linked to mental phenomena (thoughts, ideas, concepts, and images). Thinking of Mr. Carson's quarry—the palace that is Downton Abbey—this ancient and beloved technique takes on new resonance, for it is with and from Mr. Carson (and his staff) that we learn the ins-and-outs of the estate.

Film itself becomes a surrogate for our own creation of a mental memory palace; the show, with each new episode, in each new season, elongates and intensifies our familiarity with the home—and with its details. For anyone who has visited Highclere Castle in Hampshire, watching the show is an uncanny provocation to one's own first-hand, in-person memories—as if they were being stylized, lit, directed, shot, and edited anew. And an inverse experience occurs when on the grounds, as a visitor's curiosity about the downstairs at

Downton is frustrated by the fact that the company shoots all of the downstairs scenes at Ealing Studios in London! Thus, as the actors perform in the London kitchen then take the stairs to the Hampshire countryside, so the visitor enters Highclere Castle but must repair to her memory of the show in order to "visit" the kitchen and the bustling life underfoot.

Many histories and philosophical accounts of the memory palace—and its affiliate tropes—have been written, as noted, all the way back to classical Rome, and we find the metaphor still in vogue in the years when *Downton Abbey* is said to take place, beginning in the nineteen-teens. Here are a few lines from T. S. Eliot's celebrated, well-known "Gerontion" (1919):

> Think now
> History has many cunning passages, contrived corridors
> And issues, deceives with whispering ambitions,
> Guides us by vanities.

At Downton Abbey, there are, of course, so many "passages" and "corridors," and on any given day, perhaps even more "vanities." So often too, we hear of remembering as an activity akin to walking "memory lane"—another geographical space to be traversed, commonly in a linear fashion like a road or pathway, perhaps by steps, backward in time. Similarly, remembering is described as "retracing one's steps," thereby emphasizing the sequentiality of memory: one thing after another (not unlike the way history itself is comically lampooned). Thus, the spatial metaphors of palace and passage, corridor and lane, are all consistent and complementary.

In the generation before Eliot, we find Ralph Waldo Emerson (1803–1882) writing of the literal Cabinets of Natural History that he encountered in Paris, but also see how he adapts the "cabinet" as a symbol for collection, composition, arrangement, and analogy. In "The Method of Nature," Emerson appeals to a naturally constituted space—the cave—when he writes of the "cave of memory." More recently, the memoirist, James McConkey has written *Court of Memory*, the title of which is meant to return us, once again, to the use of the spatial descriptors for the art of memory creation and reclamation, in this case from St. Augustine in his *Confessions* (10.8): "All this I do inside me, in the huge court of my memory. There I have by me the sky, the earth, the sea, and all the things in them which I have been able to perceive. . . . There too I encounter myself; I recall myself. . . . I can contemplate all these [things I've remembered] as though they were in the present."

Mr. Carson would likely find Augustine's account deeply appealing because it includes the twin processes of collection and contemplation: as the business of life at Downton Abbey is the care and custodianship of the estate, so the business of life for Mr. Carson's personal experience is the collection and contemplation of his experiences as he finds them in the "court" of his memory. And as with McConkey's memoiristic reclamation—and re-use—of Augustine, we find contemporary journalist, Joshua Foer, not only commenting on Augustine's legacy, but also devoting an entire chapter of his book *Moonwalking with Einstein* to the art of memory storage and retrieval. There Foer reminds us of the *Ad Herennium*—a rhetorical text from 90 BCE, once attributed to Cicero—that tells us about the "treasure house" of memory, and about two kinds of memory, one "natural" and another "the product of art." And it is to the art or discipline of memory that the author of the *Ad Herennium* turns his attention in this treatise:

> When we see in everyday life things that are petty, ordinary, and banal, we generally fail to remember them, because the mind is not being stirred by anything novel or marvelous. But if we see or hear something exceptionally base, dishonorable, extraordinary, great, unbelievable, or laughable, that we are likely to remember a long time. . . . We ought, then, to set up images of a kind that can adhere longest in the memory. And we shall do so if we establish likenesses as striking as possible. . . . The things we easily remember when they are real we likewise remember without difficulty when they are figments, if they have been carefully delineated.

Aristocracy and Acquisition

The preceding accounts of the spatial metaphors of memory—figured as they were by palaces, pathways, lanes, cabinets, corridors, caves, courts—find a complement in the aristocratic context of *Downton Abbey*. That is to say: it didn't occur to rhetorical theorists to propose a "memory hut" or "memory hovel"—rather a *palace*, a place of great ornament and splendor, of sparkling detail and wondrous expanse. One of the underlying themes of *Downton Abbey* is the pressure exerted by industrial capitalism on the customs and traditions of the aristocratic lifestyle. A titled family, it would seem, can no longer live off the interest of the estate's wealth: rather, money must be made, the land must be worked.

When it comes to our thinking about memory—and the metaphors that are used to define it—the millennia-old memory-palace technique finds a counterpart in the acquisitive nature of capitalism. And as Mr. Carson so aptly illustrates in talking about "business" (while still very much part of an old-order aristocratic hierarchy), even the worker-class subscribed to a shift into acquisitional motivations. After all, Mr. Carson does not—as he is so often quick to do—make a distinction between the business of the Lord's life and his own when it comes to memory-making; rather, Mr. Carson presumes this activity of collection is also collective, something shared across the range of ranks. And the bourgeois industrialist—who owns the means of production; who is occasionally featured as a guest, and thus a *visitor*, at Downton; and who can be said to occupy the space between the "upstairs" and the "downstairs"—is a perfect emblem of the new economic order that sees acquisition (of property, of money) as its chief pursuit. Why not include memory in this frenzy for ownership?

Thus, treating memories as "things" one might collect, possess, or otherwise accumulate is very much in keeping with the spirit of this age-in-transition. As the show offers an abbreviated time register of the 1910s and 1920s, it is squarely situated between the first stirrings of modern industrialism in the midlands of England in the mid-nineteenth century and what leads robustly to the 1970s, when the dawn of computers seemed to herald the end of the industrial model as it was known early on in Manchester, Liverpool, and Birmingham. The acquisitional model of memory is illustrated in *Downton Abbey* in at least two prominent forms.

First, since memory is here analogized to property (albeit mental property), recall the very definition of property insists not just that a thing can be owned but that it can also be disposed of. If one's memories can be "had," then, if this model is consistent, one ought to be able to be liberated from them. We might just call this *forgetting*. So this is clearly a complication for the analogy, since memories do appear to be "ownable" in a certain sense, while they are at the same time not so easily gotten rid of. As a result of the difficulty of forgetting, we can go back and re-read Mr. Carson's lines, and realize that he didn't specify the *type* of memories being acquired, and yet, one can't help but presume he meant—or wished—that they'd all be pleasant ones. By contrast, consider the emotional pain Mr. Carson suffers in the second episode of the first season when he is forced to remember his former life as part of the "The Cheerful Charlies." Mr. Carson is at once embarrassed to have been a song and dance man—an identity very much at odds with the stiff and strident propriety he demands of himself at Downton—*and* deeply nostalgic, as Charlie Griggs's return reminds Carson of his love—and loss—of Alice Neal. While the "business of life" may involve all manner of pain and turmoil, loss and hurt, the hope is that the memories being acquired will be happy ones.

Downton Abbey, like any great melodrama, seems bent on maximizing trauma and lending only the slimmest moments of light and levity. The series is a catalogue of miseries—beginning with the death of the estate's heirs on the *Titanic*, and running through to Lord Grantham's loss of family wealth in the stock market, Hugh "Shrimpie" MacClare's unhappy marriage, Edith's jilting at the altar and subsequent troubled love with a married newsman, Sybil's death, Lady Grantham's miscarriage, Mr. Bates's wrongful imprisonment, Anna's rape, Matthew's paralysis and then his death, and so on in enumerable variations. In a turn fitting her character and temperament, it seems only the Dowager Countess is free of such dramas (that is, until Kuragin appears)—and is instead called in to sort and deliberate on them.

Second, *Downton Abbey* takes place when photography has become a common, familiar part of daily life—from newspapers to family picnics, from postcards to posters. Periodically—and pointedly—throughout the series, we find characters admiring and reflecting on a photograph of a beloved other: Tom looking at a curio of his now dead wife, Lady Sybil; Mr. Carson admiring an image of Alice Neal—the woman he loved, but never confided in. And since mental images may be hard to "delete" from one's memory, photographs—with their stubborn persistence, and uncanny likeness—do much to keep, motivate, and even animate memory. In this respect, photography acts as an unanticipated method not so much for remembering as for re-traumatizing. Where at first, the photograph can seem a comfort—a surrogate for the loved and lost—it can just as well call to mind just how much one has lost, and how unaccountable the loss is and must remain. Perhaps the notion of "time healing wounds" is predicated on the mind's natural capacity to forget; if so, then photography—as the capture, preservation, and re-presentation of time—seems a cruel invention, a sure way to never be able or allowed to forget.

One of the effects of the show, then, is to cause viewers to think back (or think anew *with* the show) about what it may have been like when photographs began to be treated as memories, or like prompts to memories, or even in some cases as *creators* of memories—for example, when an image of a dead loved one is shared with another, it can seem that the photograph *is* the memory, the keeper of a reality now forever absent. The photograph is, then, variously the source, surrogate, stimulant, or cause of memories. And as the show develops, so do the photographic expressions therein—the framed pictures on various tables, desks, and mantles; and worn on the body, kept in pockets and lockets. For a group so accustomed to stocking and sorting a household, the notion of populating the place with photographs seems a logical next step, especially when one has such a place to display them in. From this angle, Downton Abbey itself becomes a memory palace.

The New Science of Memory

What is perhaps most surprising about the evolving discoveries of contemporary neuroscience is that the old, old spatial metaphors—of palaces and the like—are being replaced by new, new spatial metaphors—of neural circuits, pathways, and synapses. If these phenomena are empirical, however, there is a very real reason that we need not say these are metaphors at all (or at least not solely), but rather are descriptive of real things, real processes, real spaces. Memory, it would appear according to the findings of the new cognitive sciences, has a location and it is a place one can navigate (albeit, at present, with a still nascent familiarity). When John Searle, for example, writes of consciousness being a biological process, and uses the word "gap" to describe, say, the space between one's imagination and one's action—and thus the space of freedom—he does not seem to be speaking in strictly metaphorical language. And yet, "gaps" and "neural networks"—especially insofar as these can't be seen with the unaided eye—retain something of a double status, so that "circuitry" seems at once a tangible entity *and* a metaphor (tangible when seen on an MRI; a metaphor when imagining the "space" of these synaptic processes).

Viewers of *Downton Abbey* may or may not have noticed how remarkably well and abundantly it engages with the technologies of its day, drawing them into the narrative and even the melodrama. From the opening scene of the first episode with wires delivering vital news, and thereafter in the opening credits, the telegraph is a signature motif—as if announcing the arrival of a new kind of modernity—to the automobile that delivers Matthew to his death, several seasons later, the interventions of technologies elementally shape the narrative instead of being mere set decoration. Daisy's skepticism about turning on a light switch, in the first episode of the first season, is met by Gwen's condescending correction—"electricity's not the devil's handiwork." When, in turn, Gwen wants to study to become a secretary—by learning how to use a typewriter—others are shocked by the notion that she'd dismiss her appointed position, no matter how lowly it may be, and seek to train into an elected profession. When a blending machine arrives in Mrs. Patmore's kitchen, she immediately takes the presence of the contraption as a threat to her livelihood—not as something to make her life easier, but as something to replace her. Tom Branson is perhaps most emblematic of the radical transitions underway on account of technology and social change: he, of course, goes from plebian, immigrant chauffeur—the person who operates "the motor"—to a person who is, despite a lack of pedigree, an accepted (if still occasionally controversial) member of the immediate aristocratic family. Upward mobility, indeed. Of course the photograph and moving pictures come in for their roles in the narrative as well—often as keepsakes (in the former case) or as entertainments (in the latter).

A haunted house, even if it is the grand, stately Downton Abbey, presumes that the spirits are there forever, but the new science of memory increasingly suggests that memories are not permanent, but malleable, and so not only are memories not fixed in content but also our relationship to them is indeterminate. In the current stage of neuroscience, we're discovering how the old metaphors are being replaced by new models and metaphors, yet as part of that process we're learning how some tropes correlate to actual structures of brain activity, while some do not. For instance, when we speak conventionally about personal (or private) truth, or even historical (in other words, shared) truth, the malleability of memory presents some significant problems. Instead of having or holding a memory in mind as one would a photograph in hand, memory—on the new reading—is anything but fixed and finished. Thus, to appeal to one's own memory, or even to a shared experience, is troubled. The metaphors of memory palaces and photographic memory lose their accuracy; and in turn, they seem, well, old-fashioned. But how did we get here?

In *The Shallows*, Nicholas Carr provides a survey of some recent neuroscientific research on mind and memory. Carr finds an apt analogy in Friedrich Nietzsche's desperate purchase of a typewriter (Nietzsche's eyesight was failing so he needed a machine to help him write), and concludes that "the tools we use to write, read, and otherwise manipulate information work on our minds even as our minds work with them." Meanwhile in "Technologies as Forms of Life," Langdon Winner writes, "technologies are not merely aids to human activity, but also powerful forces acting to reshape that activity and its meaning." Most of *Downton Abbey* takes place between 1913 and the mid-1920s, when photography has become commonplace, but also before it has become an art form in its own right. In short, photography is, at this point, a technology—much in the same way as the telegraph, telephone, and electric light. They are utilities. But the representational nature of photography—thought of here as a technology—was not illuminating the night (as the lightbulb was) but shaping human consciousness about time and space, duration and expiration, and perhaps most of all, the cognitive content of memory. Did I experience this, or did I just see a photograph of it?

Transforming Memories

Daniella Schiller is among the vanguard of researchers who are exploring the chemical, biochemical, physical, and even light-sensitive aspects of the neurons that contribute to memory formation, retention, and recall. Her research is representative of a wider trend in brain and memory science; in her work, for instance, she addresses the ways in which the acquisitional model (in which we say we "have" a memory or have "lost" a memory) doesn't line up with what's happening in our heads. Consequently, Schiller is contributing to a re-education in appropriate metaphors for memory, and in that capacity is helping us find our way to the science that expresses the image we *should* have of mind and memory. Schiller's research is poised to refigure our relationship to memory: where once we imagined that painful memories ("caused by war, trauma, rape") would be permanent—something we would be forced to live with throughout our lives—Schiller's experiments point to a process known as "reconsolidation." In this process, one remembers a painful memory in order to re-write it, in effect, to transform—and perhaps diminish or delete—its mental content.

At present, with the work of Schiller and others, we're now poised for a new model of memory, where a memory can't be acquired in the sense of coming into one's possession once and for all, because it is itself *perpetually evolving* (not an object so much as a set of habits of thinking that are themselves under negotiation through a series of biological, chemical, and mechanical processes). Here memory and imagination suddenly draw together as tandem forces. Memory is no longer linked strictly to empirical, historical events, but is something—like imaginings—that can arise and disappear, can be molded by inputs, reshaped, and emerge in some new form, *or not at all*.

Thinking again of Mr. Carson's sentiment—that life's business is the acquisition of memories—in the wake of the latest proposals from neuroscience complicates his view both that we should be *collecting* memories at all, and that once collected such memories are *permanently* fixed (like built-in shelves in Downton's downstairs library). Mr. Carson meant to suggest—like so many others before and since—that memory is crucial not just to one's pleasure (at least in remembering the good times) but also to the nature of one's personhood. Who one is seems caught up, on Mr. Carson's view, with what one can remember about one's experience. Those promoting a new neuroscientific approach to memory suggest another narrative, namely, that while "We are nothing without our memories . . . sometimes they also make us less than we could be." In short, traumatic memories can interfere with our development as individuals.

In the End . . . There Is No End

The acquisitional model of memory reinforces a nostalgia for pleasant memories, but it doesn't offer any reassurance for painful ones. Instead—like Mr. Carson and his company at Downton Abbey—one is meant to have a stiff upper lip, and suffer the defeats, the deaths, and dire circumstances that arrive periodically. Unlike the model of memory that has held Mr. Carson captive, like so many others, the new neuroscience offers a competing—and perhaps hopeful—account of memories-as-malleable. On this view, painful memories can be rewritten—fade, be altered, go missing. In the shift to neuroscientific accounts, nostalgia can find its proper object with appealing memories, while traumatic memories may be unseated—in effect, expunged from the Lord's mental manor. The authority and appeal of the past is not inherited but instead negotiated. Memory as such is of less value overall—and perhaps especially with regard to individual identity and personal happiness—since it is not so much acquired as created (or altered or deleted). Instead of making the business of life the filling, cataloguing, and caring for objects in a memory palace, one is liberated to travel light (something the Crawleys have yet to master).

16
Female Integrity in Times of Change

MELANIE ABBOTT

The microcosm of Downton Abbey is fascinating in that it contains three generations of women. The young Crawley sisters, although their youth may offer them more promise for future choices, are not the only ones dealing with the rise and fall of various social expectations and practices. Cora and Violet also must maneuver their way through the changing tides while holding on to their beliefs. That is, *all* these women must struggle to show integrity in the midst of powerful societal change.

Identity and Integrity

The term "integrity" can be used in a multitude of ways, from describing the consistency of someone's actions to the structure of King Edward's chair. Philosopher Bernard Williams (1929–2003) argues that integrity is based on standing up for the beliefs that make you, you. But the key here is not merely standing up for beliefs, but *how* you stand up for your beliefs; you must be *open* and *honest* about what those beliefs are and stand up for them *publicly* and act on them with some measure of consistency. Obviously, integrity itself can be misapplied; think of the fanaticism of the Germans we hear about in *Downton*'s second season. But on the whole, most would agree that integrity itself is good. Maybe it's the binge watching that helps to highlight it, but *Downton Abbey* seems to me to stand out as a TV show that does a fine job of showing realistic character development.

Lord Grantham, for example, sometimes seems like he's moving right along with the times, supporting—or at least accepting—some of his daughters' more controversial choices (such as when he welcomes back Sybil and Tom after their scandal), yet in other places, he reverts to his more conservative nature, such as when he attempts to withhold power of estate from Mary in season 4. Tom Branson, too, wavers, most obviously after Sybil's death when he must deal with living the life of a bourgeoisie when he's been fighting against that type of lifestyle his whole life. Compared to a one-directional, upwards slope of character development, the residents of Downton Abbey move up and down like a stock market graph, making them all the more interesting and a better reflection of our own human character.

According to philosopher Immanuel Kant (1724–1804), good will is one thing that can be considered genuinely good in and of itself; that is, it is good without limitation. A person without a good will is someone who can be considered lacking a proper human constitution. A person's integrity is a close cousin of good will. They are keys to the formation of the human spirit and condition, both in the individual and in how others surrounding them perceive them and receive their actions. Despite all the adages about how it's best to not care what others think and to do what you want, this can only take a person so far; without caring about how your actions and beliefs impact life around you, the delicate system will implode instead of develop. Imagine if most of us were like Violet Crawley and refused to change and expand; her stubbornness might seem like a type of integrity—after all, Violet and others like her are holding fast to their beliefs and acting on them—but there is little room for flexibility or change. If you need any evidence of the cons of an attitude like that, look at any civil uprising.

Integrity, if we merge Williams's and Kant's interpretations, isn't merely holding fast to a belief, but doing so when one ought to do so. That is, perhaps real integrity has to do with the right sort of holding fast, and maybe this helps to separate the fanatic from the person—here, the woman—of virtue. To test this out, let's look at the lives of five women from *Downton*.

Sybil

In the Crawley family, the youngest generation—the three sisters—are the ones who must learn for themselves how to act in these new times that are increasingly different from those that Cora or Violet grew up in. Without a role model who has been in their situation, each sister handles the waves of change in different, sometimes inconsistent, ways.

Sybil, as the baby of the family and the closest to the change in times, has, arguably, the least trouble and the fewest internal conflicts to work through as she matures. This sometimes causes uproars amongst her family members, which can lead them to see her as a rebellious spirit that may be in need of taming. However, her broader outlook on morality makes her sense of integrity one of the most interesting shown in the series and influences her sisters to act more independent themselves as the show progresses.

Although Sybil faces fewer mental obstacles than her sisters in regards to being involved in the women's rights movement, she still lives in a highly patriarchal society. The aura of patriarchal restriction not only comes from her culture and country, but also from her family—such as when she witnessed the fiasco of the rapid search for a suitable heir for sister Mary because she is not allowed to inherit herself. Even Sybil's riches don't protect her from gender-specific restrictions. Despite eventually casting her vote, Sybil struggles mightily against a conservatism that would suppress egalitarian movements such as socialism and feminism. But Sybil stands up for such movements because she thinks they are at the heart of her—and human—identity.

And this is tied up with integrity, as we know. Despite obstacles, Sybil never wavers in her beliefs and goes out of her way to act on them; but it is not just any beliefs she sacrifices so much for. She is willing to elope with Branson—a like-minded believer—at the end of season 2 and leave her family for her moral beliefs, namely, love-choice and equality. This is integrity with good will or, perhaps, we could say proper integrity since Sybil holds fast for good moral purposes, as opposed to, say, mere aesthetic purposes like what sort of hats she wants to wear. Sadly, her life was cut short, but hints of her fierceness are sometimes revealed in her sisters and husband.

Edith

The rivalry between Mary and Edith Crawley is a story line that evolves throughout the series. Although the two sisters are only one year apart in age, that one year has affected their standing in society quite significantly. Mary is in charge of marrying someone who can be an heir or provide one, while Edith is just another child in the eyes of those around her. Mary starts out the series by learning that her husband-to-be has died in the *Titanic* disaster; to Edith the death of Mary's fiancé means that the love Edith lost once already to Mary she has now lost forever to death.

Edith is also said to be the "forgotten" sister because she's not as independent as her younger sister, Sybil, nor does she have the role of wife-to-heir that Mary, her elder sister, has. Edith and Mary's relationship appears to be on a ruinous path at the beginning of the show with Edith doing things like sending out a gossipy letter to the Turkish embassy concerning the sexual scandal between Mary and Mr. Pamuk. However, things change over the years, as does the integrity of both sisters.

One thing that contributes to this positive change—and the promise of future moral integrity—is Edith's outlook on love. Although obviously wrong, Edith's brief love affair with a married farmer leads her to a deeper appreciation for the work and vocation of the lower class. Love stimulates her sense of wanting to find a place—her place—in the world. As a result, she joins Sybil in the hospital, and later on becomes more Sybilesque both by becoming a journalist and through her romance with a commoner, Michael Gregson.

Edith's evolution of integrity is only noticed by other characters if it affects them. For instance, the Crawley family reacts with some horror to the idea of Edith's having a career, and, despite their attempts to dissuade her, Edith sticks to her guns because she thinks this is not merely right for her, but also her right. Moral integrity grows and adds a valuable stabilizing element to Edith. This adds even more intrigue as her story line develops, including such occurrences as the disappearance of Mr. Gregson and the subsequent (secret) birth of their child.

Edith's emotional pushes and pulls in season 5, after she relinquishes her child to the care of Mr. Drewe (and eventually his wife), present an interesting conundrum. Her moral integrity is being tested in two conflicting ways; she wants an active role in her child's life, but if she pushes too hard too fast, she may cause serious problems for the Drewes' marriage. The fact that so much of the truth about Edith's child is hidden even from the child's mother figure (Mrs. Drewe) means that Edith was not acting with integrity according to Williams's definition, since she was not open about her actions and beliefs. I would argue that clearly Edith's role as an active mother shows some level of moral integrity—after all, she does want to be an involved parent—but her failure to go public with her moral feelings brings them into question. It is easy to bring up the time period when thinking about this and the conversation would be incomplete without it. How much do we as viewers expect someone in Lady Edith's position to give up regarding her secrets? This question has been a reccurring theme of the show since season 1 when Violet says that half of ourselves remains hidden when we walk down the aisle. We've seen women of lower status, like Ethel, who've had a child out of wedlock, lose their jobs and any standing they once had as well. Perhaps the problem that Edith faces is meant to provide a question for us all to ponder: How much truth is necessary for moral integrity?

Mary

It is in season 2 that Mary's real character development starts. In the second episode of that season, Mary insists that the moral high ground can't be left only to Sybil. While engaged to Richard Carlisle, she begins to put love ahead of the largely non-moral opinions of outsiders. Despite Richard's money and status, he treats her with disrespect and even abuse; at the same time, she also begins to fall sincerely in love with Matthew. She even puts her feelings of love ahead of her own happiness when she wishes Matthew to be with Lavinia over her in the early episodes of season 2. This is especially meaningful because she does so for moral reasons and not merely because of custom.

Although her time spent married to Matthew is short, it is a precious time and made more precious by the child (George) they have together. For a few episodes, the audience gets to see her happy and out of the "waiting room." But ironically her integrity really starts to shine when she embraces her role as a mother. As a mother she (eventually) recognizes she has a moral obligation to do what she can for her child. In the second episode of season 4, Matthew's will is found and determined to be valid by several people, and is also supported by Cora and Violet (their support, of course, carrying no legal weight). This leaves Mary with half of the estate, and a chance to step up and safeguard her and George's estate by being an active, competent woman, not merely an aristocrat with the integrity of custom, but rather a woman with the integrity of the moral right. She eventually rises to her new role, and continues to deepen in this respect.

Mary proves that she will walk the walk as she learns more about the estate from Tom. She stands up to her father and expresses her disagreement with his plans to sell part of the land. With Tom, she ventures into pig farming as a way to earn money for the estate. Mary is also the lone person to speak out and ask Tom to stay when he wants to leave for America, knowing that they all would suffer without him there at Downton. From season 1 to season 4, Mary transforms from a woman of her time quietly accepting her limits to one who has grown into herself, and has gained the courage necessary to stand up for her beliefs. By the first episode of season 5, she and her father are even able to joke about it. After Mary remarks that she's been thinking about the grains on the estate, Robert jokes, "Oh I know every man (these days) hears that from his daughter," and they share a knowing smile.

Cora

As an American dropped into England's aristocracy, Lady Cora displays a unique perspective that we don't get to see in the other characters. Despite the similarities between England and the United States, the differences in how women are treated—especially noble women—are striking. For one thing, she must give up her family fortune to her husband and male heirs and for another, she must in turn give up a part of her voice.

That lack of voice burdens her more and more as the show continues. In seasons 3 and 4, she stands up for the rights of her daughters to pursue their own dreams and follow their hearts and even encourages Rose to be less formal with her

(4:6). In the third episode of season 4, she flares with anger and disappointment when she learns that Robert has not been entertaining the singer they have visiting and snips at him, "Am I the only member of this family that lives in the twentieth century?" She is also less fazed by Ross, the black jazz singer, than Violet or even Edith.

A scene with Robert shows how much she has followed in her daughters' footsteps, becoming more interested in the increased role she could have as a woman. Cora tells Robert how she misses some aspects of the war because she was running more of Downton, but he quickly tells her not to talk about it (5:3). The expression on her face paints a portrait of disappointment. Like her daughters, she, too, wants more freedom and more choices, yet she doesn't fight the current in the same way they do. In this way, she can be seen as a stepping stone between Violet and the Crawley sisters.

Violet

If there is any word that accurately describes Violet, it is authentic. Early in season 1, she says to cousin Isobel, "Why do you always have to pretend to be nicer than the rest of us?" Putting aside her ambivalent relationship with Isobel, she displays her appreciation of honesty and genuineness to others, even if she doesn't always recognize it from others (as with Isobel). In a less meaningful way, she also shows her genuine, immovable personality by the clothes she wears. While the younger two generations of women in the house make noticeable changes in fashion as time goes on, Violet does not. In fact, it takes her until the 1920s to really "loosen up," and take some pressure off of her waist, but even then her fashion looks noticeably more Victorian than Cora's or the Crawley sisters'.

Yet in many later episodes, Violet becomes more complex, at once amazing the viewer with her change or, more often, startling us with the lack thereof. For example, at one point, Mary states that Sybil is entitled to her own opinions, to which Violet responds, "No, she isn't until she is married. And then her husband will tell her what her opinions are" (1:6). But several seasons later, in season 4, it is Violet herself who influences her son, Robert, to let Mary control more of the estate and even sticks up for the rights of her granddaughters.

The Sybil Effect

In the first season, Sybil was arguably the only woman of the five I've discussed who showed genuine female integrity or moral strength through change. Nevertheless, her legacy was far-reaching. Over time, all five of the women—even Violet, though less so—demonstrate this sort of moral growth in their female personhood in a believable and enjoyable way, which, in my opinion, is at least one factor in *Downton Abbey* 's greatness.

17
Downton Abbey as Eternal Recurrence

CHRISTOPHER KETCHAM

Primogeniture, the passing of the estate to the firstborn male child, has kept Downton Abbey in the family for generations. Primogeniture is cemented even further by the common law practice called *entail*, putting into trust the *entire* estate, which means even a rightful heir cannot sell the estate or pieces of it to anyone else.

Primogeniture and entail are the principal mechanisms that ensure the continuity of Downton Abbey as an entity that stays within the family. Of course, as Cora, the Countess of Grantham, has only produced female children, and Robert, the Earl of Grantham, has no brother, it is a distant cousin of Robert, Matthew Crawley, who is the designated heir. But Matthew dies at the end of the third season of the series, potentially leaving the estate to his newborn son.

"Continuity is the thing" to paraphrase Hamlet from his eponymous play. It is continuity that we will use to discover the nature of the Abbey's eternal recurrence as did Hamlet use a play to reveal his stepfather King Claudius as the murderer of his father. But we will not be channeling this continuity, this eternal recurrence through Hamlet's creator, William Shakespeare (1564–1616), but through the late-nineteenth-century German philosopher, Friedrich Nietzsche (1844–1900).

Spiders and Moonlight

Those who know the slightest thing about Nietzsche's work might think of this effort to equate the eternal recurrence with the continuity of the Abbey as completely misreading his work and dismiss it entirely as pure bunk. After all it was Nietzsche who tried to kill the idea of God, calling on us to erase God's shadow from the wall of humanity. Here was a man who believed the noble creates the moral code; that "The good are a caste, the bad, a mass like grains of sand"; that there is a "master morality" and "slave morality" (partly produced by the Christian church, which peddled self-subjugation and voluntary abstaining as nothing more than scare tactics to get one to behave).

For Nietzsche nobility has its roots in barbarism, the picking upon and subjugating of the weak not just through strength but through what they represented themselves as: "At the commencement of the noble caste was always the barbarian caste: their superiority did not consist first of all in their physical, but in their psychical power—they were the more complete men (which at every point also implies the same as more complete beasts.)" It's the stronger will of the noble that prevails—but for how much longer at Downton?

After railing against God, God's moral code, the noble, and the eternal soul—Nietzsche came up with and embraced a concept that he called the *eternal recurrence,* which he said was "The greatest weight":

> What, if some day or night a demon were to steal after you into your loneliest loneliness and say to you: "This life as you now live it and have lived it, you will have to live once more and innumerable times more; and there will be nothing new in it, but every pain and every joy and every thought and sigh and everything unutterably small or great in your life will have to return to you, all in the same succession and sequence—even this spider and this moonlight between the trees, and even this moment and I myself. The Eternal hourglass of existence is turned upside down again and again, and you with it, speck of dust!"

Some of us might think this sounds dreadful, boring. But is this not what the aristocracy wants with its common-law entail, the preservation and recurrence of place, the same place from generation to generation, without change, without *any* revision? More than once Nietzsche proclaimed the importance of the eternal recurrence:

Zarathustra is a dancer—how he that has the hardest, most terrible insight into reality, that has thought the "most abysmal idea," nevertheless does not consider it an objection to existence, not even to its eternal recurrence—but rather one reason more for being himself the eternal Yes to all things, "the tremendous, unbounded saying Yes and Amen. Into all abysses I still carry the blessings of my saying Yes."

This *abysmal thought* is the eternal recurrence that permeates Nietzsche's work—it's *sticky* and it's Zarathustra's eternal "yes saying." *Stickiness* is a kind of eternal recurrence in human knowledge structures. Stickiness implies adherence, attraction, and connectivity and, in a cosmic sense, that the fundamental forces of atoms can be bonded over vast periods of time if not in penultimate perpetuity. Yet at the same time, stickiness implies that the bonding is not a seal or a permanent adhesiveness but is something that could be dramatically altered given the right conditions. Yet this eternal recurrence is conditional and depends for its existence upon the stickiness of its knowledge in the face of competing facts, ideas, and understandings. Because knowledge is sticky and possesses the ability to recur over vast durations, change requires a process of unlearning and new learning. Because belief systems are often systemic throughout populations, Nietzsche's slowly-fading-shadows-of-God-on-a-cave-wall metaphor is an appropriate description of a systemic unlearning and new learning required to remove stickiness—and metaphorically may be required to erase the continuity that is the Abbey.

Certainly Nietzsche's life was no picnic. His was no royal progeny tucked away in a warm and inviting Abbey. His body was wracked with pain and illness and he became insane during the last few years of his life. He lived in rented rooms and moved from place to place when money ran out. He was as penniless as the most ascetic monk and when he died few were familiar with his work. And what, too, is an Abbey without a little intrigue and eccentricity bordering on the manic because, Dear Reader, the continuity of the Abbey is threatened.

Palace Intrigue

The intrigue of discontinuity—the unstickiness period—well, when did it begin? Many centuries ago. Like virtually all the landed estates in Britain, Downton Abbey has always been in the business of agriculture. Tenant farms, some with families who have tilled the same soil and raised animals for generations, provide the means and the revenue for continuing the maintenance of the Abbey and its heirs and staff. But, as you can imagine, primogeniture has not always produced the most astute business leader. As we have seen with the present earl, Robert, rather than invest in improving the business of the estate, his misadventures into speculative investments all but bankrupted the Abbey and even drained the wealth his American wife, Cora, brought to the marriage. But Robert is not novel in this respect. Many other estates in Britain in the early twentieth century were also challenged as the nation rumbled into high-gear industrialization and nascent globalization, which served to depress local agriculture. Combine this with the advent of what Robert calls the "death tax" (an inheritance tax), and we have the real possibility that the estate might fail.

But these are stalwart people and not used to being denied their pomp and circumstance or their necessary complement of services. So the family in its own inimical way, led by the bumbling Robert, have it in their mind to restore the eternal recurrence of the Abbey. But the problem is, how do they do it?

Turning the Eternal Hourglass of Existence

The trouble is that Nietzsche did not lay out his concept of eternal recurrence in a way that we might say, "Ah, there it is, that's what he means." So there have been all sorts of different interpretations of what eternal recurrence means. In *Nietzsche's Life Sentence*, Lawrence Hatab groups these interpretations into five categories. So, if we want to consider how the family might preserve Downton Abbey's stickiness and engender its eternal recurrence, we, too, should develop alternatives from these five separate categories.

The first category is concerned with the eternity of time itself. The idea of royalty is a theory that certain individuals by accident of birth are different from everyone else, deserving of respect because of their family name and entitled to deference and certain trappings of wealth and pageantry that others simply can never have because they are not born into it. Given this theory, then, the Abbey, as part of the estate of such a family, is entitled to remain as such, intact, and to serve as evidence of the grand symbolism that is the designated birthright of all who follow. Thus there is a real eternal recurrence because while the estate is always already an eternal entity, it is renewed with each new generation. The Abbey becomes the evidence, the frontispiece for a theory of cosmic time that is both eternal and cyclical. But there are forces chipping away at this theory because there are those pesky and unpredictable humans meddling in this cosmic force. The House of Commons repeatedly passed higher and more invasive estate taxes, heirs squandered wealth, and while the idea of perpetuity of name and rank in society is maintained and recorded in *Burke's Peerage*, there is no such eternity guaranteed for the property that underlies the estate. It appears that this cosmological category of eternal recurrence is not of much help to our quest.

The Abbey Grounds as Life-Affirming and Renewing

Certainly as a place of agriculture and animal husbandry, the Abbey is an existential place that both affirms and renews nature and as such is better tuned to the natural world than if it had been turned into a factory that belches smoke and fouls streams. It is the nihilism of capitalism that the Abbey is stalwartly positioned to thwart. That capitalism as a nihilism serves to downplay tradition in favor of competition clashes regularly with Britain's aristocracy even to this day. The nihilism of dog-eat-dog is at long odds against the maintenance of tradition which serves to temper if even to eliminate competition (wars aside) in the countryside. The Abbey is a positive affirmation of the status quo, encouraging its eternal recurrence in the face of nihilist pleasures in the tearing down of a once impenetrable fortress. And it is not by direct frontal assault that the nihilists are winning the battle. Rather, it is through the erection of a new god of wealth through commerce that provides incentives for the tearing down of the other. For this new nihilistic tradition is to serve up fad after fad.

And the royals, the people so designated, have proved not to have served their cause most righteously; for remember it was three cousins, the king of England, the tsar of Russia, and the kaiser of Germany who aligned themselves as allies or enemies for war, the Great War, the war to end all wars, World War I. The burgeoning capitalism movement, which had jumped all over itself to fuel the debilitating engine of war, has seriously compromised the existential argument for a life-affirming and renewing hereditary estate. War has sucked dry both the life of heirs and their estate's finances to feed the maw of world discord. Rather than the perpetuity of the paradise of Eden promised by God, the royal cousins and industrialists have embraced Darwin and his survival of the fittest.

The Categorical Imperative of Royal Continuity

The Great War ended and with it the empires of Russia, Germany, and Austria-Hungary. Certainly great books of heraldry will continue to name the names that once held great prominence, but the categorical imperative of their continuity has been severed as easily as the Gordian knot. And it was Immanuel Kant (1724–1804) who first proposed the idea of the categorical imperative but in the context of ethics. His idea was that there are certain ethical imperatives which, on their face, have no interpretive ability. "Thou shalt not lie" does not allow one to tell a white lie or even lie to save another's life. Any lie is unethical, period, full stop. And so, for us here, is the idea of royal continuity as categorically imperative.

Of the *major* European powers, only Britain has maintained this royal categorical imperative of right and perpetuity. Yet this royal imperative is in a weakened state. While royalty is permitted to exist and is even admired and treasured, it proves to be subject to the same forces that everyone, even the abject poor suffer through—legislative compromise and economic forces that could care less who one is or what title one has. The world can take or leave royals. But unfortunately royalty is not like the cinema where the eternal recurrence of youth and beauty is guaranteed with each new generation of actors. The royals are an aging bunch, relegated to bit parts and matronly or dowager roles, shells of what had been admired as chiseled marble, that are now tarnished in the toxic winds of change.

Pomp and Circumstance vs. Reality

If Nietzsche felt so strongly about eternal recurrence, why would he relegate it to the symbolic? When millions of commoners line the streets to view royals passing by in their bulletproof sedans or line up to walk through some old retired manor house, perhaps pomp and circumstance is a form of bread and circuses that mollify the masses without otherwise recognizing their day-to-day needs—a kind of soda fizz in the belly whose only appetite reduction is the belch. The peoples' dreams take form in the flesh of the aristocrats who can maintain their aloof pageantry—despite the encroachment of the "new society" who are well costumed in ever fresh technology, hype, and the latest fashion fad, and are brimming over with consumer confidence.

We look at the bones of dinosaurs and marvel at how something so stocky, so substantial, so frightfully regal could be snuffed out by a simple stroke of the cosmic pen. Likewise, we marvel at the clinging to life of the aristocracy even as some are relegated to apartments in their once sumptuous mansions. Still the heralds in the great room of such bygone residence shine in spite of the fact that there are water leaks all throughout the south wing so to speak.

I ask you, then, is the symbol enough? Is the listing in *Burke's Peerage* recognizing the locus of a long extinct mansion and grounds that is now the suburban Middlington Development of small homes and a rather bland apartment complex adequate to consider the estate eternal? And again we must ask if Nietzsche thought that symbolism for eternal recurrence was good enough. Really, why massage the idea and come back to it so many times? But isn't that so with the dream? We come back and again to the same story because it is familiar and comforting. But Nietzsche was not really about comfort. His Zarathustra said, "What good is my happiness! It is poverty and pollution and wretched contentment."

The Anthropomorphic Abbey

We have run out of real estate; we're down to the final category of interpretation of Nietzsche's eternal recurrence. And so far it has been less than filling, more like an English tea where the crusts on the bread have been shaved off and the conversation is banal, mostly gossip and rumor.

But enter Violet Crawley, Dowager Countess of Grantham, respectfully late to high tea but full of that acerbic wit which we look forward to hearing at least once per episode. She, the others of the house, the servants, and the tenants have become one with the property itself. They create the anthropomorphic structure of Downton Abbey. They have become the organs and skin and blood which course through the skeleton that is the structure of the Abbey itself. Without the earl and his eccentric family and the generations of bones in the graveyard and generations yet to come but little imagined, the Abbey is nothing but an edifice, a shell, an empty cup. So, if it were not for the personalities, there would be no Downton Abbey and the servants know this and so does Violet.

But is that not also true of mythology—that the gods of prior ages were the same then as they are now? That there is a cosmological-fixedness to the mansion because paintings and pictures down through the ages paint the same structure, firm, tireless, shiny, and always there. But the bones of the structure are like that of a T-rex in a museum—token representations, the ossification of an entire genus of life that could not adapt. And so the question put forth for consideration is whether physical existence is an adequate explanation of the eternal recurrence? The fact that dinosaurs have not returned but their bones have recurred in the form of fossils—is that what we mean by eternal recurrence? And even if these ossified bones remain until the end of the earth is that enough to meet the requirements of eternal and recurring?

Of What Then, Eternal Recurrence?

Perhaps then it isn't possible to place our foot firmly on to the bog of culture without sinking into it and disappearing; or perhaps by wishing to preserve our footing we drain the bog, thus changing its nature and sacrificing what was the engine that drove its ultimate destiny towards peat. Society has evolved as has the bog. We have harvested the peat and drained the bog for progressive purposes but we miss the warmth of its heat in the cold of winter and the earthy smell that permeates walls and clothing and reminds us of our own natural roots.

Similar to the bog is the landscape of the aristocrat. Drained are its coffers and redeveloped are its lands to where only a few true bogs of primordial hereditary estates remain. And will this be adequate to maintain the eternal recurrence, another reason to redraft *Burke's Peerage* once again for profitable distribution? Or will the aristocratic dwindle to the point where its recurrence is but a whisper of what it has been? Only time will tell.

War

18
Wondering What It's All For

TRIP McCROSSIN

"We've dreamed a dream, my dear, but now it is over," Lord Grantham says to Lady Grantham, in the closing moments of the third episode of season 2. "The world was in a dream before the war," he continues, speaking not just of social change in general, but of warfare as its catalyst, "but now it's woken up and said goodbye to it. And so must we." World War I has come home to Downton Abbey, both as a newly minted convalescent facility, and in the many particular ways it adversely affects family and staff. The warfare story line not only reconnects us with this period in the history of the enterprise, but also engages us with the many moral questions that haunt it.

The story line is most central to the first two-thirds of the second season, spanning the second half of the war. Still, the rest of the seasons, spanning roughly the first year of the war's aftermath, and subsequent seasons, moving farther into the early decades, see it continue to arise periodically. In this spirit, we follow out here a particularly provocative portion of it from seasons 2 and 3.

We begin with Lord Grantham's rumination above, which sets the stage for Matthew and William to go mysteriously missing in action shortly thereafter, only to reappear, seemingly miraculously, and with truly brilliant timing, back at the Abbey. This sets the stage for both to be critically wounded in action, at the Battle of Amiens, the first of the Hundred Days Offensive, which, ironically, brings the war to an end. This sets it in turn for William to die tragically from his wounds while Matthew struggles with his own. And so the stage is set, finally, for Matthew to die nonetheless, even more tragically than William it seems, less than two years later, as season 3 comes to a close.

Along the way, the story line provides a timely warning against complacency regarding the plight of combatants in warfare, in addition to that of civilians, who have become the greater moral concern in the post–World War II era. And it warns us as well, in an equally timely manner, against a more general complacency, increasingly entrenched in our day, regarding warfare's seeming inevitability.

The Lord's and the King's Dreams

We can hear in Lord Grantham's turn of phrase an allusion to a much older one, King Nebuchadnezzar's, in verses 3 and 5 of chapter 2 of the Book of Daniel: "I have dreamed a dream, and my spirit was troubled to know the dream," the king complains, but the "thing is gone from me." As the story goes, the king awoke from his troubling dream demanding that his advisors not only explain it, but, as he could no longer recall it properly, reveal it to him in the first place, threatening to execute them otherwise. Naturally they balk. Only the gods can do such a thing, they insist, but of course they live nowhere among us. Daniel, determined to demonstrate God's power to the king, prayed through the night, and in the morning was able to reveal the king's dream to him. The king's realm, Daniel reports, would be succeeded by others, each breaking and replacing its predecessor, to yield eventually one divinely inspired and perpetual. If we're to imagine that Lord Grantham is indeed channeling Nebuchadnezzar, then are we also to imagine that he and Lady Grantham, the Abbey more generally, and "the world" more generally still, awoken by warfare from their shared dream, need to have their dream not only explained, but also somehow revealed to them? And if so, by whom?

Channeling Daniel

The answer is in part simply that the overall story line is of a bygone era. Lord Grantham, the Dowager Countess of Grantham, and Mr. Carson busily protest to the contrary, but it had to have been obvious to most everyone at the time that their realm was being succeeded by a new order. "Things are changing," Ethel exclaims, for example, approving of Lady Sybil's desire to learn to cook, for "her lot and us," just as Lady Sybil does to the Dowager Countess later on, "surely you can't want things to go back to the way they used to be" before the war. That things are moving forward, not backward, is clear enough, but toward what?

King Nebuchadnezzar is fortunate to have Daniel to step in, but remembering that even the forward-looking Tom sees his self-confident predictions regarding the Russian Revolution dashed, the Abbey seems clearly without a Daniel to guide it. The parable of Daniel wouldn't be much of a parable, however, if it was just about how prophetic he is. Rather, it's surely just as much about how we all have it in us to be Daniel. The king's advisors, that is, even though they can't do what Daniel does, are nonetheless right about something important. The king's dream is *his* dream, which he would surely have access to if he'd only pay proper attention, and allow it to be revealed to him, as Daniel does. If the dream is *our* dream, as Lord Grantham suggests, then *we* have it in us to be Daniel if *together* we pay proper attention, and help to reveal the dream to one another, even if only in bits and pieces at a time.

And this we've seen happen at the Abbey, little by little, as the seasons have gone on. Family and staff have struggled with the various ways the war has affected them, individually and together. And they've also struggled in the process with their attitudes for and against the war, and warfare generally, led most conspicuously by Tom and Lord Grantham. The warfare story line is a plea, in this sense, that as proponents and opponents of warfare we struggle with one another in a more *familial* way, that we recognize more than we usually do that in spite of our differences, we've considerably more in common. Lord Grantham may be channeling Nebuchadnezzar, but together with the Abbey's family and staff, they're collectively channeling Daniel, and in the process channeling the spirit of what a beloved US president would come to remind us, at a later crossroads in history, which is that our "most basic common link is that we all inhabit this small planet. We all breathe the same air. We all cherish our children's future. And we are all mortal."

What's Going on Over There

The force of Lord Grantham's allusion to Nebuchadnezzar lies also in the obscurity of the king's dream in the first place, before Daniel ever steps in.

Warfare isn't a spontaneous event. It results rather from a myriad of conditions coming to a head. And while the immediate cause may appear to be clear enough, the extent of these conditions is less so, if at all. "The main topic [at the Abbey] is the murder of the Austrian Archduke," Mrs. Hughes tells Mr. Carson, who replies pithily, but also accurately, "Here and everywhere else." Even a quick look at the history of the warfare reveals that this is only part of the story. For present purposes, what the broader story is in retrospect is less important than its general obscurity at the time, together with the obscurity of the conditions that await combatants in battle—obscure to them beforehand, and to civilians before, during, and after.

"When I think of my life at Downton," Matthew says to his soldier servant Davis, for example, in season 2's opening moments, as their dug-out trembles from exploding shells, it "seems like another world." And what he says, he says as something that cannot help but make more sense to the two of them, than to anyone not part of such horrible circumstances, if they could ever really make any sense of them at all. The sentiment is confirmed later on, when Mary asks, "What's it been like," and Matthew answers, visibly anguished, "The thing is, I just can't talk about it." It's Mr. Lang, though, who's been "invalided out" of military service, for shell shock we later learn, who represents most tangibly the ravages of war, and who adds substance to what we learn from Matthew. He does so in his confrontations both with William, as he's enthusiastically off to the front, and then with Mrs. Patmore, whose nephew Archie, as we've learned, but Mr. Lang has not, has been executed for cowardice.

Early on, we find William struggling with his father, who doesn't want his only child to enlist, and struggling likewise with Daisy and Mrs. Patmore, who are struggling with one another in turn over how Daisy should respond both truthfully and kindly to William's courtship. He's called up finally, though, departs for training, and has just now returned to the Abbey, proudly in uniform, he and Daisy are now engaged, and he awaits transport to the front. Everyone present seems sincerely proud of him, except of course for Mr. Lang. "So," he says, mockingly, "still full of the joys of war?" "I'm not sorry to be part of it," William answers, visibly enthusiastic, "and I can't pretend I am." In response, Mr. Lang is incredulous, but also seems to want benevolently to educate him, to send him off to war at least disabused of his illusions.

"Oh, yes," he says, "you're part of it. Like a metal cog is part of a factory, and a grain of sand is part of the beach." In response, surprisingly, William also agrees in part. "I understand," he says, and "I'm not saying I'm important or owt like that. But I believe in this war. I believe in what we're fighting for, and I want to do my bit." "Then God help you," is all Mr. Lang can say in response, though with apparent sincerity. What's ultimately telling about the scene is the look of confusion on William's face, not knowing whether Mr. Lang means this in the encouraging sense of "farewell," "godspeed," and such like, or in a rather more discouraging sense, that in his ignorance of what he's about to confront, only God can help him. What we take away from this is a more substantive sense of what Matthew had already suggested to Lady Mary, which is that the gulf is truly forbidding between those who've experienced warfare and those who would try, but ultimately fail to imagine it.

This idea is at the core of, and given additional substance by, Mr. Lang's later confrontation with Mrs. Patmore. "I sometimes feel," he complains to her, that "I'm the only one who knows what's going on over there. You all wander around ironing clothes and cleaning boots and choosing what's for dinner, while over the Channel men are killed and maimed and blown to pieces. Have you any idea how scared they are? How scared they all are?" "We know more than you think," she objects, and the example she offers indicates what precisely *she* knows, or rather *infers*, which is that the circumstances of war must be for some, her nephew in particular, incomprehensibly awful. Archie would still be alive, that is, "if he hadn't been half out of his mind with fear." "Don't blame him," Mr. Lang pleads in response, seeming to want to comfort her. It was him," he adds, "but it could have been me. It could have been any of us."

Mrs. Patmore's not as visibly confused by what Mr. Lang's said as William seemed earlier to be, but she's also not obviously comforted either. Perhaps this is because we hear in Mr. Lang's attempted comforting a certain ambiguity. Does he mean that "it could have been any of us [*soldiers*]," or does he mean "any of us" more generally? In the latter sense, he would be meaning to include not only soldiers, but also officers, and finally citizens as well, were they ever placed in such psychologically devastating circumstances as Archie faced, and as Mr. Lang himself did, sharing the tragically damaging experience of legions over the course of the war. Given his earlier conversation with William, it seems perfectly conceivable that Mr. Lang means the latter. If so, Mr. Lang's challenge, to bridge the above gulf—separating those who've experienced warfare and the rest of us, who would try, but ultimately fail to imagine it— is one we've long struggled with, and do still today.

Shall We Be But Ghosts

Looking back to the close of the first season, as its final episode airs, it's been a little over two short months since President Obama announced that the "combat mission in Iraq has ended," and, with soldiers returning from the war, many of them deeply scarred by the experience, the national and international conversation about the human and material costs of the war has taken on new urgency. It's also just a few days before Remembrance Day in Britain and Veterans Day in the US. At the Abbey's annual garden party, it's Lord Grantham's great "regret to announce . . . that we are at war with Germany," and only a few days later, on Remembrance and Veterans Days, we hear from Colonel Herbert Hayden.

Colonel Hayden was ordered in November of 1918 to make his way to the front, resulting in "months of the most perfect and unmitigated hell," and afterward years of the hell of shell shock, which he records movingly in "Shell-Shocked—and After," published anonymously in the December 1921 issue of the *Atlantic Monthly*. When we hear from him more recently, it's in the form of a dramatic reading of excerpts from his essay in the 2010 HBO documentary, *Wartorn—1860–2010*, which testifies broadly to the legions of fellow soldiers who suffered the same hell, not only in World War I, but in the wars before and after. In concluding his essay, Colonel Hayden asks, "Shall we help back those thousands of humble men who trod the rocky pathway of the Front in France? Shall we give them the little boost that they need, to come back? And what of those other men who have suffered, whose minds are gone? Shall we be but ghosts for those unburied dead—who did not die?"

Granted, the timing is very likely coincidental. But still, this part of the warfare story line, and its continuation in season 5, with Mrs. Patmore's efforts to resist Archie's exclusion from Downton's war memorial, and Lord Grantham's assistance in memorializing him nonetheless, are a welcome continuation of the questions that Colonel Hayden raised almost a century ago. And welcome attention to the sad fact that, hearing them spoken to us again so recently, we can't help but be troubled that we've yet to provide a proper answer.

In part this is because a strategy initiated modestly in World War I, the aerial bombing of cities, would become a far more dominant strategy in World War II, as it has been since, with far more devastating effects on civilian populations. With this, the dominant concern in the ethics of warfare became the massive scale and seeming inevitability of civilian casualties. What *Downton*'s warfare story line helps us to see, especially with the assistance of *Wartorn*, setting Colonel Hayden's voice alongside voices from the Civil War, World War II, Vietnam, and Iraq, is that the moral concern we rightly have for civilians caught in warfare, shouldn't come at the expense of moral complacency regarding combatants. Surely, that is, we can walk and chew gum at the same time.

A Long Business

It's "a long business," the Dowager Countess declares in the first months after the war, and there's "no getting out of it for our kind of people." Granted, she's talking about marriage. But given what we know now about World War I, that it failed utterly to live up to its billing as "the war that will end war," her "long business . . . there's no getting out of" might just as well refer to warfare. And the longer the business, the more complacent we become about its apparent inevitability. The warfare story line has something interesting to tell us here as well.

Mr. Lang is not alone in trying to prepare William for what awaits him. Lord Grantham is also doing what he can, arranging to have him assigned to Matthew, to stand in for Davis as his soldier servant. His safety's not guaranteed, but warfare's without guarantees anyway, and it's a gesture that has to seem far better than nothing. But when Lord Grantham learns that they've been declared missing, family and staff can't help but fear the worst, as we can't either. After a few days of hand-wringing and furrowed brows, though, they turn up, seemingly miraculously, during a concert for the Abbey's convalescing soldiers. Mary and Edith leave off mid-song, and rejoicing ensues, topped off by Matthew insisting on finishing the song with Mary, and how perfect that it happens to be Ayer and Grey's 1916 "If I Were the Only Girl (in the World)."

It's a very nice moment, but it also lulls us into imagining, when later we see William and Matthew lying injured on the battlefield, in the Battle of Amiens, that eventually they'll turn up again miraculously mid-song at the Abbey. Sadly it's not to be. William has managed to save Matthew's life, but has fatally damaged his lungs in the process, leaving him to perish slowly, but inevitably. And while Matthew lives, paraplegia is his grim diagnosis, all the more so for his having, he believes, not only to break off his engagement to Lavinia, but to swear off married life altogether. And of course we must have suspected that it wasn't to be, from a key difference between Matthew and William going missing in episode 4 and being injured in episode 5, which is that in the latter case we witness the moving premonitions that Daisy and Mary have at the moment they're injured.

Matthew does recover, though, again seemingly miraculously, jumping up from his wheelchair to catch Lavinia, who's stumbled. As before, there's much rejoicing, the marriage is back on, but again, it's not to be. The Spanish flu comes to the Abbey and kills Lavinia, and Matthew is robbed yet again of his happiness, as he's been robbed time and again.

When we first meet Matthew, he's a happy middle-class lawyer, at tea with his mother, reading a letter from Lord Grantham. "He wants to change our lives," he tells her, having learned that he's to be Sixth Earl of Grantham. And as we expect, he and Lady Mary are soon courting, and finally he proposes, and it seems likely she'll accept, or so at least we hope. But of course, it's not to be.

Instead Matthew's robbed of his happiness by what he sees as class-snobbery, Mary's in particular, scuttling their marriage plans, and, we sense, sending him off to war. He recovers, and begins to build a new life with Lavinia, but again he's robbed, by the war, injuring him in a way that scuttles their marriage plans. Again he recovers, and their marriage plans are restored, but now disease is the thief, killing Lavinia, under circumstances that are all the worse for scuttling also, he believes, any thought of eventually reconciling with Mary. Yet again he recovers, and manages to reconcile with Mary after all, and they marry, and eventually start a family, and it's a son no less, ensuring the Abbey's survival through yet another generation. "Do you ever wonder how happy you've made me," he says to her, as they dote over little George, as we'll come to know him, Mary sitting up in bed cradling him, Matthew joyfully sitting beside them. All's well finally, it seems. But yet again, and this time finally, and tragically, it's not to be.

"Life is strange, isn't it?," Lord Grantham muses, to family members gathered to celebrate, as we've just seen Matthew driving back to the Abbey, ecstatic, having just left mother and child. "In so many different ways," the Dowager Countess agrees, enjoying perhaps one of her many humorous moments. "No," he replies, struggling to voice something deeper, "I mean, I think of all the uncertainty between Matthew and Mary; when the money was lost, and everything was so dark." In the audience, our view now returns to Matthew, still driving, still ecstatic, looking up as if to the heavens, to the side as if to the Abbey. But we also see what he doesn't, which is that a truck is approaching from the opposite direction, which we can't help but fear is on a collision course. "Yet now here we are with two healthy heirs," Lord Grantham concludes, "an estate in good order, and I wonder what I've done to deserve it."

"I agree," the Dowager Countess says, as we return to those assembled back at the Abbey, her expression making clear that she hadn't meant to be humorous at all. "But then," completing prophetically her son's thoughts, "we don't always get our just deserts." She's reminding those gathered, that is, that they live under the specter of an old, but persistent problem, and reminds *us* in the process that *we* do as well. A problem as old as another book in the Old Testament, the Book of Job, the "problem of evil" haunts us still—in the words of Colonel Hayden, for example, given new voice by modern media—as we ask, time and again, why ever good things happen to bad people, and bad things to good? And the Dowager Countess reminds us of this precisely as we return to the side of the road, to find Matthew pinned and lifeless beneath his over-turned car.

The last we see of him is his face in close-up, as we watch in disbelief, almost as if we were lying next to him—his eyes open, but sightless, blood trickling down his lifeless cheek. What we see next can't help but move us all the more then. Mary is sitting up in bed still, cradling George still, just as she was when we last saw her, albeit without Matthew at their side. We know what she doesn't yet, which is that Matthew has been killed, and we're glad for her to have a last few moments of happiness before it's stolen from her once again. As we've seen Matthew subjected to fortune's merciless peaks and valleys, so it's been for Mary as well. For the moment, though, she's at peace and happy, bathed in white, seemingly angelic, smiling down at her newborn, marveling at how he grips her thumb. We're moved, but in a way also surprised.

As we watch, that is, we also wait for her to have again the sort of premonition she had when Matthew was injured in battle. But she doesn't, and we can't help but wonder why. There're no doubt different perspectives to offer. One of them, though, is presently of particular interest.

Matthew survived the perils of class, romance, disease, and war, and found happiness nonetheless, joy even in his last hours. Finally, though, it's the trivial confluence of human contrivance, imprudence, and bad luck that kills him—nothing grand or cosmic, no premonition, no nothing. We're reminded of what Thomas's fellow stretcher-bearer says to him in the trenches in episode 1 of season 2. "I think it comes down to luck," he says, because if "the bullet's got your names on it, there's nothing you can do." "If not," he continues, "then thank God you were lucky," just as he's shot in the head and killed instantly. Both he and Matthew are feeling lucky, and then both are suddenly dead, their sightless eyes facing us, but not quite in our direction, as if transfixed by something distantly in back of us.

If Matthew's death and the stretcher-bearer's seem equally meaningless, and together they seem as meaningless as Lavinia's and Sybil's, one reaction to *Downton*'s warfare story line is to wonder why we should worry *particularly* about warfare in the first place. It's just one of the many things that happen regularly in the world, that is, all of which are very, if not entirely likely to rob us of our happiness—people are born into this or that class, fall in love with this or that person, contract this or that disease, enlist in this or that war, drive along this or that road—and in particular war's just one of these inevitably occurring phenomena that may kill us. Maybe we should try to reduce warfare's destructiveness, just as we should try to make class, disease, traffic, and romance less destructive. But, according to this line of reasoning, they'll always be around, even if a bit more tolerable, and so let's just live with that.

The better reaction, it would seem, is this. Even the best doctors and medical researchers don't aspire to rid humanity of disease altogether. We admit easily, given the sort of creatures we are, that this would be an unreasonable expectation. Likewise, however convincing their commercials, however "scientific" they may aspire to be, outfits like eHarmony will never produce only successful romances. The heart wants what it wants, as Emily Dickinson wrote long ago, and Selena Gomez sang more recently, and this might make us happy, or it might make us miserable, it might even kill us, but in any case the outcome's at best only a little bit in our control. Class, on the other hand, however entrenched, is still just a particularly unfortunate attitude, which can be ameliorated, and in the end, we hope, eliminated. "Things are changing," Ethel rightly predicts, for the family's "lot" and also the staff's. This too may be a "long business," but the idea that class is artificial, undesirable, and ultimately eliminable follows simply from the very first of the truths we hold to be self-evident. Likewise, the persistence of traffic fatalities is less a function of not knowing how to reduce them, than of what we do know to this effect being outpaced by the unreasonable proliferation of cars, which is something we can surely do something about, and so an aspiration we should just as surely not allow ourselves to be discouraged from having.

The destructive power of warfare is more akin to the destructive power of class and traffic. But why then does Mary have a premonition of warfare's threat to Matthew, but not traffic's? Because unlike traffic, warfare, beginning with World War I, is "total," encompassing all aspects of humanity, making possible this sort of connection. What the premonition reflects, then, is the sheer difficulty we face in accomplishing in the future what World War I was supposed to have accomplished already long ago, which was to be the "war that will end war." As it turns out, not surprisingly, it's not up to warfare to bring about its own end. "Do you ever wonder what it was all for," Lord Grantham asks Jane after the war, which is a very good question indeed, even if posed only in retrospect, especially given the change it reflects in him. How much better it will be if next time he asks it *in advance*. When a few of us dream up wars in the first place, that is, it's up to the rest of us to band together as Daniel, interpret their awful dreams in full and gruesome detail, and not stand by and allow them to come to be. This too is something we can surely do, and so again, as *Downton*'s warfare story line helps us to imagine, it's an aspiration that we should absolutely not allow ourselves to be discouraged from having.[1]

---

[1] I would like to thank Gina Pearson for helping to pique my interest in *Downton Abbey* in the first place, a season or so in, and for many provocative and helpful conversations since. I would like to dedicate this essay to the memory of her mom, Virginia (Ginny) Mary Pearson, who passed away peacefully, in her home, with family at her side, during the final weeks of writing it. My interest in and perspective on the problem of evil derives from Susan Neiman's body of work on the subject, in her 2002 *Evil in Modern Thought* and related books and essays before and after, and so thanks are naturally due to her as well. My interest in and perspective on the ethics of warfare derives primarily from Howard Zinn's body of work on the subject, in his 1990 *Declarations of Independence* and related books and essays before and after, which I would have been much less likely to come to if not for the help and encouragement of Marina Sitrin, many years ago now. I am grateful to her for, among other things, helping to make it possible for me to be grateful to him

19
Of Downton and Drones

Jai Galliott

When we tune in to watch *Downton Abbey*, we revel in the Crawley family's finery, posture, and ability to make the sharpest remarks in tempered rhetoric. We marvel at their access to servants who specialize in their every need. Many of us find this polarized class system antithetical to our modern democratic values and culture. But in one major way, the *Downton* world is less class-stratified than our world, namely, with respect to who fights and dies in war.

When the show faces the grand rupture of World War I, grief is rained on all classes; indeed, historically the upper classes of this time suffered just as much if not more so than the middle and lower classes. But today, war is fought largely from afar with aerial weapons called "drones," which are piloted by people from the lower and middle classes. World War I helped propel this technological change in terms of driving unmanned systems development. But with these weapons have come new ethical concerns about the use of these "honorless" killing machines rather than arguably more honorable one-on-one combat. When we abandon the sort of symmetry and equality that characterizes the conflict depicted in *Downton Abbey*, we begin to experience serious difficulties interpreting and applying Just War Theory, an ethical theory that concerns the rules of engagement.

More specifically, when the degree of divergence from chivalric war of bygone days reaches a certain point, universal principles of justice and their practical application are brought into conflict, or at least into competition, with the aims of technological war. It's important to think about these matters now, because in the same way that Mrs. Patmore says that "nothing can stop her [Lady Grantham—the American] from dragging us into the new age," nothing will stop us being dragged into the drone age.

The Downton Tech Revolution

Set in the years leading up to WWI, and detailing the threat and promise of a technological revolution that would change almost everything, *Downton Abbey* pays homage to forces that transcend early twentieth-century Britain and apply just as well to the twenty-first-century world. The signs of the tech revolution are most obvious in the Downton household. The upper floors have recently received electricity, even if the servants downstairs are still using candles and oil lamps. There's a great scene with the Dowager Countess of Grantham—who is of course part of the upstairs lot—saying that she can't bear electrical lights because she thinks they give off glare and a bad smell. But given that Lady Edith carelessly set fire to her bedroom sometime later by leaving a book too close to an open flame, electricity is arguably the least of *her* problems! Mrs. Patmore has what she thinks are bigger problems and her new electric mixer-beater, to which Daisy has taken so well, is just the beginning of it all. The new sewing machine and refrigerator, which she is told will help reduce costly waste, soon come to irritate her. Then later a telephone arrives—imagine the weird sensation it must have been for them to be able to speak with someone they can't even see.

But technology's impact is rarely limited to the domestic sphere and the Abbey folk weren't the only ones struggling with new technology. The Great War was the first major conflict in which technology entered into the fighting and old-fashioned military tactics no longer worked. It was the first war to use telephones, wireless communications, armored cars, tanks, and aircraft, and even ushered in the development and use of the first generation of unmanned systems. Michael Gregson's German friends built a dozen large gas-powered tele-operated motorboats for use against the Brits. These carried explosives that detonated on impact and were initially tethered to a land-based control tower and, later, an overflying seaplane. Later again, they were able to be radio-controlled. As you can imagine, there were difficulties coordinating the warship, seaplane, and land station. These difficulties, coupled with engine troubles, resulted in a lack of confidence surrounding the use of these unmanned vessels.

Sadly for us and our ancestors, Germany instead displayed a preference for the well-tested U-boat, which went on to kick some serious behind. Toward the end of the war, an American engineer with the Caterpillar Tractor Company designed one of the earliest tele-operated unmanned ground vehicles, called the "Land Torpedo." From patents, it is known that the design of this tracked-and-tethered vehicle was motivated by a desire to avoid the horrors of early trench warfare as depicted in season 2 of *Downton Abbey* and was thus designed to deliver communications cables from trench to trench, minus the human. It was also capable of levelling terrain between trenches prior to infantry advances, or delivering explosives directly to enemy trenches.

It was roughly during the period represented in the second season that Elmer Sperry made one of the most important aeronautical developments with the creation of a levelling device known as the gyrostabilizer, which is at the heart of most modern autopilots and many modern robots. Later, in 1917, the US Navy gave Sperry's son a grant to build an aerial torpedo, with the name again indicating the fact that they were designed to deliver weapons which would detonate on impact, destroying the device itself. This led to the development of the Curtiss N-9 catapult-launched seaplane, which was capable of basic self-guided flight, but had a pilot to carry out the more complex take-off. It was a flight of this kind that claimed the life of Joseph Kennedy, the elder brother of the future US president, John F. Kennedy. A radio-controlled version was later made, but it was just as crude, with its analogue instruments not allowing precision flight or weapons delivery. Those on Cora's side of the world designed a similar aerial torpedo in 1918, named the "Kettering Bug." The British also had several programs underway, mostly based on existing aircraft frames retrofitted with expendable (read: "cheap") engines. All of these systems were rather unreliable.

Toward Class-Stratified Technological War

The unreliability of these early unmanned weapons is part of the reason why William Mason and Matthew Crawley had to take to the trenches, ultimately costing the former his life. As British novelist William Boyd said in a *New York Times* piece, while WWI is overshadowed by WWII, it is unique in more than just the sense that it ushered in the first generation of (unreliable) military robots or "drones." There was just so much death involved, and gory death at that. It left what is the deepest the scar on the British people, even to this day: In just one single day of the Battle of the Somme, for instance, more than 50,000 British soldiers met their demise—butchered largely by forms of conventional technology that they did not yet have the ability to overcome. Tanks and howitzers, tear gas and hand grenades—these were not weapons that the average Yorkshire boy or member of the nobility would have ever confronted or seen, let alone been prepared to survive. But it wasn't just the dirtiest war in which England had ever fought, for the Axis also suffered a tremendous number of casualties. This dirty war also signaled the beginning of the end of a class system that had stood the test of time.

World War I was arguably the last war in which the upper classes would suffer their fair share of the mental, physical, and financial harms that accompany conflict. The aristocrats did their bit in this war primarily because the lower classes had, during the late nineteenth century, come to the opinion that they were no better than idle parasites, living off the proceeds of their land monopoly and abusing their inherited political power. The war in 1914 gave them a chance to combat the Miss Buntings of the world and, as David Cannadine wrote in *The Decline and Fall of the British Aristocracy*, "to demonstrate conclusively that they were not the redundant reactionaries of radical propaganda, but the patriotic class of knightly crusaders and chivalric heroes, who would defend the national honor and the national interest in the hour of its greatest trial." There's evidence that they harnessed this opportunity in the fact that not since the War of the Roses had so many aristocrats died so suddenly and violently. Proportionately, their losses were far greater than those of any other social group. During the first few months of the war, six peers, sixteen baronets, ninety-five sons of peers, and about eighty sons of baronets perished in the slaughter.

How many children of our economic elites fought in Iraq or Afghanistan? Not many. That's partly because there's an economic crisis going on and times are tough all over, so while many of our best minds and bodies go into private enterprise, military forces are left to select from those for whom military service is one of few options. Even at Britain's Royal Air Force, which is struggling in these times of austerity and looking to save a penny or two itself, they intend to replace some combat pilots with . . . gamers—young gamers, usually in their twenties. Thankfully, we're not talking about real warfighters here, so rest easy, people of Britain. You're not going to have a snotty-nosed kid crashing a fighter jet into your backyard. You may, however, find one crashing a Reaper drone—an armed unmanned drone—into some poor Afghani's backyard, given that these systems are not without their technical problems. Nevertheless, the PlayStation generation probably stands the best chance of flying these aircraft successfully, and the military knows this all too well.

Concerning who is sacrificed in war, the Western world has become more class-stratified since the *Downton Abbey* days. This is particularly problematic for the United States, given that the "American Dream" largely revolves around overcoming its undeniable history of inequality and class stratification on all levels. Poaching the young and enlisting them to fight war via proxy is likely to perpetuate cycles of inequality, if anything.

After drone operators leave the military, they are often plagued with psychological problems related to this unique form of combat. The American Dream is an ideology in the United States (similar concepts exist under different names in Great Britain and Australia) in which freedom includes the possibility of prosperity and success for all, regardless of social or economic class. Rooted in the ethic of equating success with morality, the American Dream is the idea that anyone can succeed by working hard. The same idea pervades the thoughts of the downstairs lot at Downton. But can one really have a chance of making something of oneself after having engaged in this troubling form of conflict? While drone warfare may not compare to hauling one's behind from trench to trench and seeing all the death that this entails, killing people and then going home to have dinner with your loved ones isn't exactly stress free, either. Many drone operators experience post-traumatic stress disorder akin to that suffered by conventional pilots. It seems unfair to place the burden of communal defense largely upon the shoulders of one social group, even in a capitalist society. General Stanley McChrystal has suggested that conscription could be implemented both to limit the unjust recourse to arms and more fairly spread the burden of defense.

Technology, Morality, and the Death of Chivalric War

In any case, this isn't the only problem faced by Western military forces. There seems to be something else that is unfair and unjust about our departure from bygone days of chivalric war, as depicted in *Downton Abbey*.

It has something do with the morality of the technological asymmetry that has been developing ever since Henry V started preparing for the Battle of Agincourt. It was at Agincourt that the English achieved victory over the numerically superior French army. It is thought that the English were outnumbered by almost six to one, with the French having troop strength of approximately thirty thousand men. Yet what is striking is that due to the longbow, which allowed its users to launch a barrage of powerful arrows at a greater than normal distance, the English suffered only a few hundred war dead, while the French lost many thousands. William Shakespeare later depicted this conflict as ruthless and unchivalrous in his *Henry V*. According to Shakespeare, ruthless and ungallant conflict was essentially one of the paradoxes for the king—something he had to wrestle with when protecting his empire.

Another engagement that reflected technological asymmetry was the one that took place between well-armed colonial forces and an army of traditional African warriors at Omdurman, on the upper Nile, at the end of the nineteenth century. Under the command of General Horatio Kitchener, the colonial forces fought a vastly larger armed force and managed to achieve a decisive victory, which was critical to the British conquering Sudan. The Egyptian forces under Kitchener's command carried breach-loading rifles and the British machine guns and field cannons. Their opponents, on the other hand, had only spears, swords, and muskets. Unsurprisingly, the Anglo-Egyptian casualties were few and far between, while their opponents lost approximately ten thousand troops. Showing his concern for such "asymmetric war," Winston

Churchill, who fought in this conflict, later wrote about his disillusionment with modern technology and how dishonorable the Omdurman slaughter was.

Churchill's distaste for modern technology might explain why WWI was essentially reduced to a matter of trench warfare (remember the gruesome scene that opens the fourth episode of season 2). However, recent American leaders obviously don't have the same distaste for emerging warfighting technologies. The Gulf War was another key point in the progression toward radical technological asymmetry in the more modern sense of the term. Executed by a United Nations coalition force, led by the United States and financed mostly by Saudi Arabia, the Gulf War was waged against Iraq primarily in response to its invasion and annexation of Kuwait. While the Iraq of the 1990s was far from a defenseless state, its weaponry was out of date. The Gulf War saw the introduction of advanced networked technologies including fighter jets, surveillance aircraft, and so on. It was widely portrayed as a "tele-present" war conducted by armchair generals via satellite. There was little contest here and few coalition losses. It served as a template for conducting modern asymmetric warfare, and the Kosovo War was its corollary.

This war, aimed at bringing down the Milosevic regime and protecting Kosovo from Serbian aggression, was dominated by precision-guided munitions attacks, aided by drones. Because of the technological asymmetry, NATO's allied forces suffered no military casualties. Accordingly, some theorists have labelled both Kosovo and Iraq as being "no risk" wars. In each case, this is an obvious misnomer. No war, at least no war that we can conceive of today, can be totally risk free. War will always pose *some* harm to both combatants and non-combatants. What these theorists mean to convey is that the states that wage this sort of technologically asymmetrical warfare are taking significantly less risk, and that such warfare has progressed significantly from the (relatively) level playing field we saw in WWI. Sure, at that time women didn't have the right to vote and pursuing a career wasn't really an option, but Crawley family chivalry in the context of war is something we sorely miss today.

When I say "chivalry," I mean a sense of justice—especially the justice of treating an equal (one combatant) as an equal (to another combatant).

All's Fair in Love and War

When the technological imbalance reaches a certain level, which is when war becomes *really* unfair, said imbalance may override any justification for war. What do I mean by "really" unfair? As already suggested, while WWI conflict was horrendously violent, the playing field in was relatively fair and level—the justice of treating an equal as an equal was still largely present. Yes, the Germans had some big tanks. Yes, they had better guns. But at least there were troops on the ground. Fast forward to today and we see conflict where the soldier is completely physically removed from the battlefield. We're now at a point in history where it is possible to wage war entirely from afar. We can send in reconnaissance drones to survey an area and provide intelligence. This information can be transferred via satellite networks and then analyzed by supercomputers which can in turn determine bombing locations, and then send combat drones to kill the combatants and destroy the infrastructure of a state or group that has virtually no means of retaliation. Iraq, anyone?

There's an interesting article called "The Paradox of Riskless Warfare" by Paul Kahn. In it, he says that any fighting between combatants needs to be qualified in terms of the mutual imposition of risk. Kahn's paradox occurs at the level of individual combatants or groups of combatants and is underpinned by a belief in the idea that soldiers can fight each other justly regardless of whether they are fighting for the objectively "bad" side. He is saying that the right to engage in potentially lethal conduct only holds where there is some degree of mutual risk involved. He seems right in using the notion of risk, and thus threat, as a condition. Philosopher Robert Sparrow discusses this idea in "Building a Better WarBot" and deploys it at the level of individual responsibility. He notes that in wartime, wounded soldiers are generally considered immune from attack, as they no longer pose an immediate or near-term threat. Similarly, those who raise the white flag and surrender are also generally considered immune from attack, because they likewise pose little threat. In both cases, threat is at the core of their immunity.

But I think things are more complex than this. Where there are such high levels of asymmetry created by technology, as in the case of most US military interventions, war surely cannot be considered a last resort. In most cases, technologically strong states would presumably have other less-lethal options available. For example, they could make clear the fact that they possess significantly superior technology, perhaps by putting on a non-lethal display of their technological capabilities. This may result in both states reaching some sort of peaceful political negotiation and settlement. Additionally, there is the principle of proportionality. This principle asks us to look at the harm our proposed military action is likely to cause and weigh it against the harm that we hope to avoid. But, where the technological imbalance is so radical—that is, where those on the receiving side of an attack are virtually unable to retaliate—it seems that the harm that the technologically superior state hopes to thwart will in many cases be so insignificant that it would present dire problems for the proportionality calculus.

Back to the *Downton* Days?

Where to from here? Well, war can be more limited in nature and need not cross the symmetry threshold that presents the problem. That is, war doesn't necessarily need to be a perfectly symmetrical fight all the time. But war arguably needs to be *a fight*. It should also be made clear that none of this is to advocate a return to the days of *Downton Abbey* and the violence and savagery of WWI. There's no joy in seeing Matthew crippled and William killed, just as we wouldn't want to see today's soldiers purposely put at risk because a state needs to lower its protective measures to make war seem more fair. Nor would we want to "go easy" on the enemy and allow for transgressions of the laws of war. What, then, might a war that abides by these stronger norms look like? Kahn suggests that, in cases of such high asymmetry, the solution is for the application of any military force to be very restrained and for it to be more like a form of international policing. That is, military forces may need to become more like a cop on the beat that is governed by standards that are more restrictive than those guiding regular war. Whatever the eventual solution, we need to start thinking about how we adapt to technological change, especially in the deadly context of war. Just as Mrs. Patmore was forced to come around to the idea of the electric mixer, we're being dragged into a drone age that we can't escape.

20
Masters and Servants and Soldiers

CARL SOBOCINSKI

Not very well known in the US, and a fading memory in Europe, World War I remains one of the most important events of the past century. The war had a massive impact on much of the world, and even a century later we can still see its effects. Downton Abbey, too, was affected by the war, leading to many developments. Many of these developments are apparent from the very first episode, but as the series progresses they all come together via the catalyst of World War I, also known as the Great War. But, do these changes actually carry a degree of continuity? Certainly, the world of *Downton Abbey* sees much change resulting from the Great War, but did the war instigate these changes, or did it merely accelerate changes that were already present?

Change and Continuity

Change and continuity are essential concepts for philosophers of history, and yet it can be very difficult to distinguish them. Change certainly does happen, but a degree of continuity is almost always present. When changes come radically, or when people try to accelerate them, the result is often disorder, and sometimes disaster. In such situations what frequently happens is that older patterns re-assert themselves, and some form of continuity stabilizes the situation. Sometimes a period of radical change lasts decades, as in the Russian Revolution, which *Downton Abbey* sees gaining momentum toward the end of the Great War. These themes of change, continuity, and even constancy appear in many of *Downton Abbey*'s characters, and no more so than amidst the World War.

Downton Abbey is set amongst themes of uncertainty right from the beginning. Hints of change are apparent, though most of the characters see only limited aspects, if they are even aware of them at all. One of the most important themes is the decline of the traditional nobility. This was not a new trend in 1912, when the series begins. Far from the nobility's original function as a hereditary warrior and ruling class, which had emerged over a thousand years before, by the mid-nineteenth century noble families had less and less purpose in society. Large estates, far from being a source of wealth as had been the case in medieval times, now generated little income. By this time Britain's true wealth was in industry and commerce, but the landed aristocrats clung to their traditions and desperately sought ways to preserve them, as careers in business or professions were considered unworthy. (Think of Lord Grantham's reaction when Matthew Crawley tells him that he has taken a job.)

Lord Grantham's marriage illustrates this situation nicely. A rapidly growing American economy during this "Gilded Age" (as American historians describe it) created a very wealthy upper class, many of whom had pretensions of aristocracy. As such, an ideal solution for "land-poor" English noblemen was to marry daughters of these families. Such events were fairly common, as illustrated by Winston Churchill's wealthy American mother, *née* Jennie Jerome. The heiress's wealth could preserve the estate, she could pretend to enter the aristocratic ranks, all while traditional English aristocrats quietly ignored her lack of any true noble pedigree. In this way Cora Crawley—Lady Grantham—embodies the social shifts which even at that time had already been in place for many years. The Great War would accelerate them dramatically. By 1918 Cora's daughters, who represent the succeeding generation of aristocracy, would come to see that the old life had lost much of its purpose.

Another uncertainty, much more apparent to the characters, was Lord Grantham's lack of a son as heir, reminiscent of Jane Austen's *Pride and Prejudice*. The loss of two prospective heirs on the *Titanic* complicates the situation, news of which provides *Downton Abbey* its opening scenes. While traditional aristocracy was declining quietly, this epitome of maritime tragedies was a blatant sign that perhaps their society had exceeded itself and was now facing decline. As *Titanic* Second Officer Charles Herbert Lightoller remarked in the classic 1958 movie *A Night to Remember,* after surviving the disaster he doubted that he could be certain of anything ever again. Such uncertainty would grow dramatically via the Great War, which by 1918 would signal the undeniable decline of the Empire while seriously fracturing the confidence enjoyed in Victorian and Edwardian Britain.

Hints of the coming war gradually appear through the first few episodes, though the characters generally fail to notice their significance. The scandal of the Turkish ambassador Kemal Pamuk is actually tied quite closely to the coming of the Great War. While his scandalous death certainly captivates viewers, what is scarcely mentioned is that he was in Britain for diplomatic talks concerning events of the First Balkan War, which began late in 1912. This war, and its sequel, the Second Balkan War, the following year, are widely regarded as the preludes to the much greater cataclysm that arrived in 1914, which itself has sometimes been described as a Third Balkan War.

An earlier war a decade before *Downton Abbey* provides the setting for the relationship between Lord Grantham and his valet John Bates. The origin of their relationship is mentioned in the first episode, just as Bates assumes his new duties, and is referred to at scattered moments, but its great significance is not explored in great detail. However, some understanding of it provides a fascinating glimpse into the class relationships and the aristocracy's self-image, themes which permeate the entire series and play a part in the coming world war. Instead of falling into the neat classifications of change or continuity, some of these themes demonstrate constancy.

Lord Grantham and John Bates served together in the Boer War (1899–1902), one of the British Empire's last colonial conflicts prior to 1914. Little discussion of it appears, aside from a few passing references to "the South African War." If many Americans are unfamiliar with World War I, the Boer War is almost totally unknown. Fought between the British Empire and Dutch settlers in southern Africa, the British eventually achieved a nominal victory. Far from being a limited affair, as were so many of Britain's colonial conflicts, the Boer War cost some 75,000 British lives and was often conducted with a ruthlessness that belied the romanticized image of war as often imagined in Victorian society. Clearly acting from the conviction that privileged aristocrats have a moral duty to behave honorably by serving the nation and society, a concept captured by the term "noblesse oblige," Lord Grantham served in the Royal Army. And, at one point early in the series, Bates is briefly referred to as having been the Lord's "batman" in South Africa.

This passing reference, which a viewer might easily overlook, actually says a great deal about both men. In Royal Army tradition, a "batman" is an enlisted man who acts as an officer's personal aide. Officers select batmen from their regiments' ranks, and in addition to regular military duties such as driving an automobile or running messages in combat, a batman also attends to his officer's quarters and maintains his uniforms—many of the same duties as Bates would later perform as a valet.

Downton Abbey makes no mention of Lord Grantham's and Bates's early acquaintance, but often an officer and his batman had known each other prior to their service, as British regiments sometimes recruited both officers and soldiers from the same district. Thus, it is possible that their relationship was older than the war. Officers and batmen were often quite devoted to each other, and there are many stories of remarkable courage of each trying to protect the other. Indeed, J.R.R. Tolkien of *Lord of the Rings* fame, who had been an officer in World War I, based the character Sam Gamgee—one of the most heroic in all his works—on the unassuming, courageous, and devoted batmen he knew during the war.

Bates fits this image very well. Self-sacrificing, faithful to his duty, intensely loyal, Bates's quiet manner gains little attention at first. But, this conceals a great inner strength, and in a just cause he could become the most dangerous of enemies. He demonstrates this nicely when he threatens to drive the footman Thomas Barrow's teeth out the back of his neck. Much to the viewers' disappointment, it remains merely a threat. Lord Grantham's and Bates's fine qualities and mutual loyalty find a counterpart after the Great War begins, when the Abbey's prospective heir Matthew Crawley finds his own batman in William Mason, a far more praiseworthy footman than Thomas Barrow.

Superficially, Lord Grantham and John Bates are almost exact opposites. One, the refined successor of old traditions; the other, a man almost from the gutter. At an earlier time a drunkard and felon, John Bates nonetheless emerges as one of *Downton Abbey*'s most honorable characters. Rather than opposites, perhaps Grantham and Bates should be regarded as mirror images. Amidst the surrounding turmoil they both retain their moral integrity and maintain a close friendship. They play their parts in society, the Lord and Servant, but more so they provide a sense of constancy, balancing between the change and continuity of a human disaster such as the World War.

From this general setting the journey to war progresses, with some foreshadowing references but few that worry any of the main characters. This is perfectly fitting with the history of the time. While high-ranking European statesmen had been expecting some sort of war following the succession of diplomatic crises beginning in 1908, few of them expected the horrific cataclysm that did come—much less would the servant class have expected any such conflict. Lord Grantham shows significant interest in the assassination crisis of the summer of 1914, but that is to be expected from one of his social rank and personal acquaintance with high government officials.

Although the possibility of war certainly became common knowledge by July 1914, it is unlikely that Thomas Barrow would have had any suspicion of its duration or severity. When Thomas inquires of Dr. Richard Clarkson about the possibility of military service in the medical corps, he tells of his concern that a coming war will encompass all of British society and that he wants to be prepared. His motives are to avoid combat through an imagined cushy job in a hospital far from any shooting. As Thomas has a contemptible personality, it is quite satisfying to the viewer when he ends up in a trench tending to wounded in the thick of the fighting, which is certainly accurate historically. But in July 1914 he would have seen little to concern him, since few envisioned a long war and the British Army traditionally did not practice conscription. Even though it broke this precedent during World War I, conscription did not even begin until 1916.

Downton Abbey addresses little more of the war until the end of the final episode of the first season, as Lord Grantham follows the succession of crises through the summer of 1914. In that concluding scene Lord Grantham announces Britain's declaration of war. For many, it is disappointing that the first two years of World War I are not addressed at all. When season 2 begins the viewer is thrust directly into 1916, one of the bloodiest years in history.

Widespread Change

An emerging theme at this point is the war's progression toward affecting everyone's lives. Lord Grantham has once again donned his country's uniform, but is given few actual duties beyond public appearances directed at national morale. In fact, he yearns for active service at the front. Such aspirations are perfectly in keeping with the values of the times. At one point Lord Grantham refers to how Winston Churchill, after resigning his cabinet post in 1916, requested and received orders for active service. Churchill subsequently spent several months in the trenches. Today, this would be the equivalent of an American Secretary of the Navy resigning his office to go to war alongside ordinary soldiers.

This definitely demonstrates great change, not within the confines of *Downton Abbey*, but between the early twentieth century and today. Such ideals are now difficult to imagine, though our countries might well benefit if our higher leaders behaved in similar fashion. This is unquestionably a major change compared to today's values. In contrast, during World War I the British aristocratic and gentlemanly classes suffered a very high proportion of casualties. Nearly all of them strove greatly for active service, as illustrated so well in the 2007 film *My Boy Jack*, based on the true story of how Rudyard Kipling's son was lost in battle in 1915.

Matthew Crawley fits this ideal well. As season 2 commences, we find him in a trench under heavy fire during the Battle of the Somme, a conflagration still remembered in Britain. Few other details of the war appear, however. Nor need they, for *Downton Abbey's* purpose here is less a description of the specific campaigns and more a portrayal of the war as an amorphous presence that inexorably erodes traditional class distinctions.

No conflict since the civil wars of the 1640s had so great an impact on English society. Neither the imperialistic wars of the nineteenth century, nor even the Crimean and Napoleonic Wars so deeply affected English daily life. A good comparison is the 1995 production of *Pride and Prejudice*, one of the best known dramatizations of the Jane Austen novel. Although set amidst the Napoleonic Wars, there is almost no reference to the conflict. Napoleon is never mentioned by name, and the only evidence of any war at all is the constant presence of soldiers, whose main dramatic purpose is to provide opportunity for the romantic scandal which concludes the production. Not so *Downton Abbey*. The great numbers of men in uniform, the enormous number of the deaths and casualties, and the response of English society in dealing with these ordeals draws almost everyone into it. Next to this, the dalliances of the younger Bennet sisters of *Pride and Prejudice* appear trivial.

The great number of men in uniform is one of Britain's greatest catalysts of change. In previous conflicts, British soldiers tended to come from lower, sometimes disreputable classes. Simultaneously, the officer ranks were almost exclusively drawn from the aristocracy. Their relatively small numbers resulted in little direct impact on the common British subject. By comparison, the Great War saw hundreds of thousands of British volunteering out of patriotic duty, and later, serving via conscription. Many of them were ordinary men, like footman William Mason, who otherwise would have been very unlikely ever to see uniformed service.

Concomitantly, the rising need for troops led to a need for more officers than the traditional social hierarchy could support. Accordingly, officers' commissions began to be awarded to middle-class men who otherwise would not have been considered acceptable candidates. Even the concept of an enlisted man working his way through the ranks and attaining a commission, previously quite rare, became increasingly more common. This contrast between changing times appears in one of the Sherlock Holmes stories, *The Crooked Man*, which refers to a regimental commander as embarrassed by his past as a common soldier. But, as the Great War dragged on and consumed ever more lives, such occurrences became increasingly ordinary, and men previously of low social rank came to exercise significant power.

Take the case of Thomas Barrow, who midway through season 2 is a sergeant in the Royal Medical Corps. In his military capacity he is put in charge of Downton Abbey's convalescent facility. Thus, a once low-ranking servant comes to wield authority over his former superiors, even confronting Lord Grantham himself. This would have been unimaginable before the war. But, such a drastic change could only continue so long as extreme circumstances permitted. Doctor Clarkson, by then a major in the Medical Corps, puts a stop to this radical social shift and places the lines of authority back in aristocratic hands.

But are these changes a matter of novelty or degree? Great wars between world powers had occurred before, as against Napoleon a century earlier. The scale of national mobilization may have been unprecedented, but the principles behind it were already visible prior to 1914. Promotion of officers from the enlisted ranks, however rare, was not a new concept, but its prevalence and social acceptability were. The Boer War, which did not lead to conscription, did see massive recruiting campaigns which the Great War would replicate on a much larger scale. Both wars received much patriotic support initially, but by their conclusions much of the idealism had dissipated. From this perspective many of the changes the Great War brought can be regarded as enlarged continuations of trends already apparent before 1914.

Shaking the Abbey's Foundations

The scale of the Great War would further shake the Abbey's foundations. When the enormity of casualties overwhelms the local hospital, the mansion itself is converted into a hospital-like rehabilitation facility, hard to imagine prior to 1914. Yet if the scale is greater, the concept is perfectly in keeping with the principle of noblesse oblige. Dowager Lady Violet is a good example. Early in the series she did support the local hospital, but from behind the scenes. But by 1916, the thick of the war, she actually gives her support to Sybil, the youngest Crawley daughter, in her ambition to become a nurse. In Sybil we see an aristocratic woman serving a hospital, not as a committee leader or board member, but as an actual hands-on medical professional deeply entrenched in the unpleasant but necessary realities of treating war casualties.

The cases of Sybil Crawley and Tom Branson present challenges to the theme of continuity. Here we see serious social changes. The war made Sybil's nursing profession acceptable, as national mobilization during wartime blurred earlier social conventions. Some of her inclinations were already well-developed before the war, such as her growing interest in politics, especially the women's suffrage movement. But, had the war not happened, her suffragist aspirations might have been limited by social restrictions in the face of significant family pressure. Her disillusionment with life as an aristocratic lady had already begun, but the changes the war brought provided an opportunity to act on it.

Her counterpart Tom Branson, the estate chauffeur, is a socialist teetering on the edge of becoming a revolutionary. More than any other character he embodies the prospect of profound social changes. He welcomes the Russian Revolution early in 1917. He laughs in the face of a young woman when she hands him the white feather—an accusation of cowardice—and is actually disappointed when he is declared medically unfit for the army, as it deprived him an opportunity to make a political statement by resisting.

The genteel environment of Downton Abbey and his friendly/romantic relations with Sybil may well have tempered Branson's revolutionary tendencies. Had he spent the war in a different environment, such as Ireland, he might have become a dangerous radical. Ireland was indeed a hotbed of instability, which Branson sometimes mentions in reference to the Easter Rebellion of 1916. Instead, he comes to respect many of the Crawley family as individuals, while maintaining his opposition to traditional class structures.

Had the war not occurred, and had Branson remained at Downton Abbey, it is likely that he would have remained largely unchanged. His romance with Sybil might not have occurred, but his ideology would have remained. He may actually have become more radical. Without the war the Bolshevik revolution might not have happened, depriving him of the opportunity to be disturbed by the assassination of Nicholas II and his family. He did say that perhaps great sacrifices are necessary for world progress, as many socialists of that time truly believed, but he gives little appearance of approval. The horror of the war's upheavals, and the tempering of his perspectives on the nobility as he began to see them as individuals rather than symbols drew forth his inherent humanity.

The most serious shift in social values can be seen in the relationship between Branson and Sybil. Actually, it does seem unlikely, and it may well have been included for dramatic purposes rather than historic authenticity. It seems more likely that Sybil, dissatisfied with her aristocratic life, would have remained unmarried rather than risk so drastic a leap over social boundaries. In comparison, Lady Edith's dalliance with the farmer for whom she drove a tractor is much more plausible. Wartime needs brought them together, they shared an attraction, but soon both returned to their former stations. Even so, such events do demonstrate that severe breaches of the social order are more likely amidst massive upheavals.

"There were masters and servants and servants and dogs . . ."—such a quote might describe Downton Abbey prior to 1914, but this line was actually written by Englishman Joe Strummer, leader of the British rock band The Clash, in the classic 1980 song "Something about England." This song, aside from being one of The Clash's best, provides a striking counterpoint to the world of Lord Grantham, John Bates, and the dog Isis. The song tells the story, via an old man's reminiscence, about England through much of the twentieth century beginning with the First World War and ending with the punk-gang riots of the late 1970s. "They say it would be wine and roses if England were for Englishmen again" is one early line. Such might have been the sentiments of Lord Crawley had he managed to survive to the late twentieth century. But, Joe Strummer's old man tells a different tale. While acknowledging the changes the twentieth century brought, he concludes that, for his class, things were never really very good. An era which brings great changes to one man may reveal very few to another.

Change, continuity, and constancy are challenging concepts for the philosopher of history, and ones that will forever have conflicting interpretations. "It was a transitional time" is a common joke amongst historians, in that all periods can be described as "transitional" and denoting one as such is a just lazy way of appearing profound without really saying much. Continuity has its appeal, but it must not become so prominent that the real changes are ignored. In *Downton Abbey* change and continuity are most apparent during and after the Great War, with change ultimately coming out on top.

Love and Belief

VI

21
God-Talk at the Abbey

SAMUEL KLUMPENHOUWER

If there's one thing you can rely on the Downton crowd for, it's good conversation. Whether they're eating at the dinner table, sitting around the reading room, or out having a stroll, they're always having a good chat. But there are some things they don't talk about much. One of those things is religion. Oh, there's the odd bedside prayer (2:1) and mention of having attended church (2: Christmas Special), but usually everyone keeps their religious beliefs to themselves.

In the third season this momentarily changed when the fiery Tom Branson announced to the rest of the house that his baby would be baptized as a Catholic. His announcement sparked controversy because almost everyone else in the house was an Anglican. For a short time, everyone started talking about religion. Lord Grantham in particular wasn't too happy with Tom.

But whereas the folks at Downton are never at a loss for words when it comes to things like how to manage the estate, their religious conversations don't get very far. During one of the servants' dinners we hear them talking about the Catholic Church and religion in general (3:6). Anna wasn't too keen on the topic, saying, "I don't like discussing religion. We'll only fall out. And surely it's our private business." Mrs. Hughes gave a hearty "Amen" to Anna's sentiment.

The boys tried to keep the conversation going. Thomas slyly asked Alfred, "what about transubstantiation?" Thomas was just trying to show how smart he was. And Alfred, like most of us, didn't understand what he was talking about. He could only reply with a baffled "What?" Then the butler cut in and basically ended the conversation, saying "Never mind, Alfred, your heart's in the right place."

Why is it so hard for the people at Downton to have a good religious conversation? We could point to a few issues. Maybe it's because they are lacking in knowledge—that they don't know what things like "transubstantiation" are. Some people like Anna and Mrs. Hughes think that religion is too controversial or impolite, and believe it should be kept to oneself. Mary has doubts about whether God exists. Others might simply have nothing to say since God does not have an important part in their life.

Let's start with Mary's question of whether God exists (2:1). But even if she believed He existed, there would still be more problems. She would still be left wondering what God is like and whether He cares about the daily lives of people. Still more, how can people even talk about God? What does Matthew Crawley, for example, mean when he calls God "Father" at Lavinia's grave (2: Christmas Special)? Is God able to be described using human language? These are just some of the many problems of talking about God.

But before we get too bogged down, let's bring in some help to clear up a few issues.

The Other Thomas

Saint Thomas Aquinas (1225–1274) lived back in the Middle Ages, in a time of great change. People were busy building Gothic cathedrals and founding universities across Europe. Aquinas himself taught at the University of Paris, one of the oldest and greatest schools on the European continent. He was especially concerned with how people could know and talk about God (and, like Barrow in *Downton Abbey*, was also interested in transubstantiation).

Aquinas held that there are two ways to know God— through reason and through revelation. According to Aquinas, people can know a few things about God simply through using their reason alone. One of these knowable things is that God exists. But how can someone know God exists through using only their reason? To answer that question, Aquinas provided five different rational proofs to demonstrate that God exists. One of these proofs is called the argument from design.

Aquinas's argument from design is often mistakenly said to be the same as William Paley's argument for God's existence. Paley presented God as some kind of divine watchmaker. You might have heard of his argument. It begins by having you imagine that you were walking along the beach and you came across one of those old mechanical pocket watches. In the same way that you would suppose the watch had been designed and created by someone, so too does the complexity of things like the eye or the universe as a whole (or *Downton Abbey* for that matter) suggest a designer and creator.

Paley's argument is popular, in part because it's relatively easy to understand. It presupposes a certain mechanical view of the universe that almost everyone holds these days, regardless of whether they believe in God or not. Whatever the merits or faults of this argument, it's a bit different from Aquinas's argument, which does not arise from a mechanical view of universe, is not really interested in the complexity of things like watches or the universe as a whole, and presupposes a world view that most of us don't hold.

Candles and Causes

Aquinas's argument from design begins with a simple observation of nature, namely that some things regularly or always cause other things. The flame of a candle, for example, always causes light and heat to be produced. (Think back to before electricity came to Downton.) But why does the candle flame always produce light and heat? Why doesn't the burning of the candle sometimes produce cold or darkness or thunder? Why does that effect (light and heat) always follow that cause (the burning of the candle flame)? One might be tempted to answer like a modern scientist and start talking about the chemical processes going on in the burning of the flame. But that doesn't really answer what Aquinas is asking. It only changes the terms of the question. The fundamental question about why some things regularly or always cause other things remains unanswered.

Some philosophers have answered this question by stating that there is no essential relationship between cause and effect. The burning of the candle doesn't actually cause light and heat to be produced. To put it simply, we just think it does.

Cause and effect are something that people think they perceive, not something essential to the universe. But Aquinas saw an essential relation between cause and effect. The production of light and heat was an essential part of the flame. The flame had a purpose, a goal which it was always heading towards—namely, to produce light and heat. Aquinas then wondered how something like a flame, which lacks intelligence, could have this end that it was continuously heading towards. There must exist some intelligence that was directing the flame to that end, like an archer directing an arrow to the target. That intelligence he called "God."

Mary's Doubts

When Matthew Crawley was away during the war in season 2, Mary was deeply worried about him. In the first episode she knelt at her bedside and prayed: "Dear Lord, I don't pretend to have much credit with you. I'm not even sure that you're there. But if you are, and if I've ever done anything good, I beg you to keep him safe."

But why is Mary unsure whether God exists? She seems like a reasonable person, one of the smartest people in the house. If anyone could understand Aquinas's argument from design, for example, it would be her.

Now, it's true that even the most intelligent people do not always think reasonably. People are complex beings. We not only have the faculty of reason, but also a multitude of other desires and passions which can get in the way of using our reason. We often impulsively do things that we later regret when we think about them rationally—like watching four seasons of *Downton Abbey* in a week (but maybe that's a bad example).

That said, desires and passions are not necessarily bad. They do not necessarily get in the way of using our reason. They can have their own proper place in our lives. And in Mary's case, we don't know enough about her to say why she's unsure whether God exists. Perhaps she has never thought about the arguments for God's existence. Perhaps she has, but doesn't find them convincing.

What is surprising about Mary's prayer though, is that she desires God to exist. Why else would she be praying to Him? Not only that, she desires God to be personal, to be involved in the lives of people, to keep Matthew safe during the war. Even if Mary were to accept Aquinas's argument from design and became convinced that God exists, she would still be unsatisfied. She's not just looking for an explanation of God's existence. She seems to want to know or at least get help from a personal God.

The Reasonable Saint

Let's return again to Aquinas and see if he can help Mary out. Aquinas lived almost seven centuries ago, but we still know a fair bit about his life. He was not just a philosopher who wondered about God's existence. He was also a Christian, believing, among other things, that God is a deeply personal God. But how could he know that God is personal?

As we saw above, Aquinas taught that people can come to a knowledge of God's existence through reason alone. But people can also come to know more about God through revelation. As Aquinas believed, God had revealed Himself to people, most particularly in the person of Jesus Christ. All those teachings that Christians have about the divine nature of Jesus were not figured out simply by people using their reason. They were revealed to the Church by God.

According to Aquinas, the knowledge of God that is attained through revelation must be grasped by faith. Mary could know that God exists through reason alone, but it's through faith that she could better understand God as personal. But as Aquinas would be quick to point out, faith in a personal God is not an unreasonable thing. It does not contradict what we know by reason. For Aquinas, all knowledge comes from God, both those things known through reason, and those known through faith. If a contradiction arises between the two, then there is a problem with how we are using our reason or our faith in that instance.

The Limits of Language

All that's been said so far might help Mary and the rest of the Downton crowd with how they could know God. But are there not still more problems regarding how they could talk about God? I mean, it's all well enough to say that God exists and is personal. But what do we mean by that? Is He "personal" in the same way that Sybil or Anna Bates is personal? How can people use human language to describe God?

Let's take another example of religious talk. Let's take the statement "God is good." We see this written over the workhouse where Mrs. Hughes found Charles Grigg—Carson's former co-performer (4:1). The statement is troubling. Whoever painted the sign doesn't seem to have given much thought to the wretched working conditions that Mrs. Hughes found Grigg in. But even more than that, what does it mean to say that God is good? Is God "good" in the same way that people are good?

Like What?

Now, Aquinas taught that we can't ever talk about God directly. But there are still two ways to talk about Him indirectly. The first is to use analogies. Think about when Matthew Crawley was praying at Lavinia's grave (2: Christmas Special). He begins by saying, "Our father, who art in heaven . . ."

Here Matthew is using an analogy. He calls God "Father," but as Aquinas would point out, what Matthew really means is that God is *like* a father. Or to put it more exactly, God is *like our conception* of a father.

When we call God "Father" and our biological parent "father" we are using the same word in similar but different ways. Both God and an earthly father play a role in giving a child life. Both care for the child and teach it what it needs to know. But in other ways, God is not like an earthly father. God does not have a physical body. He will not someday die.

When we say "God is good" we are also talking analogically. We each have our own conceptions of what "good" means, but none of those exactly describes God. So when we say something like "Anna Bates is good" and then go on to say "God is good," what we really mean is "God is *like our conception* of good." He is not good in exactly the same way that Anna Bates is good. So when we saw that statement about God's goodness written on Charles Grigg's workhouse, it is right that we were troubled or confused. For we lack understanding. We do not fully understand the goodness of God, or how it could exist alongside the suffering of Grigg.

Will Aquinas Ever Stop Talking?

This brings us to the other way that Aquinas said we could talk about God: the way of negation. Through analogy, we can talk about what God is *like*. Through the way of negation, we can talk about what God is *not*—God is not a horse carriage; God is not the sun; God is not Lord Grantham. Even on a more fundamental level, you could say something like "God is *not* good," if you meant that God is not good in exactly the same way that you understand goodness. Talking in this way can help people to grasp what we can call the "divine otherness" of God.

The way of negation is an important one to some Christians. Some Christians have even said that it's the only way—that we can't know anything about what God is like. We can only say what He is not. Aquinas would disagree, and argued that we can indeed speak about God through analogy. But the way of negation remains important, and reminds us that God is mysterious and hidden as well. He is not exactly who we think He is. The butler Carson has a strong sense of how mysterious God is. When talking with the other servants about why Sybil died, he says, "It is not our place to reason why" (2: Christmas Special). He doesn't understand her death, nor does he think he should try to.

Aquinas wouldn't quite agree with him. While Carson may not be able to understand why God allowed Sybil to die, that does not mean that he shouldn't try to understand. Realizing the mystery and otherness of God should never be an excuse not to use our reason. Rather, it should help us recognize that our reason has limits.

Aquinas himself was deeply sensitive to the limits of reason and his ability to use language to talk about God. Near the end of his life, he experienced something while celebrating Mass. It is said that he heard the voice of Jesus asking him what he desired. Aquinas replied to Jesus, "Thyself." Up to that point Aquinas had been writing a monumental work called the *Summa Theologiae*, which remains one of the most influential books in Western history. But he never finished it. After this experience, his secretary urged him to do so, but Aquinas replied saying, "I cannot, for all that I have written seems to me like straw." Aquinas never wrote another word.

We should note that Aquinas did not say that what he had previously written about God was wrong. But in the face of whatever had been revealed to him, it was not enough.

Silence in the Abbey

Like Aquinas's final silence, the lack of religious conversation in *Downton Abbey* doesn't necessarily mean that the characters aren't religious. Mary is unsure about God, and maybe a couple others are secretly atheists. But still, it's a safe bet that most everyone else believes in a personal God at some level.

It's true that we saw war, the Spanish flu, and other tragedies befall the Abbey with hardly anyone turning to God. Violet Crawley's question to the archbishop of York (3:4) seems especially pertinent: "Do you find that the war has driven people back into the churches or further away than ever?" The archbishop's answer to that question seems strange at first; he says, "Behold, I stand at the door and knock." This is said partly as a pun since Tom Branson was standing at the door at the time, but it is also theologically insightful: God is always actively calling people, but people need to do something as well—they need to "open the door;" they need to search and think. And both war and peace can present such opportunities.

Yet it remains true that the things that are most personal to us are often those that we keep most silent about. Sometimes the more deeply we know something, the more keenly we realize, like Aquinas, how language fails us when we try to talk about it. The odd comment now and then, like what Carson said about Sybil, suggests a quiet faith at the Abbey.

Three Abbey Attitudes

I think we can point to three main attitudes to religion at the Abbey. The first is held by people like Carson, Lord Grantham, and Tom Branson, who know confidently what they believe in, and identify themselves with a specific religion—whether Anglicanism or Catholicism. The second is held by people like Mary, who are searching and unsure of what they believe. And the third is by people like Anna Bates and Mrs. Hughes, who may or may not know what they believe, but think everyone should keep their religious beliefs to themselves. Their approach to religion is similar to people in our own world, who think of themselves as spiritual, but not religious. These people might consider themselves to have a relationship with a personal God, but don't see any need for all that formal and organized religious stuff that Lord Grantham and Tom Branson hold dear.

But are religion and relationship so easily separated? If God exists, and is a personal God, it's probably true that his relationship with people is in some ways analogous to our own relationships with other people. And even in the deepest relationships people have with each other, even in those between a husband and wife, we see that they have a certain language and structure—set date nights every week, a common liturgy of please and thank you.

In a similar way, religion can provide a language and structure for one's relationship with God. Matthew Crawley gives an example of this when he says the "Our Father" prayer at Lavinia's grave—a prayer that he himself did not make up, but that Jesus taught his disciples to say. The prayer is often now seen as formal and religious, but if anything, that adds to its meaning for Matthew.

But religions like Christianity do more than provide a language and structure for a person's relationship with God. More importantly, they also make claims about truth. In particular, they make claims about how God has specifically revealed Himself to people.

22
Lady Edith and the Trials of the Modern Woman

GORDON HAWKES

When Lady Edith decides to get an abortion, she's in a desperate situation (4:7). She's pregnant, unmarried, and her lover, Michael Gregson, has gone missing in Germany. To carry and give birth to the child would mean scandal and shame for both her and her family. She would be a social outcast. But to go through with the dangerous and illegal abortion would, in her words, mean, "killing the wanted child" of the man she loves. "I just can't see over the top of this," she says, while waiting in the clinic for the procedure. After hearing a patient crying in the other room, she abruptly changes her mind and leaves.

Immediately following the airing of the episode, the Internet debate factory went into production. Many viewers claimed *Downton Abbey* was making a pro-life statement, since Edith ultimately chooses not to have an abortion. Others, including writers for *Time* and *New York Magazine*, countered with articles claiming the episode was, in fact, pro-choice, since she courageously chooses what she thinks is best, independent of what anyone else thinks.

Few topics arouse more passion in the public square than abortion, but Julian Fellowes, the writer and creator of *Downton Abbey*, managed to present the topic in a subtle, nuanced way that avoided any overt moral judgments. Fellowes, with proper English reserve, did not reveal his hand. His focus, no doubt, was on creating good drama, not advancing a moral argument.

But behind the drama, the question remains: Would it be morally permissible for Lady Edith to get an abortion? Would an abortion be morally justified in her circumstances? Proper etiquette might frown on such a question in the drawing room, but since we find ourselves safely at leisure, let's look at some of the arguments philosophers have made both for and against abortion.

Intentionally Killing a Main Character

The natural place to begin is with the classic argument against abortion. Chances are, if you've ever read or heard a case against abortion, you've come across some version of this argument:

1. It is generally wrong to intentionally kill an innocent human being.
2. The unborn entity (the entity in Edith's womb) is an innocent human being.
3. Therefore, it is generally wrong to intentionally kill the unborn entity.

This is what logicians call a *valid* argument. The form of the argument is such that the conclusion necessarily follows from the premises. Just as importantly, though, if both premises are *true*—that is, if they "correspond with reality"—then the conclusion must also be true, meaning it would be generally wrong for Lady Edith to have an abortion. If either premise is false, however, then the argument is as effective as Mr. Molesley on the cricket pitch.

The first premise seems uncontroversial at first glance. If intentionally killing innocent human beings isn't generally wrong, then what is? Normally we call that murder. We consider killing even wretched villains like Vera Bates and Mr. Green a crime of the most serious order. Even so, an obvious question arises: do abortion opponents oppose *all* killing of the innocent? The answer is most often no.

For example, if someone happens to kill another without the intention to do so, then it isn't necessarily an immoral action. For instance, in the heart-breaking last minute of season 3, the truck driver who drove into Matthew's AC Roadster killed an innocent human being, but arguably did nothing immoral.

Along these same lines, abortion opponents almost universally allow for abortion to save the life of the mother. Lady

Sybil's death in episode 5 of season 3 is a tragic example. Lady Sybil, suffering with pre-eclampsia, might have survived childbirth along with her baby had she been given, following Dr. Clarkson's advice, a Caesarean section. But, as Sir Philip stubbornly argued, "A Caesarean is a gamble which might kill either or both of them" (3:5). Nevertheless, even if the operation were to kill the baby, abortion opponents agree the Caesarean would be justified because the primary intention would be to save the life of Sybil and, if possible, her baby, not to kill the baby directly. In contrast, the primary intention behind most abortions is, as Edith states in her own case, "to get rid of it" (4:7).

Her Ladyship's Soap

But, when Edith tells Aunt Rosamund, "I've decided to get rid of it," what is the "it" that she's getting rid of? If the "it" is not a human being, then there's most likely nothing wrong with killing it, and Edith wouldn't need any special justification to have an abortion. How, then, do abortion opponents defend the second premise of the classic argument, the claim that the "it" in her womb is, in fact, a full-fledged human being?

Some might try to defend the claim that it's a human being by pointing to the way people talk. In episode 7 of season 1, Cora has a miscarriage about four months into her pregnancy, caused by a bar of soap and Miss O'Brien's misplaced revenge. Mrs. Hughes sighs, "That poor wee babe." Lord Grantham, in his grief, tells Mr. Bates, "It was a boy." Thomas, who is at first unsympathetic, calls it an "unborn baby" (1:7). Even Edith, as we've already seen, calls the entity she plans to abort a "child." Since language is far from neutral and is often important not only in helping us think about things but also in revealing how we think about things, the language of *Downton Abbey* strongly suggests that the entity in Edith's womb is a human being, at least in the minds of the characters or in the mind of the show's creator. Nevertheless, these people could be wrong. But are they?

Those opposed to abortion in all but the most serious cases often appeal to science to make their case. Dr. Clarkson, given his medical and scientific training, would almost certainly have believed that human life begins at conception: among physicians and scientists of the time, the old belief that life begins at "quickening," the first discernible movement of the fetus, had been replaced by the mid-nineteenth-century view that human life begins at conception. In modern embryology, the claim that human life begins at conception is not seriously disputed. And although Lord Grantham would not approve of more medical details, some biological evidence can be given to support this claim.

After Edith's egg and Michael Gregson's sperm come together to form the zygote—a single cell—that newly formed cell has its own unique genetic code. Left alone, that cell, unlike a sperm or an egg on its own, will grow and mature provided it has adequate nutrition and a proper environment, through all the same stages the Dowager Countess has already passed through—doubtless, though, without the same panache. Unlike other individual cells in Edith's body, the entity that begins as a single-celled zygote, and which expands into a many-celled embryo, and so on, functions as a whole organism. All of its parts or cells work in tandem and are coordinated to its growth and survival, much like all the staff are coordinated to the proper functioning of Downton. The organism's biological development is continuous from conception through birth through infancy through childhood through young adulthood, finally culminating in full adult maturity. No sharp dividing line in that continuous, organic growth exists, except at conception. If we could rewind the tape of Marigold's biological development, there would be no distinct break until the very beginning. In other words, Edith's daughter, Marigold, did not come from an embryo. She once *was* an embryo.

Here someone might, in the face of the biological facts, insist that we can't know when life begins. If that were true, however, it would count as a reason against most cases of abortion. For example, suppose after the fire breaks out in the Abbey in the premiere of season 5, Lord Grantham is checking rooms, and Thomas tells him a particular room may or may not be occupied. If he were to reply, "Well, since we don't know for sure whether someone is in there, we can just let it burn," we would consider him highly irresponsible, if not grossly negligent, to allow for the possibility that someone might die. Likewise, if we don't know whether the unborn is a human being or not, our ignorance is generally a strong reason not to kill it, lest we risk killing an innocent human being.

Defenders of the classic argument against abortion believe if the unborn is a human being, then almost none of the common reasons used to justify abortion are adequate. For example, Edith tells Rosamund her reason for choosing an abortion: "I don't want to be an outcast. I don't want to be some funny woman living in Maida Vale people never talk about" (4:7). Her fears are not misplaced. If word got out that she had a child out of wedlock, she would not likely be welcome in any house of standing. But the need to escape social disgrace wouldn't justify killing Marigold as a three-year-old, so the same reason wouldn't justify an abortion, unless we assume the unborn is not a human being. Similarly, Ethel Parks becomes destitute because she cannot get work as an unwed mother (2:5). She eventually resorts to prostitution to support herself and her son (3:2). Undoubtedly, much hardship could have been avoided had Ethel had an abortion. But, again, she wouldn't be justified in killing the infant Charlie in order to escape poverty, so she wouldn't be justified in having an abortion for that reason either, unless we assume the unborn is not a human being.

The most emotionally difficult challenge to the classic argument is pregnancy in the case of rape. The horror of this crime, and the deep suffering of its victims, became disturbingly real for many *Downton Abbey* viewers during episode 3 of season 4, in which the valet Mr. Green rapes Anna Bates. Asked by Mrs. Hughes what she would do if she is with child, Anna answers, "I'll kill myself" (4:4). If Anna were impregnated by Mr. Green, she would indeed bear an onerous physical and psychological burden beyond the grievous harm of the attack itself. Having the offspring of a rapist inside her for nine months would be cause for suffering, to say the least. But would it be permissible for Anna to kill an innocent third party to ease her suffering? Mr. Green must be punished for his horrific crime. And, as a victim, Anna needs the reassurance, which Mrs. Hughes gives her, that she is not "dirty" or "soiled." Yet, if the unborn is a human being, an abortion would make it a victim, and one arguably greater than Anna.

They're No Bigger than a Hamster at That Stage

As it turns out, most philosophers who defend abortion in general concede that the unborn is, biologically, a human being. In other words, they concede that if Edith were to have an abortion, she would be killing a member of the species *Homo sapiens*. This may surprise some readers, since this concedes the second premise of the classic argument. "How, then, can these philosophers say abortion is morally permissible?" one might ask.

These philosophers make a distinction between being a *human being* and being a *person*, and add that it's only wrong to kill persons, not human beings. Thus, they deny the first premise: it is generally not wrong to intentionally kill *human beings*, but it is generally wrong to intentionally kill *persons*. Since the unborn are not persons, based on their various definitions of that term, abortion is generally not wrong.

Mary Anne Warren, a notable pro-choice advocate, believes we use the term "human being" in two different senses. First, we use the term in a *genetic* sense. This sense includes every genetically human organism, from single-celled zygotes to mature adults—even Sir Richard Carlisle. Second, we use the term in a *moral* sense. This sense includes those humans who are part of what Warren calls "the moral community," the group of humans to whom we ascribe rights and protections, such as you, me, and Mrs. Patmore. Only those who are human in the moral sense are *persons*. Therefore, only persons have moral rights and moral value.

Very significantly, Warren does not believe that all genetic human beings are persons. She does not believe that all genetic human beings have moral rights and moral value. How does she determine, then, who counts as a person and who does not? Suppose, she says, someone were to travel to an alien place and encounter life forms he thought strange—say, if Lord Grantham were to travel to Ireland—by what characteristics could he determine whether the life forms were persons or not (assuming his prejudice did not blind him)? Warren suggests that a person will display at least some, if not all, of the following traits: consciousness, reasoning, the capacity to communicate, self-motivated activity, and self-awareness.

Since the human fetus possesses *none* of these characteristics (or only in very rudimentary forms in its later stages of development), it is not a person, and therefore not something with rights. This is the sentiment behind Thomas's remark about Cora's miscarriage: "She'll get over it. They're no bigger than a hamster at that stage" (1:7). Although the remark was clearly in bad taste, given the time and place, his meaning is clear: the fetus does not share the characteristics of a full *person*. It is not valuable in the same way as an adult.

Defenders of the classic argument against abortion say it is generally wrong to intentionally kill any innocent human beings. It is simply being human that grounds our rights. Warren, however, says it is only wrong to kill *persons*. It is her list of traits that grounds our rights. The dividing line, then, between those humans who have rights and those humans who don't is the list of characteristics that Warren provides. If Mrs. Patmore spoiled the fish sauce, it would be wrong for the Countess to execute her and hire a new cook because, based on Warren's list, Mrs. Patmore is a person. She has rights. Mrs. Patmore's capacity to communicate alone is enough to mark her as an exemplary member of the moral community.

On the other hand, if Lady Edith decides that she "doesn't want to be an outcast" (4:7), it would not be wrong for her to have her fetus killed because it doesn't possess the characteristics of a person. It's not conscious; it can't reason; it most certainly can't hurl witty zingers at the drop of a hat. Therefore, it has no rights. Lady Edith's right to control her own body, to protect her health, or to pursue her own interests, trumps any considerations that might be raised on behalf of the fetus.

Dogs, Chauffeurs, and Irishmen

Mary Anne Warren and others believe the classic argument includes too many human beings in the class of things with rights. In the same way, some philosophers criticize Warren for including too few.

Warren believes even fully developed fetuses do not satisfy the conditions of personhood enough to merit rights. As she explains, fully developed human fetuses are considerably less person-like than the average mature mammal, such as Lord Grantham's dog, Isis, or Lady Mary's pigs, and therefore have no significant right to life. If Lady Mary decided to get an abortion late in her pregnancy, say, in order to prolong her vacation at Duneagle (3: Christmas Special), it would not be immoral for her to do so. Furthermore, following the birth, Lady Mary's newborn baby, George, does not display consciousness, reasoning, the capacity to communicate, self-motivated action, or self-awareness to any higher degree than when he was in Mary's womb. He is hardly more a person the moment after birth than the moment before. It would therefore also be permissible for Mary to kill newborn George. While philosophers like Michael Tooley and Peter Singer, whose views are similar to Warren's, argue explicitly that baby George is not a person until some time after birth, and, therefore, that infanticide is morally acceptable, many people find this an unacceptable consequence of the view.

Philosophers like Tooley, Singer, and Warren agree that not all human beings are persons, but they don't agree on the conditions for being a person. Nevertheless, they share one thing in common: they define what it is to be a person based on *function*. For example, Tom Branson is both a chauffeur and Irish. We define a chauffeur in terms of what the chauffeur *does*, in terms of his function (he drives). In contrast, we define being Irish in terms of what someone *is*. It doesn't matter what he can or can't do—an Irishman is an Irishman. Edith's daughter, Marigold, is a human being from the moment of conception, but she does not become a full-fledged person, and does not gain rights, according to these philosophers, until she attains certain abilities, like being able to feel pain or being able to reason. Her moral rights and moral value are grounded in what she can functionally *do*, not in what she *is*.

There are two unappealing consequences of defining a person based on function. First, since something can be more or less conscious, or more or less rational—something can be more or less of a person. Being a person comes as a matter of degrees. Thus, there is no genuine equality of value or rights among human beings. Sybbie, the girl in season 5 who "can answer back" and call her grandfather "Donk" (5:1), is more of a person, and therefore more valuable, than little Sybbie the infant in season 3. An insane and irrational human being, like Mr. Gregson's wife, is less of a person, and therefore less valuable, than a sane and rational woman like Lady Edith. This runs counter to a deep conviction many have that human equality is not based on function or ability, as if Matthew were less valuable when paralyzed than he was before and after.

A second apparent consequence of defining a person by functional abilities is that a human being who is sleeping, unconscious, or in a temporary coma is not a person with rights.

When Captain Crawley is knocked unconscious by a shell on the battlefield (2:5), he cannot exercise any of the abilities that supposedly make him a person, whether reasoning or self-awareness or the ability to communicate. Yet we don't think he suddenly lacks rights or value as a human being, nor would we accept that he could be rightly killed by his mother, Isobel.

This indicates, in contrast with Warren's claims, that we don't locate Matthew's value in his present abilities, we locate it in the type of being that he is. But Edith's fetus and Matthew are the same sort of being. They're both human beings. Because both the comatose Matthew and Edith's fetus are human beings, they both have the *capacity* for reasoning, self-awareness, communication, and the rest—they simply lack the *present* ability to exercise those capacities. In order to illustrate, consider Alfred's culinary expertise. Alfred lacks the present ability to cook while he is asleep, but he nevertheless has the *capacity* to cook the whole time he is sleeping. When he wakes up, he can exercise that ability. Because Edith's fetus is the type of being with capacities for reasoning and self-awareness, given enough time to develop she will gain the present ability to exercise those capacities, as we see in season 5. Edith's daughter, Marigold, only has the traits which Warren says belong to a person because Marigold was first the type of thing—namely, a human being—that could develop those traits.

If it is true that abilities have no bearing on human beings' moral value, then some other difference between the unborn and us is needed to justify their complete lack of rights. But the only differences between even the smallest unborn entity and us are size, level of development, environment, and dependency. None of these differences is morally relevant. Size has no bearing on our value. Mr. Carson is much larger than Master George, but the butler does not have a greater value than the heir to Downton. Level of development has no bearing on our value. Lady Mary is more developed than little Sybbie, but not thereby worth more. Environment has no bearing on our value. Branson's value doesn't change with a move from the driver's seat to a seat at the dining room table. And dependency has no bearing on our value. Matthew, as an "impotent cripple" (2:5), is as dependent on the nurses as any infant on its mother, but he remains his oh-so-valuable self.

So, are Marigold's moral rights and moral value grounded in the type of being she is, or do they come from some functions or abilities she gains at a certain stage of development? If they come from functions or abilities, then some human beings, that is, unborn humans, do not have rights or value. If they are grounded in what she is, then every human being is a person, with rights and value equal to every other human being, no matter what stage of development.

The Odd Case of the Australian Opera Singer

Could abortion be justified if we agreed, for the sake of argument, that every unborn human being has all the rights and protections of you, me, and Mrs. Patmore? In "A Defense of Abortion," probably the most famous article ever written on abortion, Judith Jarvis Thomson argues that even if the fetus has full rights and protections, women like Edith *still* have a right to have an abortion.

Thomson's argument takes the form of an analogy, which has been adapted here. Imagine Lady Edith wakes up the morning after Dame Nellie Melba's performance at Downton Abbey (4:3) to find herself sitting back to back with the world famous singer. It turns out that, in the middle of the night, Dame Nellie fell unconscious, doctors were called for, and it was discovered that she had a life-threatening kidney ailment. They did some quick investigation and discovered that Edith was the only person whose blood type matched Dame Nellie's. So, without Edith's assent, they hooked up her circulatory system to the opera singer's. (There's a reason why philosophers don't write drama for Masterpiece.) Now, the doctor tells Edith, "You must stay hooked up to Dame Nellie for the next nine months. If you unplug her from yourself at any time, she will die."

The force of the analogy is clear. Dame Nellie is using Lady Edith's body without her consent. Even though the opera singer has a right to life, she doesn't have a right to use Edith's body for her survival. And while millions of fans across the British Empire might be eternally grateful, Edith has no obligation to provide her body to the singer and may unplug herself if she chooses, even if it would mean sure death for Dame

Nellie. In the same way, Edith's right to control her body means that, even though her fetus has a right to life, she can "unplug" herself from it if she so desires.

Thomson's argument is an argument by analogy, and the analogy only does the trick if the two things compared are similar in relevant ways. In Thomson's argument, there are at least two problems with the analogy. First, an abortion would not be equivalent to Edith "unplugging" herself from Dame Melba. Abortion does not "unplug" the fetus from the mother. Rather, the purpose of abortion is to kill the fetus. No medical detail is needed; we need only consider this illustration. If Edith detached herself from Dame Melba and the singer miraculously survived, Edith would have no reason to be upset. After all, she was merely concerned with her *own* body. But if Edith were to go to London for an abortion and the fetus miraculously survived after being "unplugged," the abortion would be a failure. The fetus's survival would defeat the whole purpose of having the abortion in the first place. Edith would be left with the problem the abortion was meant to solve.

A further difference is that most people think parents owe a special obligation to their own children that they don't owe to strangers (the Law of Special Beneficence). Part of what makes the character Major Bryant such a bloody scoundrel is that he leaves Ethel in the lurch, not only after causing her to lose her job, but after fathering her child (2:5). He refuses to acknowledge paternity of Charlie, and offers no aid whatsoever. He obviously didn't consent to the child, but, as the audience, we feel deeply for Ethel's suffering because we think Major Bryant has an obligation to support his own son, wanted or not. But, if Major Bryant has an obligation to a child that he had no intention of siring, surely Lady Edith has, at the very least, some obligation to protect the child in her womb, even though she didn't intend to get pregnant. The unborn child is, after all, not only a full-fledged person with rights equal to you or me, in keeping with Thomson's assumption, but also her own flesh and blood. Suppose Lady Edith woke up to find herself attached, not to an Australian opera singer, but to her own daughter, Marigold. In that case, there does seem to be an obligation for Edith not to unplug and kill her daughter, that is, if one believes the Law of Special Beneficence should take priority.

The Unwanted Epilogue

After Mary's "week of sin" with Lord Gillingham (5:2), her grandmother asks if there will be any "unwanted epilogue" to the affair (5:3). For Edith, there was an epilogue—unwanted at first, but one that continues to be written.

23
Justice in Love

ADAM BARKMAN AND NOAH VAN BRENK

Upon first viewing, *Downton Abbey* appears simply to be a show depicting the evolution of an upper-class family in England during the early twentieth century. It draws the viewer in with its depiction of rigid class structure, period costumes, and pomp and circumstance, all of which are more or less extinct—and therefore exotic—in today's society. The attention to minute details and portrayal of everyday occurrences as events worthy of formality may cause one to feel as if there is no commonality between their world and ours.

However, taking a second look reveals key similarities. Beneath the social order and the rules that govern it are humans who desire to love and be loved. And as with all times, the types of loves expressed and sought vary. According to C. S. Lewis (1898–1963), there are, in fact, four different types of loves, all of which are feelings of attraction and all of which require justice in order to be healthy and properly functioning. Our interest in this chapter is not to examine exhaustively every type of love, but one love in particular: *agape,* or sacrificial love. It is our contention that *Downton Abbey* reveals many insights about this type of love.

More than a Feeling, but Not Less

All species of love have as their genus a feeling of attraction. *Storge* love is a very broad, humble feeling of attraction; in English we call it "affection" and it is the type of love Bates might have for his cane, Lord Grantham for Isis (his dog), and

Edith for the chair she usually sits on at dinner. *Eros* is the feeling of attraction in which the lover desires a kind of unity with the beloved; here we mostly think of the love between husbands and wives like Bates and Anna, but it can also be expressed spiritually (Plato sought unity with perfect Beauty, for example). *Philia* is the feeling of attraction toward a common mind or interest; it is best understood as "friendship," such as the friendship between Bates and Lord Grantham, and is one of the loves unique to rational beings (since only they can share their thoughts and common interests). Finally, *agape* love is the desire for the best interest of another; it is the least concerned about what it can get from the beloved, even though it certainly finds happiness in benefiting the beloved.

What all these loves have in common—here, especially *agape* love—is that they require justice in order to be properly expressed feelings of attraction. Plato long ago defined justice in the *Republic* as "each performing its role," which is to say treating superior things as superior things, equal things as equal things, and subordinate things as subordinate things. Only when we first pay attention to justice can any act of love—especially acts of *agape* love—be considered genuine acts of love.

Now, when we use the terms *superior, equal*, and *subordinate* in relation to human beings, we don't mean that certain humans are inferior or "less than human" compared to others. We're instead referring to areas of differences *within humans*. The characters of *Downton Abbey* have a keen grasp of this concept; indeed, their entire societal structure is organized around this principle. For example, the servants address the members of the House of Grantham as "My Lord" and "My Lady," and many servants such as Mrs. Patmore and Daisy rarely, if ever, "go upstairs" to the main house. This isn't because the servants are inferior *as human beings* to the Granthams; they are all essentially human, having the same ultimate capacities for free will, rationality, emotion, and so on. They each have the same rights and dignities we might say, and the trial of John Bates is evidence of this, for though Bates is a servant, he is as much entitled to a fair trial as his master.

And even within the Grantham family there exists a hierarchy that evolves as the show continues into later seasons. The Dowager Countess, fondly referred to by her family as

"Granny," oversees the family with a sharp eye and quick wit, while her son, Lord Grantham, is the official head of the house. He exercises control over the estate, and when any major decisions are made by members of his family (especially his daughters), those decisions must first be approved by him. As societal roles begin to shift, the lines between who is superior, equal, and subordinate to whom become blurred, it's true, but this is beside the point. What is important to understand is that the hierarchy of justice refers to a person getting what they deserve based on their varying attributes, roles, relationships, and so on, but not based on their bare human nature.

Now, this idea of justice is a fairly rigid and impersonal concept. "Justice" means that people get what they deserve and nothing more than what they deserve. Yet *agape* love acknowledges and satisfies justice, then perfects and transcends it. It loves each thing firstly as it ought to be loved according to justice, but then extends the love further in a positive direction. As a result, this kind of love is the only kind that is able to love that which is naturally unlovable. In other words, *agape* love is able to love what the other three loves cannot. No one feels affection towards a person who is cruel and mean towards them; no one becomes friends with a person who sneers at and makes fun of their interests and dreams. I may treat such a person with the respect and dignity they deserve as a human being, but I will find it extremely difficult, perhaps even impossible, to truly love that person. *Agape* love, however, sees that person in their unlovable state and still loves them.

To Love a Molesley

So, where do we see "justice in love" at Downton? One of the first instances occurs early in the fourth season. At this point in the show, Matthew Crawley is dead, tragically killed in a car accident at the end of season 3. As a result, his valet, Mr. Molesley, is out of a job, and shortly after is relegated to doing manual labor. Molesley's shame and embarrassment at having to work menial and dirty jobs is evident, and indeed he seems to be at his wit's end. Anna Bates sees him in this state, approaches him and offers to give him some money to help him get back on his feet. Molesley refuses, indicating that he "couldn't accept that" but that he was "most sincerely" thankful (4:2).

Anna confides in her husband, John Bates, and the two search for a way to help Molesely. Eventually Bates, with the financial help of the Dowager Countess, forges Molesely's signature on a note saying that Bates owed Molesley thirty pounds, an amount that would more than cover his debts. Molesley is left completely shocked yet wholeheartedly grateful.

So, is this an expression of *agape* love, or is Anna and Bates's action simply the result of their acting justly towards Molesley? According to the definition of justice laid out earlier, Anna and Bates were under no strong obligation to help Molesley. True, we might say that generally speaking, the strong should take care of the weak, and since in this case Anna and Bates are the strong and Molesley the weak (financially speaking), Anna and Bates have a weak obligation to help him. But still, Anna and Bates are not rich and they wouldn't be expected, on justice, to help Bates out to the extent they did. And since the help they gave Molesley didn't cause moral harm to others—since giving money to Molesley doesn't cause Anna and Bates to violate their financial obligations to other people—the act of giving Molesley the thirty pounds is genuinely an act of *agape* or sacrificial love.

Going a Bit Further

Another case of *agape* love occurs over the eighth and ninth episodes of the third season. Thomas Barrow, one of the principal antagonists of the show, has developed an interest in Jimmy, the handsome footman. Led by Mrs. O'Brien to believe that Jimmy reciprocates his feelings, Thomas enters Jimmy's room one night and attempts to kiss him. Jimmy wakes up horrified, and kicks Thomas out of his room. After the incident, as he's standing in the hallway, Thomas realizes that Alfred, the other footman, witnessed the whole affair.

The subsequent actions of Jimmy and Alfred in response to this incident reveal a mindset seeking justice alone. Influenced by Miss O'Brien, who desires to bring Thomas to ruin, Jimmy and Alfred attempt to have Thomas brought to justice in various, and perhaps misguided, ways. Alfred initially reports the incident to Mr. Carson, who confronts Thomas and warns him of the seriousness of his actions. Then Jimmy attempts to convince Mr. Carson to give Thomas a bad reference. Finally, Alfred again contacts someone about the incident, but this time it's the police. They interrupt the estate cricket match looking for Thomas, who seems destined for downfall but for the actions of two singular characters: Bates and Lord Grantham.

Bates, having seen Thomas in his pitiful state, is moved to help him. Bates does not want to condemn Thomas to life in prison, the horrors of which he knows firsthand. Thomas is taken aback by this offer of help, noting, "Prison's changed you; there was a time when nothing was too bad for me as far as you were concerned." Here it is clear that Thomas notices—perhaps for the first time—not only the quality of Bates's character, but, more importantly, what real *agape* love looks like, for Bates helps out his enemy; Bates loves the unlovable.

One of the ways that Bates helps Thomas is by convincing Jimmy to stop demanding Thomas get a bad reference letter. This certainly seems loving to me, but still one might wonder if Bates is acting *lovingly* (going beyond justice in a positive way) or *unjustly* (failing to keep justice and passing it off as "love"). After all, doesn't Thomas *deserve* to receive a negative reference for what he has done?

Carson, who all would agree is very much a "rules" man, deemed justice satisfied in strongly reprimanding Thomas for his actions and then fairly dismissing him. Carson's reasoning is that the crime—a minor indiscretion on Thomas's part—doesn't warrant a major punishment, such as never working again as a servant (if a bad reference were written) or going to jail (if the then-illegal homosexual activity were reported to the authorities). Justice means treating each thing as it ought to be treated, and, according to Carson, the just punishment for Thomas's crime is a strong warning and fair dismissal. Since Bates seems to agree with Carson's sense of justice here, Bates would have wanted to make sure that justice is satisfied—that Thomas accept some of the consequences of his indiscretion, including his fair dismissal; yet if Thomas can be given a chance at start again (such as by not going to jail and by finding servant work elsewhere), then this is potentially a good state of affairs for Thomas, and since this good state of affairs is not a matter of pure justice, then it must be a matter of *agape* love, indeed, mercy.

Lord Grantham, too, shows *agape* love toward Thomas when he prevents the police from arresting Thomas. The police had been called there by Alfred, who genuinely agrees with the laws of the land at the time that all homosexual activity is immoral and should be illegal. Lord Grantham, though he doesn't tell us specifically what he thinks a just punishment for Thomas should be, does think that *agape* love needs to temper justice here. In defense of his allegedly unjust action of sparing Thomas, Lord Grantham tells Alfred: "I'm not asking you to abandon your beliefs, Alfred, just to introduce a little kindness into the equation" (3:8).

What we should take away from this is the insistence of Carson, Bates, and Lord Grantham—all men that we generally admire in the show—that justice be tempered by love, and that there be justice in love. Of course, we should also note that good men can sometimes disagree about how this theory translates into practice. For example, while Carson and Bates might think that Thomas should be fairly dismissed (justice), yet mercifully spared a life of unemployment (love), Lord Grantham might think a strong reprimand is fair (justice), followed by a merciful reinstatement in the estate's service (love).

A Proper Sacrifice

Of all the instances of *agape* love being embodied throughout the show, perhaps the most poignant example comes not from a principal character, but one who is present in the show for less than a season. In the fifth episode of season 2, Matthew Crawley lies severely wounded in a room of the Abbey-turned-makeshift-hospital, suffering from a severe spinal cord injury he received while fighting on the Western Front. His fiancée, Lavinia Swire, visits him and insists that they will still marry in spite of his injury. Matthew, however, thinks that they should not marry. He reveals that his injury has not only made him lame, but impotent as well. He feels that it would be cruel to force Lavinia into a life where she can't have children and where she would have to take care of a crippled spouse. Lavinia protests, but Matthew is adamant: he urges her to "think of me as dead" and to never contact him again.

Distraught, Lavinia complies. However, in the next episode, she returns with renewed vigor. Now she is the adamant one, and she makes this clear to Matthew: "You won't frighten me away, whatever you do." This emphatic sacrifice is one of the purest examples of *agape* love in the entire show and, further, it reveals a little of the persistence of this love—of its refusal to have one's beloved reject its beneficial advances.

Now arguably, Matthew was acting and thinking purely in terms of justice. He understood correctly that Lavinia, as his fiancée, was his equal and therefore deserved certain aspects of a marriage that he could not provide. Sending her away was, if this is all there is to it, a just act. Lavinia understood this, and while she acknowledges that it "won't be easy," she also makes clear her desire to be his wife, regardless of their circumstances. She is ready to sacrifice a normal marriage in order to be with Matthew because she loves him for his own sake, dismissing whatever faults or disabilities he has and what he can or can't provide for her in return. Lavinia sees Matthew in his broken, hopeless, and unattractive state, and chooses to sacrifice for him.

While we have already commented on Matthew's "justice-only" attitude, there is potentially an additional dimension to this. Matthew's fierce opposition to Lavinia's desire to stay with him points to one tendency in human nature, which is to react angrily at being offered *agape* love. Now in some cases this anger might be out of reciprocal love for the other as one person doesn't want to see the other suffer by sacrifice. Sure; but there is also the tendency for many who receive *agape* love to resent its offer since secretly the recipient doesn't believe that this offer is *agape* at all but rather justice (something owed) or even injustice (an insult more than anything else). Now, Matthew's anger is likely out of justice (Lavinia isn't being treated fairly and she should be) or even reciprocal *agape* love (she is sacrificing for Matthew, and Matthew wants to sacrifice for her), yet still: more than a few chapters in the volume in your hand suggest that Matthew could have less honorable motives throughout, and so it's at least possible that his anger could be out of a sense of wanting to be treated justly (she *does* owe me marriage) or even a sense of being treated unjustly (she *insults* me by insisting on marrying me, for she owes me this and yet pretends as if this were more than that). As philosophers, we'll stick with the hypotheticals, the morals, and the arguments, however, and leave the psychoanalyzing to the psychotherapists.

Aping Agape Love

Up to this point, we've largely been looking at actions and decisions by characters of the show that embody true *agape* love. But it's also helpful to look at cases of false *agape* love. Here we're looking for cases that ape *agape* love, rather than are *agape* love.

As a character on the whole, Thomas Barrow has many of these moments, though one in particular stands out. It occurs in the first episode of season 4—the primary episode dealing with Matthew's death. A nanny has been hired to care for Baby Sybil and Baby George. Thomas and the nanny are both stubborn by nature, and they butt heads on a regular basis throughout the episode, each trying to exert authority over the other. Eventually, Thomas slyly intimates to Lady Grantham that the nanny is neglecting the children, feigning interest in their well-being. He does this neither out of a desire to see justice achieved, nor because he loves the children for their own sake. Instead, he does it in an attempt to get the nanny into trouble for no other reason than to triumph over her. Ironically, the nanny was indeed abusing one of the children and as a result of Thomas's false information, Lady Grantham catches the nanny spewing vulgarity at Baby Sybil and promptly fires her. Justice was achieved, but this was not Thomas's original intention.

A more shocking example of false *agape* love is demonstrated by the life of Vera Bates, John Bates's former wife. Throughout the show, she is a constant thorn in Bates's side, harassing him and threatening to steal his happiness by various means, one of which involves using her knowledge of Mary's affair with the son of a Turkish diplomat to blackmail Bates and prevent him from marrying Anna. She claims "love" for Bates, but all her actions are fuelled by a frantic desire to possess Bates—to treat him, in effect, as a thing, and therefore something below her. This is not the just desire to see husband and wife keep their marriage vows toward each other, and so, since it's not concerned with justice, her efforts for "love"—sacrificing herself through her various efforts to be reunited with Bates—can't be seen as acts of genuine *agape* either. Indeed, by the seventh episode of the second season, we discover that Vera actually committed suicide in a manner that makes it look as if Bates himself killed her—far from a just and loving act.

The Greatest of These Is . . .

The folks at Downton, as with us all, are concerned with the desire to love and be loved. These desires of love are expressed in many forms—affection, erotic love, friendship, and sacrificial love—and all need to be rooted in justice in order to be their true selves. But of all these, the greatest is sacrificial or *agape* love. *Agape* love is able to move the hearts of people to aid those to whom they owe nothing but naturally love (such as Lavinia for Matthew), those to whom they owe little and don't know well (such as Anna to Molesley) and those to whom they owe nothing, and, indeed, naturally hate (such as Bates for Thomas).

24
Climbing the Ladder of Love

BRENDAN SHEA

Like other great TV shows, *Downton Abbey* isn't just "about" one thing. Instead, its themes concern social class, friendship, politics, aging, the role of community, and the importance of place in our lives. There is, however, one central concern that unifies this broad variety of themes and which both motivates the characters' actions and gives us viewers a reason to care about them. I am talking, of course, about love, and especially romantic love. It is the relationships, more than anything else, that keep us interested. We want to know whether Mary will ever get together with Matthew, despite all of the missteps they both make. We root for Sybil and Tom to overcome their differences in class, nationality, and religion. When Sybil and Matthew die, we sympathize with Mary and Tom, and hope that they can find a way forward. We admire Bates and Anna for all that they are forced to overcome, and can even sympathize with Thomas for the special difficulties that love presents for him.

How might the lives and loves of Downton Abbey residents look to the characters of Plato's *Symposium*? In this famous dialogue, a group of prominent Athenians gets together for a celebration. The topic of conservation turns quickly to love, and each of the guests offers a speech giving his own view of love. The accounts they provide range from the comic to the tragic, and from the pragmatic to the deeply philosophical. While it might seem odd to consider what this distinguished group of ancient Greek philosophers, playwrights, and lawyers would think about a modern TV show, this is just the sort of thing that would have interested them. In fact, the occasion for their party is the conclusion of a theater festival, where the host of the party (Agathon) has just won a prize. For the characters of the *Symposium,* just as for modern fans of *Downton Abbey,* there is something peculiarly powerful and satisfying about love stories. Love is, after all, a hugely important part of our lives, and it's something that we deeply want to get *right.*

Thomas the Brave?

If one were to ask the residents of Downton Abbey their opinion on their most heroic acquaintance, it is unlikely that many would pick Thomas Barrow. This is understandable—he is usually self-centered and vain, and frequently schemes against both his fellow servants and the Crawleys. As regular viewers know, however, Thomas is capable of bravery in the right circumstances. In particular, when robbers attack Jimmy Kent in the season 3 Christmas Special, Thomas comes to Jimmy's aid and helps him escape. However, Thomas himself is beaten up for his efforts. Thomas does this, of course, because of his romantic love for Jimmy. Were Thomas not in love, these actions would be almost incomprehensible for him. Among other things, Thomas knows that Jimmy does not return his feelings. However, when Jimmy gets attacked, Thomas forgets all of this. Instead, he courageously sacrifices himself to save Jimmy.

According to Phaedrus, the first speaker of the *Symposium,* the most valuable aspect of love is precisely its ability to inspire ordinary people to heroic action. Thomas's actions provide a perfect example of Phaedrus's thesis. First, Phaedrus would appreciate that Thomas was in love with a younger man, and that this love was not returned. In upper-class Athenian culture, homosexual relationships between older and younger men were common, and these relationships are a major topic in the *Symposium.* In general, the younger man was not *expected* to reciprocate the older man's feelings. If the younger man agreed to a relationship (and he might not), he would do so merely because he wanted the older man's guidance and patronage. Second, Phaedrus would be impressed by the way that love helps Thomas overcome his tendency toward egoism, or selfishness. Phaedrus even goes so far as to suggest the creation of a military regiment made entirely of lovers, with the idea that this would inspire them to greater bravery.

Thomas's defense of Jimmy is not the only example of love-inspired bravery in *Downton Abbey*. Phaedrus might also point out the lengths to which Bates goes to protect Anna, the sacrifices that Sybil makes when she marries Tom, or numerous other cases. Love, on Phaedrus's account, can make heroes of us all, no matter how weak we might think ourselves.

Mary's Problems with Love and the Law

Many of Thomas's problems are the result of the time and place in which he lives. Where some of the *Symposium's* characters celebrate homosexual relationships, such relationships are forbidden in the early twentieth-century Britain of *Downton Abbey*. Among other things, Thomas risks prison, the loss of employment, and abandonment by his friends and coworkers. Thomas is not the only character whose love life is constrained by social and legal barriers, of course: in their own way, characters such as Mary, Matthew, Sybil, Edith, Rose, Bates, and others must overcome social and legal obstacles to achieve successful relationships.

Pausanias, the lawyer who gives the *Symposium's* second speech, could relate to these concerns. He argues that there is a significant difference between potentially harmful "common love" directed at physical beauty and praiseworthy "heavenly love" directed toward a person's character and intellect. He then suggests that the structure of society can play a big role in helping (or hindering) the ability of citizens to find the better sort of love. To support his point, he notes that some Greek cities had forbidden homosexual relationships altogether, which he thinks had the effect of diminishing citizens' desire and ability to participate politically. By contrast, other cities had almost no legal constraints on such relationships, which he argues led to short-lived, harmful relationships in which older men pursued (much) younger men merely on account of their looks. Finally, Pausanias thinks that Athens has achieved an ideal balance, where the culture and laws present just enough difficulty for potential lovers to ensure that the relationships that do survive are based on more than a passing physical attraction.

Mary's experiences provide an ideal illustration of Pausanias's main themes. Prior to the beginning of the show, Mary seemed to have been following the path of least resistance, and to have acquiesced to her parents' wish that she marry her cousin, Patrick, and ensure that Downton Abbey would remain within the family. While the inheritance laws dictating Mary's choice of spouse may have made a certain sort of economic sense for owners of large estates, they were not designed to promote Pausanias's heavenly variety of love, and Mary barely notices when Patrick dies. After this, however, Mary decides to ignore social convention altogether, and sleeps with Kemal Pamuk, which ends up causing problems for both her and her family. As Mary painfully discovers, finding "heavenly love" requires more than just following the rules, but one cannot just ignore the rules either.

In the end, Mary is able to find happiness with Matthew only when she commits herself to playing the game of love wholeheartedly, and really trying to find a spouse that fits with both her personal life and her larger role in society. While this method takes more time and effort—wars have to be fought, injuries overcome, and other relationships ended—Pausanias would argue that this merely serves to test the lovers' sincerity, and to ensure that their love really is of the heavenly type. He might also console Mary on Matthew's eventual death, and remind her that learning to love in this way is valuable regardless of how things turn out.

Love as the Order of Life

In contrast to the turbulent love lives of Thomas and Mary, the relationship between Carson and Mrs. Hughes is a model of stability that helps to keep everything (and everyone) at Downton functioning as it should. Of course, their relationship is not romantic in the same way as those we have been talking about so far, but it would be foolish to ignore it merely on these grounds. After all, there are many types of love, and (despite what one might sometimes hear!), not *everything* is about sex.

Eryximachus, the Athenian physician who is the third speaker of the *Symposium*, argues that it is love in this broader sense that gives order to individual lives, to society, and to nature as a whole. While he agrees with Pausanias that there are two types of love, he describes the better type as a unifying force and the worst type as a destructive, dissonant force. So, where a relationship based on the first sort of love allows two people to function as a harmonious whole, the second sort ends up disrupting both the lives of the individuals involved and those around them. He argues that these same two principles of love are at work throughout the universe. In medicine, a healthy body is one governed by the first sort of love, while a diseased body suffers from the influence of the second sort. Similarly, a well-written musical composition must have the harmony of the first love, where a poorly written one based on the second love is little more than a collection of discordant notes.

Carson and Mrs. Hughes's relationship provides an exemplary case of Eryximachus's first sort of love, in several different respects. First, their relationship allows them to function as a harmonious whole, where each person knows precisely what their own duties are, and what they can in turn expect of the other person. However, this does not mean that their relationship is merely a list of duties to memorize—instead, each is able to adapt quickly to changing circumstances and to recognize when the other person needs help. Second, maintaining this sort of relationship requires *expertise,* in the same way that being a good doctor or musician requires expertise. One cannot have this sort of love merely by picturing the desired result in one's mind. Instead, it requires *practice* and *skill*, as both Carson and Mrs. Hughes continually demonstrate. Finally, their relationship produces order in the world around them. For example, their skilled intervention helps the other characters of *Downton Abbey* to form their own relationships, and keeps the Abbey functioning as it should. Without Carson and Mrs. Hughes's orderly love, *nothing* would be quite as harmonious as before—the food would taste just a bit worse, the formal attire appear not quite as impressive, the love lives of the inhabitants a little less likely to end well.

Are Anna and Bates Really One Person?

Many of the characters of *Downton Abbey* seem destined never to find a love that will last. Thomas's love is illegal, Mary's and Tom's spouses die, and Carson and Mrs. Hughes prioritize their working relationships over their personal ones. Two notable exceptions to this rule, however, are Anna and Bates, who manage to find and stick with each other even in the face of almost overwhelming difficulties. Their intense, deeply committed love provides a model that the other residents of the Abbey (not to mention many viewers of the show) aspire to attain in their own lives.

Anna and Bates's relationship is a good example of the sort of love that interests the comic playwright Aristophanes, the fourth speaker of the *Symposium*. Aristophanes presents his theory of love in the form of a mythological story. In the beginning, he says, the gods created three kinds of humans: fully male, fully female, and androgynous. These early humans were sphere-shaped with four arms, four legs, a two-faced head, and two sets of genitals. They were much more fearsome and powerful than current humans, and they even tried to challenge the gods. Because of this, the gods decided to cut them in half and rearrange them as humans in their current form. These newly shaped humans, however, were left with a deep desire to find and reunite with their "missing halves." According to Aristophanes, this explains the three different types of sexual desire: men for men, women for women, and women for men (or vice versa). What sort of human one had been *before* the split determines what one desires afterwards. Sex, on this story, is an attempt to merge back together, and to put things back the way they were originally.

Anna and Bates provide a powerful illustration of Aristophanes's idea. When people are in love, according to Aristophanes, they do their best to make their separate lives into a single life. This includes both a desire for physical closeness (as when Anna and Bates finally get their own cabin, and can share a bed), and for shared purposes (as when Anna and Bates begin to care just as much for the happiness of the other person as for their own). The lengths to which Anna and Bates are willing to go to maintain their love shows just how strong this desire for closeness can be. Consider, for example, Bates's efforts to secure a divorce from his first wife, or Anna's relentless fight to get Bates out of prison. Even Anna's rape, as terrible as it is, helps show the overall unity of their relationship, and the depth of their commitment to each other.

Even though humans can never fully become a "single person" in the way that lovers sometimes seem to want,

Aristophanes's story suggests that we can do so partially, and that it is worth trying to do so. There is, after all, something very valuable about being part of an intimate team like Anna and Bates, where each person helps the other when things get rough. The desire to find (and keep) a relationship with one's other half is a big part of what makes many peoples' lives meaningful and worthwhile. For Anna and Bates, there is never any question of "What is my life all about?" They find the meaning of their lives in their relationship to each other, and this in turn provides them the strength to get through anything.

Edith's Dangerous Love

So far, we have been talking about the many *benefits* of love: it makes us more courageous; it helps us appreciate the truly worthwhile parts of another person; it gives unity to the world around us; and it helps us find our "missing half." Of course, not all experiences of love are positive. For example, consider Edith's love life, which is filled with disappointment after disappointment, and where nothing ever seems to work as it should. What exactly is she doing wrong? And how, if at all, might she fix it?

When the host of the *Symposium,* the tragic playwright Agathon, gets up to speak, he takes a slightly different direction than the other speakers. Where they focused on the *effects* of love, he focuses more on the *object* of love; where they offer sincere praise of love, his tongue-in-cheek list of its virtues reminds us that the pursuit of love can easily lead us into disaster. He starts by claiming the god of love must be young and beautiful, and opposed to the old or ugly. He then offers an argument concluding that love must be just since people agree to be in love, and that love is temperate since love can beat out desires for things like money or food. Similarly, he claims that love must be courageous because it can make soldiers do things they otherwise wouldn't, and that it is wise because any writer, artist, or inventor must have loved something that inspired them. While Agathon intends for his speech to be a bit ridiculous, there is something revealing in it, too: when a person is in love, it really can *feel like* the pursuit of the object of love is the best possible thing to do. The problem, of course, is that this sort of blind pursuit does *not* guarantee that we will be just, temperate, courageous, or wise. In fact: it is often just the opposite: the desire for love can cause us to treat people unfairly, to indulge desires that we should not, to avoid difficult tasks, and to behave very unwisely.

To get a better sense of how this might happen, let's return to the case of Edith. As a potential object of love, she is ignored because she is not as pretty or personable as her two sisters. For example, both Patrick and Matthew choose Mary over her, though for different reasons. Edith also makes her own mistakes as a lover. For example, her decision (motivated by romantic jealousy) to tell the Turkish embassy about Mary's role in Kemal's death is hardly just, and her choice of potential romantic partners does not always demonstrate temperance. Similarly, while she is certainly capable of being courageous, she is sometimes too worried about whether her choices will look improper. Finally, Edith's pursuit of love often leads her to behave in ways that are most definitely unwise, and to ignore the advice of those who want to help her.

None of this means that Edith is doomed to be alone. As Agathon surely recognizes, there is much more to love than his speech portrays, and there is no reason that we cannot learn from our mistakes. Edith's progression as a character reflects this: in later seasons, she makes increasingly better choices (even if they sometimes turn out badly), and begins to appreciate how love works on a deeper, more philosophical level.

Just What Is Platonic Love, Anyway?

Part of Edith's desperation is due to her fear of ending up as a "spinster aunt." This same fear of loneliness affects many of the other characters, as well. For example, Daisy struggles to find a satisfactory romantic relationship, as do Tom and Mary after their partners die. To these characters, the suggestion that they should pursue a "Platonic" sort of love would no doubt sound depressing, at least if this means something like "a love between friends" or "a love without sexual attraction."

It may come as a surprise, then, to find out that "Platonic love" can be traced back to the sort of love defended by Socrates in his *Symposium* speech. Socrates's speech is much more detailed than those that preceded it, and many scholars think that Plato's own view was probably close to Socrates. At its most general, Socrates argues that love is a desire for *immortality,* and for producing something that outlives us. So, for example, the children of Downton Abbey are the result of their parents' love, and their parents respond to their birth by expanding their love to include the children. However, there are other sorts of immortality (and other sorts of love), as well. For example, the actions of a brave soldier (such as Matthew) or nurse (such as Sybil) will be remembered after they die, and their contributions will help ensure that the country they love will survive. One can even learn to love an institution such as Downton Abbey, as Cora, Robert, Violet, Carson, and others clearly demonstrate. Their quest to preserve Downton Abbey as they know it shows a desire to leave something behind after they are gone.

Contrary to popular opinion, Socrates does not criticize sexual attraction or romantic love, though he does argue that these are simply "steps" on the ladder that leads to a meaningful, fulfilled life. Tom and Sybil's relationship provides an excellent example of Socrates's idea. When they first meet, they have not established "lives" for themselves—Tom talks politics while driving a car, and Sybil's admirable moral principles seem similarly unconnected from any real world application. Then, the first "step" of love occurs, and they discover a physical attraction for *each other.* This, in turn, changes them, as they now have a concrete goal in life—to figure out how to be together. While doing this, however, they make Socrates's second "step" of love, and discover a new appreciation for the general type of person that they love—Sybil learns to understand the life of the poor, while Tom discovers an affection for Sybil's family and friends. On the third "step" of the ladder, this love for *the beauty of people in general* expands into a love of *moral beauty,* or beauty of character. Here, Sybil comes to identify with parts of Tom's politics, while Tom recognizes aspects of the Crawleys' way of doing things that are genuinely worth looking up to. On the next step, this becomes a love of wisdom in general, and a willingness to change one's life to pursue it. Sybil serves as a nurse and gives up her inheritance to marry Tom; after her death, Tom commits himself to his life as a single father and estate manager, even though it is far from what he had originally envisioned.

On Socrates's account, this is how love is *supposed* to work, at least if we do it correctly. A romantic love for a person can never remain *merely* a love for that person; instead, the object of our love continually grows and expands, and forces us to change our lives in ways we never would have thought possible. And this, in turn, is what provides meaning to our lives. In the end, Socrates hints that love will make philosophers of us all, as we begin to direct our attention toward the nature of love itself. On this view, Tom and Sybil's relationship, however difficult it may seem to them, is exactly what we should aspire to.

While Socrates describes the final object of this sort of "Platonic love" as perfect and unchanging, this does not mean that *we* must be perfect or unchanging. Instead, we must allow love to transform us, in the same way that it transforms nearly all of the characters of Downton Abbey. This account reveals the common ground between all of the earlier speeches: love can make us braver, like Thomas, and more attentive to true beauty, like Mary. If we carefully cultivate our relationships, we can develop some of Carson's and Mrs. Hughes's skills, and feel some of Bates and Anna's closeness. We can recognize the important things that Edith gets right, as well as those she gets wrong. Finally, we can embrace the changes the love makes within us, and strive to become the best versions of ourselves.

References

Aquinas, Thomas. 2006. *Summa theologiae.* Ed. Brian Davies and Brian Leftow. Cambridge: Cambridge University Press.

Augustine, St. 1991. *Confessions.* Trans. Henry Chadwick. Oxford: Oxford University Press.

Bachelard, Gaston. 1964. *The Poetics of Space.* New York: Orion Press.

Bellah, Robert, William M. Sullivan, Ann Swidler, and Steven M. Tipton. 1991. *The Good Society.* New York: Alfred A. Knopf.

Belliotti, Raymond Angelo. 2001. *What Is the Meaning of Human Life?* Amsterdam: Rodopi.

Boyd, William. 2012. Why World War I resonates. *New York Times,* January 21.

Brown, Irene Coltman. 1991. The historian as philosopher: Hegel and the plan of history. *History Today,* November.

Burke, Edmund. 2009 (1790). *Reflections on the Revolution in France.* Oxford and New York: Oxford University Press.

Buss, Sarah. 1999. Appearing respectful: The moral significance of manners. *Ethics* 109. 4 (July): 795–826.

Campbell, James. 1988. *The Power of Myth.* New York: Doubleday.

Cannadine, David. 1990. *The Decline and Fall of the British Aristocracy.* New Haven, CT: Yale University Press.

Carr, Nicholas. 2010. *The Shallows: What the Internet is Doing to Our Brains.* New York: W. W. Norton & Company.

Chesterton, G.K. 1933. *Saint Thomas Aquinas.* London: Hodder and Stoughton.

Churchill, Winston. 1899. *The River War: An Historical Account of the Reconquest of the Soudan.* London: Longmans, Green and Co.

Cohen, Deborah. 2012. Will to work: Disabled veterans in Britain and Germany after the First World War. Chap. 12 in *Disabled Veterans in History,* ed. David A. Gerber. Ann Arbor: University of Michigan Press. Kindle ebook.

Crary, Jonathan. 1990. *Techniques of the Observer: On Vision and Modernity in the Nineteenth Century.* Cambridge: MIT Press.

Csikszentmihlyi, Mihaly. 1990. *Flow.* New York: Harper and Row.

Dennett, Daniel. 1991. Real patterns. *Journal of Philosophy* 88: 27–51.

Douthat, Ross. 2014. I love Lena. *New York Times*, October 4. http://www.nytimes.com/2014/10/05/opinion/sunday/ross-douthat-i-love-lena.html (accessed June 2, 2015).

Downton Abbey. 2011–2015. (DVD). Seasons 1–5. Writ. Julian Fellowes, Shelagh Stephenson, and Tina Pepler. Studio: PBS.

Elgin, Catherine Z. 2008. Trustworthiness. *Philosophical Papers* 37.3: 371–87.

Emerson, Ralph Waldo. 1904. The method of nature. In *The Complete Works of Ralph Waldo Emerson.* Boston: Houghton, Mifflin and Company.

Epictetus. 2014. *Discourses, Fragments, Handbook.* Trans. Robin Hard. Oxford: Oxford University Press.

Fellowes, Jessica, and Matthew Sturgis. 2012. *The Chronicles of Downton Abbey: A New Era.* St. Martin's Press.

Fellowes, Julian. 2013. *Downton Abbey: The Complete Scripts: Season One.* New York: William Morrow.

———. 2013. *Downton Abbey: The Complete Scripts: Season Two.* New York: William Morrow.

———. 2014. *Downton Abbey: The Complete Scripts: Season Three.* New York: William Morrow.

———. 2012. *The World of Downton Abbey.* St. Martin's Press.

Feser, Edward. 2009. *Aquinas: A Beginner's Guide.* Oxford: One World.

Foer, Joshua. 2011. *Moonwalking with Einstein: The Art and Science of Remembering Everything.* New York: Penguin.

Fourier, Charles. 1996. *The Theory of the Four Movements.* Cambridge: University of Cambridge Press.

Frayn, Michael. 1998. *Copenhagen.* London: Methuen.

Galliott, Jai C. 2015. *Military Robots: Mapping the Moral Landscape.* Farnham: Ashgate.

Gettier, Edmund. 1963. Is justified true belief knowledge? *Analysis* 23.6: 121–23.

Hatab, Lawrence J. 2005. *Nietzsche's Life Sentence.* New York: Routledge.

Hayden, Herbert B. 1921. *Shell-Shocked—and After.* Boston: Atlantic Monthly Company.

Hegel, Georg W. F. 1991. *Elements of the Philosophy of Right.* Trans. H.B. Nisbet. Cambridge: Cambridge University Press.

———. 1991. *The Philosophy of History.* Trans. J. Sibree. New York: Prometheus Books.

Hume, David. 1955. *An Inquiry Concerning Human Understanding.* Ed. Charles W. Hendel. New York: Liberal Arts Press.

Huxley, Aldous. 2014. What exactly, is modern? In *Bohemians, Bootleggers, Flappers, and Swells: The Best of Early Vanity Fair,* ed. Graydon Carter. New York: Penguin Press.

James, Henry. 1904. *The Golden Bowl.* London: Methuen.

Kahn, Paul. 2002. The paradox of riskless warfare. *Philosophy and Public Policy Quarterly* 22.3: 2–8.

Kandel, Eric R. 2006. *In Search of Memory: The Emergence of a New Science of Mind.* New York: W. W. Norton & Company.

Kant, Immanuel. 1998 (1785). *Groundwork of the Metaphysics of Morals.* Trans. Mary Gregor. Cambridge: Cambridge University Press.

———. 1996 (1785). *The Metaphysics of Morals.* Rev. ed. Trans. Mary Gregor. Cambridge: Cambridge University Press.

Kuhn, Thomas. 1962/2012. *The Structure of Scientific Revolutions.* Chicago: University of Chicago Press.

Lackey, Jennifer. 1999. Testimonial knowledge and transition. *Philosophical Quarterly* 49.197: 471–90.

Langtree, Ian C. 2010. Definitions of the models of disability. http://www.disabled-world.com/definitions/disability-models.php (accessed July 2, 2014).

LaRocca, David. 2013. *Emerson's English Traits and the Natural History of Metaphor.* New York: Bloomsbury.

LaRocca, David, ed. 2011. *The Philosophy of Charlie Kaufman.* Lexington: University Press of Kentucky.

LeDoux, Joseph. 2002. *Synaptic Self: How Our Brains Become Who We Are.* New York: Penguin.

Lipton, Peter. 2004. *Inference to the Best Explanation.* 2nd ed. London: Routledge.

Lomasky, Loren. 1987. *Persons, Rights, and the Moral Community.* New York: Oxford University Press.

Longmore, Paul, K. 2003. Film reviews. In *Why I Burned My Book and Other Essays on Disability.* Philadelphia: Temple University Press, 119–33.

———. 2003. Screening stereotypes: Images of disabled people in television and motion pictures. In *Why I Burned My Book and Other Essays on Disability.* Philadelphia: Temple University Press.

Lowrey, Annie. 2014. The wealth gap in America is growing, too. *New York Times,* April 2. http://economix.blogs.nytimes.com/2014/04/02/the-wealth-gap-is-growing-too (accessed May 15, 2015).

McConkey, James. 1983. *Court of Memory.* New York: E.P. Dutton, Inc.

Marino, Gordon. 2014. A life beyond 'do what you love'. *New York Times,* May 17. http://opinionator.blogs.nytimes.com/2014/05/17/a-life-beyond-do-what-you-love/ (accessed June 2, 2015).

Marx, Karl, and Friedrich Engels. 2011. *The Communist Manifesto*. Trans. Samuel Moore. London: Penguin Books.

Marx, Karl. 1992. *Capital: Vol 1: A Critique of Political Economy*. Trans. Ben Fowkes. London: Penguin Books.

Navratilova, Martina. 2009. Quoted in Ian C. Langtree, Disability quotes: Collection of quotations regarding disabilities. http://www.disabled-world.com/disability/disability-quotes.php (accessed August 6, 2014).

Neiman, Susan. 2002. *Evil in Modern Thought: An Alternative History of Philosophy*. Princeton: Princeton University Press.

Nielsen, Kim E. 2012. Three generations of imbeciles are enough: The progressive era, 1890–1927. In *A Disability History of the United States*, 100–130. Boston: Beacon Press. Kindle ebook.

Nietzsche, Friedrich. 1966 (1886). *Beyond Good and Evil*. Trans. Walter Kaufmann. New York: Random House.

———. 2000 (1887). Ecce homo. *The Basic Writings of Nietzsche*. Trans. Walter Kaufmann. New York: Modern Library.

———. 1974 (1882). *The Gay Science*. Trans. Walter Kaufmann. New York: Random House.

Nozick, Robert. 2008. Philosophy and the meaning of life. In *The Meaning of Life: A Reader*, ed. E. D. Klemke, 224–31. Oxford: Oxford University Press.

Owen, Robert. 2007. *A New View of Society and Other Writings*. London: Penguin Books.

Paley, William. 2006. *Natural Theology*. Ed. Matthew Eddy and David Knight. Oxford: Oxford University Press.

Pieper, Josef. 1963. *Leisure: The Basis of Culture*. New York: Pantheon.

Pippin, Robert. 2001. *Henry James and Modern Moral Life*. Cambridge: Cambridge University Press.

Plato. 1997. Theaetetus. In *Complete Works*, ed. J. M. Cooper and D. S. Hutchinson. Indianapolis: Hackett 157–234.

———. 1997. Symposium. In *Complete Works*, ed. J. M. Cooper and D. S. Hutchinson. Indianapolis: Hackett.

Ramelli, Ilaria. 2009. *Hierocles the Stoic: Elements of Ethics, Fragments and Excerpts*. Trans. David Konstan. Atlanta: Society of Biblical Literature.

Russell, Bertrand. 1993 (1776). In praise of idleness. In *In Praise of Idleness and Other Essays*. New York: Rougledge.

Searle, John. 1997. *The Mystery of Consciousness*. New York: New York Review of Books.

Sherman, Nancy. 2005. The look and feel of virtue. In *Virtue, Norms, and Objectivity: Issues in Ancient and Modern Ethics*, ed. Christopher Gill. Oxford: Clarendon Press.

———. 2005. Of manners and morals. *British Journal of Educational Studies* 53.3: 272–89.

Simmel, Georg. 1900. *The Philosophy of Money*. London: Routledge.

Singer, Peter. 1983. *Hegel: A Very Short Introduction*. Oxford: Oxford University Press.

———. 1980. *Practical Ethics*. Cambridge: Cambridge University Press.

———. 1995. *Rethinking Life and Death*. New York: St. Martin's Press.

Smith, Adam. 1993 (1776). *The Wealth of Nations*. Oxford: Oxford University Press.

Sparrow, Robert. 2009. Building a better warbot: Ethical issues in the design of unmanned systems for military applications. *Science and Engineering Ethics* 15.2: 169–87.

Specter, Michael. 2014. Partial recall. *New Yorker*, May 19.

Strawser, Bradley Jay, ed. 2013. *Killing by Remote Control: The Ethics of an Unmanned Military*. New York: Oxford University Press.

Taylor, Richard. 1970. *Good and Evil: A New Direction*. New York: Macmillan.

Thomson, Judith Jarvis. 1971. A defense of abortion. *Philosophy and Public Affairs* 1: 47–66.

Tokumitsu, Miya. 2014. In the name of love. *Jacobin*. November 24. Retrieved from http://www.jacobinmag.com/2014/01/in-the-name-of-love/

Tooley, Michael. 2009. *Abortion—Three Perspectives*. Oxford: Oxford University Press.

Warren, Mary Anne. 1973. On the moral and legal status of abortion. 1973. *Monist* 57.1: 43–61.

Wartorn 1861–2010. 2011. (DVD). Produced by Jon Alpert, Ellen Goosenberg Kent, and Matt O'Neil. Studio: HBO Studios.

Williams, Bernard. 1982. Persons, character and morality. In *Moral Luck*. Cambridge: Cambridge University Press.

Winner, Langdon. 1986. Technologies as forms of life. *The Whale and the Reactor: A Search for Limits in an Age of High Technology*. Chicago: University of Chicago Press.

Wolf, Susan. 2012. *Meaning in Life and Why It Matters*. Princeton: Princeton University Press.

Zinn, Howard. 1990. *Declarations of Independence: Cross-Examining American Ideology*. New York: HarperCollins. Reissued in 2002 under the title, *Passionate Declarations: Essays on War and Justice*. New York: HarperCollins.

Household Staff

MELANIE ABBOTT took the Sybil approach to life and flew across the (other) pond to South Korea (Yonsei University) to get her Bachelor's degree in international studies and is now at the University of Washington getting her Master's in social work. She can be as contrary as she chooses and has interests ranging from quantum physics to Sailor Moon.

ROBERT ARP has interests in Western philosophy generally, philosophy and pop culture, and ontology in the information science sense. He has never been to Downton Abbey (obviously), but he has been to The Abbey in downtown Orlando.

ADAM BARKMAN (PhD, Free University of Amsterdam) is an associate professor of philosophy at Redeemer University College (Canada). As a C. S. Lewis scholar, Barkman keeps hoping against hope that the Oxford Don will somehow make an appearance at Downton. But he's only got one season left to dream . . .

KIMBERLY BLESSING is a professor of philosophy at SUNY Buffalo State. Her interests include meaning of life, modern philosophy, philosophy of religion, and existentialism. The question keeping her awake at night is not "what is the meaning of life?" but "what is a weekend?"

TAMÁS DEMETER has interests in philosophy of psychology, the history of early modern philosophy, and social theories of knowledge. His appetite for the intricacies of psychological interpretation and social interaction found a rich hunting-field in *Downton Abbey*.

KATHLEEN POORMAN DOUGHERTY's philosophical interests are in ethics, especially on the moral value of personal relationships and the development of moral character. Even though life at Downton holds a certain appeal, her commitments to democracy and social justice—not to mention her philosopher's income!—mean that she still dresses herself, cleans her own house, and makes her own tea.

MATTHIAS EGG studied physics at the University of Zurich, earned his PhD in philosophy of science at the University of Lausanne and now teaches philosophy at the University of Bern. His current research concerns the way in which (supposedly fundamental) scientific theories link up with our everyday world. This is just as intriguing as *Downton Abbey*: it's all about the connections between upstairs and downstairs . . .

LUCY ELVIS is a PhD student, writer, and curator from Birmingham (UK), living in the west of Ireland. She is currently studying at the National University of Ireland, Galway. Her research is focussed on the way philosophy 'deals with' architecture as an art form, particularly in phenomenology and hermeneutics. She's not acquainted personally with Lord and Lady Grantham, but she has been to the town of Grantham, where the aristocracy were few but the fish and chips were excellent.

JAI GALLIOTT holds a PhD in philosophy from Macquarie University and is currently a Research Fellow at the University of New South Wales in Australia. He researches the ethical, legal, and strategic implications of technology. Like some of the Granthams, he wishes he could retreat to a bygone era.

After watching the first season of *Downton Abbey*, GORDON HAWKES decided he wanted to become an aristocrat. But, after recognizing that he lacked any social status, wealth, or power, he decided he was better suited to become a philosopher. He is currently a master's student in philosophy at the University of Calgary.

TIM JONES has a PhD in literature from the University of East Anglia in England, where he also teaches part-time. As a Norwich City Councillor for the Green Party he should probably want to see houses like Downton appropriated and placed in the hands of the common folk, but couldn't bear to see the Crawleys parted from all of their lovely furniture.

Blimey, guv'nuh . . . Wotz all dis I hears 'bout JOHN V. KARAVITIS, CPA, MBA, writin' 'bout the philosophy of work and all that? That the posh toffs and us hoi polloi is no diff'r'nt at 'art, e'en tho we has our jelly 'n' dey has their jam?? Methinks it'll be the dog's bollocks—*pardon me*, guv'nuh, I meant *"the bee's knees"*—and you'll be gobsmacked! Read his essay, and John's your uncle!

CHRIS KETCHAM holds a doctorate in curriculum and instruction from the University of Texas at Austin. His research and writing interests are in ethics, risk management, and social justice. DaVinci said, "Small rooms or dwellings discipline the mind, large ones weaken it." Is it time for tea, yet?

SAMUEL KLUMPENHOUWER is a PhD student at the Centre for Medieval Studies of the University of Toronto. He spends his days teaching Latin and studying medieval canon law. He spends his nights dreaming about working at Yew Tree Farm on the Downton estate.

DAVID LAROCCA, PhD, is the editor of volumes in The Philosophy of Popular Culture Series, including *The Philosophy of Charlie Kaufman* (University Press of Kentucky, 2011), *The Philosophy of War Films* (UPK, 2014), and a forthcoming volume entitled *The Philosophy of Documentary Film* (Lexington Books of Rowman & Littlefield, 2016). Visiting Scholar in the Department of English at Cornell University, Lecturer in value theory and film at Ithaca College and the College at Cortland, Writer-in-Residence at the New York Public Library, and Fellow at the Moving Picture Institute in New York, LaRocca is the author of *On Emerson* (Wadsworth, 2003), and *Emerson's English Traits and the Natural History of Metaphor* (Bloomsbury, 2013). When he visited Highclere Castle, he was duly impressed by the "abbey," yet when he went looking for the kitchen, he learned that the "downstairs" is at Ealing Studios in London. Once again, foiled by continuity editing!

TRIP MCCROSSIN teaches in the philosophy department at Rutgers University, where he works on, among other things, the nature, history, and legacy of the Enlightenment. He tries to keep in mind— when grading, yes, but also as much of the rest of the time as possible—what Lord Grantham says to Jane, when she asks him whether he'll be happy, which is that he "has no right to be unhappy, which is almost the same."

ANDREW MILLS is a professor of philosophy at Otterbein University where he teaches a wide range of courses in the history of philosophy and in metaphysics. He has interests in philosophical pedagogy, the meaning and value of a liberal education, and in figuring out how to get someone to iron his newspaper for him every morning.

COURTNEY NEAL is an educator and graduate of DePaul University; her interests are in narrative study and why we tell stories. She also agrees with Mr. Carson that a day at the museum is an excellent vacation choice.

CLARA NISLEY earned a Master's in philosophy from Louisiana State University and now teaches at Oglethorpe University. Her research interests are in aesthetics and epistemology. While watching several seasons of *Downton Abbey*, she's developed an English accent, which she can't get rid of at all.

THOMAS NISLEY earned a Doctorate in political science from the University of Florida. He teaches at Kennesaw State University. Dr. Nisley has published in academic journals such as *International Politics, Politics & Policy,* and the *Journal of American Studies*. Thomas contends that he had the idea to decorate his office like Lord Grantham's study long before any member of the U.S. Congress.

AARON RICHMOND is a graduate student in critical disability studies at York University (Canada). His scholarly interests include exploring the intersections between philosophy and critical disability studies, as well as the representations of people with disabilities in English literature, on television, and in films. Aaron hopes that his contribution to this book will start discussions about the roles that characters with disabilities play in *Downton Abbey* and by extension within our society. This is because persons with disabilities should be, in the words of Mrs. Hughes, "no different to the rest of us."

BRENDAN SHEA, PhD, teaches philosophy at Rochester Community and Technical College, and has interests in applied ethics, the philosophy of science, and the history of philosophy. Like the Crawleys, he enjoys holding occasional dinner parties, though he suspects that Violet Crawley would be distinctly unimpressed with his cooking abilities, lack of formal attire, and music choice (among many other things).

DONNA MARIE SMITH is a librarian and freelance writer who has contributed to other titles in the Popular Culture and Philosophy series, such as *Doctor Who and Philosophy, More Doctor Who and Philosophy,* and *Catcher in the Rye and Philosophy*. She holds Bachelor's degrees in English and journalism, as well as a Master's of library and information science. Her scholarly pursuits have included coursework in classical, medieval, modern, and contemporary philosophy and the history and philosophy of science and technology. Like Sybil Crawley, she embraces the technological wonders of the Modern Age and the ongoing struggle for liberty and justice for all, but like Violet Crawley, she longs for the genteel trappings of the Guilded Age, where one can experience the simple pleasures of life, enjoying good companionship, witty banter, and a refreshing cup of Earl Grey tea without one's senses being barraged by—to paraphrase Mrs. Patmore—the banshee cry of a mobile phone.

CARL SOBOCINSKI (PhD) was originally a French language scholar, but after completing the degree requirements he discovered that he likes history better. World War I is a particular interest, and he hopes that someday he will figure out why it happened.

NOAH VAN BRENK, a free-lance philosopher, wishes he had been born in a time when wearing formal attire to dinner was mandatory. He also believes that enjoying tea and scones is a necessary event if one wants to have a truly productive day.

JOSEPH WALDERZAK is interested in representations of class and gender in film and television. He has been proudly correcting mispronunciations of Downton since 2010.

JAMES WILLS has spent much of his twenties being an English teacher in a secondary school, responsible for ensuring (or at least attempting to ensure) a love of all things literary. He would love to be able to pop into Downton Abbey for a look around, but might be too tempted to pinch a book or two from Lord Grantham's library to save money for the MA in literature he is currently working on.

Index